for Ros(
ui

CW00696775

Born to be Queen

Born to be Queen

DAISY SOLOMONS

Published in 2011 by Antony Rowe Publishing
48-50 Birch Close
Eastbourne
East Sussex
BN23 6PE
arp@cpi-group.co.uk

A catalogue record for this book is available from the British
Library

ISBN: 978-1-907571-20-6

www.daisysolomons.com

Printed and Bound in Great Britain by
CPI Antony Rowe, Chippenham and Eastbourne

Prologue

I wish my Mother had written the story of her early life, the years that formed her character. Here is the story of the years which formed mine: how my father died when Tanya and I were babies, and as soon as he was gone, our Mother became ill and put us into Care. We came home after five weeks, but ever since then, it seemed she was constantly making arrangements to get us out of the house. What I've written may explain how I came to be the woman I am.

But it's been a happy life. The first few years were a challenge, I don't mind telling you, but once I took control of it, things improved a lot. All the malign stuff took place when I was young, and nothing truly bad has happened to me since I was 25. It's not a misery memoir, either, there was lots of fun in my childhood, much of it thanks to Tanya. I wanted to write down everything, but should I write the truth, as I remember it, or should I try to make it a good story, which will grip you from page one?

I've decided on the truth as I remember it. However, I have changed the names of anyone who might be hurt or embarrassed at being positively identified. Because it is written from memory, my story is not strictly chronological, so the chapter on food (Chapter 14) starts in 1950 with:

'It's no good children, you will have to stop eating so much, the rations won't run to it' and ends with cake-baking almost ten years later. It's not a completely linear tale, either, because that is not how memory works.

For obvious reasons, I don't remember much of my very early years, so the first chapter is a patchwork of things people have told me; facts obtained from Public Records; my parents' letters to each other and my own memory. Billie's youngest brother, my Uncle John has read the first chapter, and wonders how I could recall all those details from when I was so young. I replied that it was because my early childhood was so eventful. Children who stay in the same place, with the same people in their early years, rarely remember as much as those of us who moved around. Imagine if you had gone on a fortnight's holiday to the seaside, with strangers, when you were four, you would remember it because everything was different from the norm.

Reedham Orphanage, where Tanya and I spent our childhood, was closed down soon after we left. We know there are still many places in the world where children are treated far worse than we were. We were allowed home for holidays three times a year, we were safe from traffic, we had plenty of room to play, and generally, the neglect was benign. Compared to, say, the suffering and deprivation of the Lost Generation of Australian migrant children, it wasn't too bad. It's just that nobody seemed to realise that I was born to be Queen.

Everyone has a story. This is mine.

To Tanya

I should like to thank all the people who read and criticised the manuscript in its various stages, and in particular:

Michéle Roberts, Vivienne Palmer, Teresa Richardson, Gillian Slovo, Linda Grant, Sarah Wood, Stanley Solomons, Brenda Berman, Tanya Rocks, Jane Sebba, Allan Watson, Jenny Christian and Dorothy Boswell.

I also want to thank Laurence Solomons, without whom...

1

Mr Mottiwalla Builds Me a House

November 1945 – September 1949

My forehead is pressed hard against the dark blue door, which leads out from the kitchen at 10 St George's Avenue. My Mother has just gone out of this door and I cannot open it. I want to go with her. Voices behind me say:

'Mummy has only gone out for a little while, she'll be back soon.'

It is impossible to make myself understood, so I scream: 'I want to go with Mummy.' For ages and ages I stand there, face up against the dark blue paint, terribly upset, while the voices keep saying that I can't go with Mummy.

I believe this was 26 August 1946, the day of my father's funeral. I would have been two years and four months old.

In November 1945, we had all arrived, from different places, at a small, rented flat on the top floor of 64 Freegrove Road, London N7. Billie, our mother, had brought our baby Tanya from Welwyn Garden City, where she had been born in October. Someone had brought me back from my Grandmother's house in Surrey, where I had been since July. Our tall, thin and clever Daddy, known to all as Lofty, was sent home from Archway Hospital.

His tuberculosis was declared incurable, and all the wounded soldiers meant a shortage of beds. The new antibiotics were very effective in treating tuberculosis, but there were limited supplies, so they were reserved for soldiers. He was told there was no point in blocking a hospital bed with someone who was going to die anyway. Christmas 1945 was to be our first and last together.

Then, in late Spring 1946 – with no money - Billie bought a house. This is how she told the story. One day, with – literally - tuppence halfpenny in her purse, enough to get some cabbage and potatoes for supper, she set out for the shops, wearing a blue and white flowered cotton dress. She knows this because she remembered that dress well, clothing had been rationed for a long time by then and it was the only dress she owned. She had made it herself, and all that summer she washed it every night and ironed it every morning. Tanya was in her pram, and – aged just two - I toddled along holding Billie's hand. Billie had completely forgotten that it was Thursday and early closing day. The only establishment open for business was the Estate Agent, who had a window full of houses so, determined not to go home empty handed, she bought one.

She saw 10 St George's Avenue, London N7 advertised for £450, walked straight in and asked to view it. As with many of the other houses on the Estate Agent's books, the owners had fled London during the Blitz and never returned, instructing the Agent to put it on the market for whatever he could get. Although the war was almost won, it wasn't over yet; bombing had only recently stopped and few people were buying property. A few doors down from 64 Freegrove Rd, at No. 50 lived Lofty's parents, our grandparents, Tom and Lizzie Wardman. Lizzie took in lodgers, so Billie immediately saw the potential of St George's Avenue and offered the asking price. She went back to the Estate Agent's office to discuss finance. Her idea was to borrow her brothers' and brother-in-law's demob pay, buy 10 St George's Avenue, fill it with lodgers and repay all the borrowed money in about 18 months. Business was so quiet, that she was able to leave me sitting on the Estate Agent's lap while she went, with Tanya in the pram, to the phone box and, using the tuppence halfpenny, rang her brothers John and Walter and her brother-in- law Jack.

To each she said something like 'How much demob pay did you get and what are you going to do with it?' And each of them replied with a variant of 'Oh about £200; I hadn't really thought about it, building society I suppose.'

'Why not invest it in me instead? I will pay you back, with interest, within eighteen months.' So, she borrowed two lots of £200 and one lot of £150, which gave her £100 over for furnishing. She went home to Lofty and told him that although there was no supper, they were now householders. He was amazed and impressed. Billie moved us all into St George's Avenue and started to take in lodgers, many referred to her by Lizzie. She paid everyone back on time, with interest, as she had promised. And that was how we all came to live at 10 St George's Avenue.

It is the house in which our father died, in August 1946, in the first floor back room, aged thirty. He had not been fit enough to fight in the Armed Forces, but he was no pacifist. A passionate socialist, in the thirties he fought Mosley's men in the East End streets, returning home to his mother covered in blood, satisfaction and glory. Now the long, hard war was finally over, the fascists - at home and abroad - were beaten, and he was finally united with his wife and family. Britain had elected a Labour government with a huge majority, there was to be a Welfare State, a National Health Service and an end to poverty. And he was to see none of it. His room overlooked the back garden, but Lofty was so angry thinking of all he was losing, that he never looked out of the window. He would not let Billie open the curtains. He refused to witness Spring 1946.

Autumn 1946

A few weeks after our father died, Tanya was sitting up in her pram in the front garden of 10 St Georges Avenue. She wore a white knitted bonnet and jacket, and a neat white blanket covered her. Her round, pale face was expressionless as usual, as she watched me play. She looked just as a baby should, and I loved her. Remembering Hansel and Gretel, who were covered with leaves by the birds of the forest as they lay sleeping, I gathered leaves from under the trees and put them all over my little sister's blanket. As I did so, I told her the fairy tale, explained what I was doing. Billie came out and laughed, but she said the leaves were making the blanket dirty, and took them off.

It was a big house - the Electoral Roll for 1947 shows 14 people, including Billie, living at 10 St Georges Avenue. That is people over 21 who were eligible to vote in the UK, there were certainly more. It seemed we could never get Billie to ourselves. However, there was usually a lodger around to take an interest in us. Mr Mottiwalla was my favourite.

Once he gave me a piece of chocolate. I said no thank you, but he said go on take it. I was not supposed to accept sweets from those men but they would sometimes put their heads around the door of our bedroom when my mother was downstairs and say:

'Would you like some sweeties little girl?'

Once it was:

'Would you like some chewing gum?'

The chewing gum man was African. I had never seen chewing gum but I had heard of it. I held the wrapped strip of gum and said nothing. He spoke gently.

'You must unwrap it first' he said 'then chew it, but don't swallow it.'

'What happens after?'

'After you've chewed it, then you throw it away.'

He said goodnight and I got into bed with the chewing gum and thought about it. You chewed it and then you threw it away. It made no sense. I put it under the pillow, where my Mother found it. She said I was too young for it, and the man should not have given it to me. She said:

'Now, you mustn't take sweets or chewing gum. Just say 'No thank you.''

Which is what I said to Mr Mottiwalla when he offered the chocolate.

'Go on, have it later.' and he uncurled my fingers and placed the chocolate in my palm, re-curling my fingers round it.

I said nothing and got into bed. I had said no thank you but I had still been given the chocolate. The best thing to do was to save it and ask my Mummy in the morning. I slept.

I woke in the night with a very wet, sticky hand. What was wrong? I sat up and inspected my hand by the light of the street lamp which shone in from outside. It was covered in something dark, runny and sticky, which had a dark, sweet, familiar smell. Was it blood? It was frightening, horrible, and I put my hand on the wall, wiping my palm over and over until all the muck was off my hand. When I felt clean again, I slept.

'What's happened to the wall?'

I looked at the wall above my head

'Penny, what's that brown stuff?' she sniffed it

'Chocolate! How did you get chocolate on the wall?

I answered truthfully 'I don't know.'

She questioned me gently and together we arrived at an explanation. She picked me up and cuddled me.

'Of course it melted in your hand, silly billy, you must never go to sleep with chocolate in your hand, it will melt in the night.'

Months later, I realised it was not the night that had melted the chocolate, it was holding it in my hot little hand.

Mr Motiwalla was one of the men who offered to marry Billie and be a father to Tanya and me. She laughed when she told me of his proposal. He was a delightful man, she said, and very well educated, but he was Indian, so of course there was no question. Billie might not have taken him seriously, but I did. I loved him, and would have married him myself, but he never asked. In his room, he had real plasticine, not the silly little coloured strips you got in children's packs, but a big, grey chunk which you could see had been carved from a larger piece.

'This is what grown ups use for modelling' he told me, kneading and softening it with his warm and elegant brown hands, their thumbs exquisitely bendy.

'Now then, you can make something really big with this.'

I made a series of grey animals, crushing each one up to create the next, and each time he helped me knead and soften the plasticine. He told me he was double jointed, and let me bend his thumbs and fingers back as far as they would go, insisting it did not hurt. We tried with my fat little white fingers, but they did not bend back at all.

He also had the first sellotape I had ever seen, and used it to construct a cardboard house for me. It stood in its own cardboard grounds, with a sloping roof, windows and doors hinged with sellotape. I watched him measure, use his ruler to draw the lines, cut it out and construct it, then together we drew grass and flowers all around it with crayons. His name was Kaikabad Motiwalla. When Billie contracted jaundice, Tanya and I went into care and all the lodgers had to leave. Mr Motiwalla and I never even said goodbye.

January 1947

Someone was packing our suitcases, which were not really suitcases, but cardboard laundry boxes, one blue, one brown.

'Why do we have to have a box each?'

'Because you're going to different places. You're going to Essex and Tanya is going to Hertfordshire.'

The boxes were on the kitchen floor, under the window, and the woman was kneeling down, folding clothes into them.

'Will Mummy be there?'

'No, Mummy is ill in hospital. She's got jaundice. You're

going away till she gets better and can look after you again.'

Essex was a place where they took your clothes away and made you sleep in a cot, the type with sides you let down with a latch to get out of. I had not slept in one of those since Tanya was born, and now considered myself far too mature for anything but a bed. I was almost three, for goodness sake.

Essex was some kind of big house with neon strip lights instead of lampshades. I arrived wearing a green dress with white spots and white piping round the collar, black patent shoes with straps, which started behind the heel and buttoned in front of the ankle. I was very proud of those shoes, and considered the strap far more stylish than the more common 'Mary Jane' button over type. These clothes disappeared and I had to wear some dungaree things, which were hard to put on and smelt yeasty, like wee-wee or stale bread.

The other children were boys and girls of different ages. They all seemed to cry a lot. In the clattering neon gloom of the dining room, we collected our food from a trolley, then sat at several round tables. One girl said I was sitting in her place, so I moved to another place. But then, someone else said it was their place. Nobody told me where I could sit, so although I found another place, and sat there every mealtime thereafter, I was never quite certain that it was my place. After the meal, you had to collect the plates from your table when it was your turn, but I never knew when it was my turn. Someone always had to shout:

'Penny Wardman, it's your turn to collect the plates'

So I would collect and pile the plates up, cutlery on top, as I had seen others do, and carry them carefully to the trolley. I tried not to let the spoons and forks slip off and go clattering on to the green lino floor, but usually they did.

Essex smelt of bed-wetting and despair. It didn't feel clean and I had nobody. Since August last year, I had lost my entire family. My father Lofty had died of TB, my mother Billie was in hospital somewhere, and my little sister Tanya, who could not even walk yet, was in Hertfordshire, wherever that was. Nobody visited me and I had no idea when I would see my loved ones again.

One night I woke up, needing to use the toilet. I disliked the arrangements: one potty at the centre of the room, an arena where you did your business in full view of everyone, but stood up to let the side of the cot down and get to the potty. Somebody had locked the side of the cot in some way, making it impossible for me to get out. I shouted for help:

'I want to go to the toilet.'

I shouted, for what seemed like hours. I knew they were out there, in a lighted room at the end of the dormitory. I could hear them talking. Eventually I could hold out no longer, went to the furthest corner of the cot and, reluctantly, shat. Then I started to cry. I didn't think of it so much as crying, as calling, but of course to an adult, it would have sounded like crying. A woman with two buns on her head (one on top, one at the back) came and smacked me hard across the back of my legs. She then wiped my bottom, turned the dirty sheet, turd and all, over and told me to lie down on it. Filled with rage, disgust and scorn, I squeezed into the opposite corner of the cot from the turd, and cried myself to sleep. It was the first time I had been hit. I suppose I had seen other children hit before, but it had no connection with my own life, it seemed pointless and didn't interest me much. Now I understood that it was not about pain or punishment, but power and humiliation.

Spring 1947

One morning, before it was light, a woman came to my bed and said 'Get dressed, you're going home today'. She held my spotted dress and proper shoes. The adult who collected me must have been Billie, but I don't remember that reunion. The one I remember is with Tanya - a front door opened and there she was, in the arms of the woman who had opened the door, her fat little legs at my eye level! That's when things started to feel all right, when the world once again seemed properly organised. Somebody had a bunch of daffodils – I think Billie gave them to the woman who had looked after Tan.

'And look – she can walk!'

Christmas Eve 1947

We had another house now. Billie had sold 10 St George's Avenue, and bought 27 Carleton Road, which was much bigger. Sometimes our bedroom was a sitting room, and I think that's why Tanya and I had a Christmas Tree in our bedroom. We woke up in the night, and under the tree was a doll in a box, covered with cellophane. I told Tanya it was a Mama doll, because that's what I wanted it to be. A Mama doll cried Maa-maaa when you turned it over on its tummy. We had just got out of bed to look at it properly, when a woman came in and we did not even know her.

'Get back into bed and don't touch what doesn't belong to you.'

The doll was not hers either, but I didn't say that. I said

'The doll is for us from Father Christmas.'

'Might not be. Might be for someone else - you don't know, do you? Now get back into bed.'

'It must be for us - who else could it be for?'

'Your Mother. It might be for your Mother.'

I knew she was wrong. I knew she was mad and she didn't belong in our house. Grown-ups didn't have dolls. Or if some of them did, our Mother wasn't one of them. This strange woman, whom I never saw after that night, was one of the growing number of unreliable and foolish adults who appeared ever more frequently. Billie always made sense, but she seemed to have less and less influence over what happened. As soon as I was big enough, I was going to rescue her and Tanya and seize control of our lives. We were going to live properly, in a house with just us, and have a real Daddy.

New Year 1948

I am asleep on this side and Tanya is asleep on the other side. Deep at night is grown ups' time, and it is naughty for children to be awake at night, because it's dark. Outside the window the big London sky is dark blue. And inside our bedroom, a bright wedge of light opens the door into a big, bright triangle. Here is Billie, in a turban, its knot tied in a bow on top of her head, so she looks like Mummy Rabbit. She creeps in to kiss me and wakes me up. Unless I am already awake, which I might be. She bends over and says

'Happy New Year, darling.'

I can taste her lipstick. There is another grown up outside. I cannot ask what Happy New Year means because it is night and I am a child.

Summer 1949

Uncle Frank comes to stay, and looks after us. He shows us the trick with the flannel on the side of the bath. Tanya and I sit in the huge bath in our high and gloomy green North London bathroom, Uncle Frank holds up a towel for me.

'Are you ready?'

'Yes.'

'Right, young lady – out you come – wheee!'

And he wraps me in the towel, catches me under my arms and lifts me, like an angel and giggling with joy, up over his head and - wheee – down on to the towel he has folded on the green lino to serve as a bath mat. Uncle Frank and I go 'wheee' and Tanya, still sitting in the bath, joins in and we are all laughing. Then he dries me, puts my pyjamas on and I sit on the chair, because now it is Tanya's turn.

Up goes the towel.

'Are you ready?'

Of course she is, but Tanya is only little, so she forgets to say 'Yes' and goes 'wheee' and he lifts her high over his head.

We love Uncle Frank, he stays for a few weeks, and then, like Daddy, Mr. Mottiwalla and all the other lodgers, he is suddenly gone.

I went briefly to a Nursery School where there was a sandpit, then it was time to start Big School. As soon as I turned five, I was enrolled at The Grafton School, Grafton Street N7. Billie was very busy cooking breakfast for the lodgers in the mornings, and had Tanya to look after as well, so taking me to school was a problem. The first day she took me herself, showing me the way and making sure I knew how to cross the Holloway Road. In 1949 the Holloway Road was nowhere near as busy as it is now, but it wasn't a sleepy country lane either, so she told me to look right, left, then right again before crossing the road. The next day she sent me off to school by myself, but to be sure I was safe, followed me. When I reached the Holloway Road, she watched me step straight out into the traffic and under a lorry. Fortunately, it was a big lorry and the wheels went either side of my small body. I have a vague memory of being on the ground with the smell and roar of traffic, black sticky road in my face and big wheels either side of me, nothing more.

So, because there was nobody to take us to school, in October 1949, Tanya and I went into Care permanently. I asked my Mother a few times over the years, for the real reason. At first, she maintained that it was my failure to negotiate traffic unaccompanied, when I was just five, and for many years this was the official version. Throughout my childhood, I accepted and believed that therefore it was my fault that Tanya and I lost our Mother and our home.

Even in those days, when children were not nearly as protected as they are now, few people would have expected a child of five years and one month to cross a busy main road alone. Not until my late thirties did I start to think about it properly. Surely, someone among our many lodgers could have walked me to school? Were there no other children going to the same school whose mother could have taken me? What about my Nanna and Grandad, my Uncles Bill and Jack, all of whom lived just around the corner?

And if that was the real reason why couldn't we come home again once we were old enough to walk to school alone?

Later Billie said different things. Her sister Marie had told her Reedham was a very good school, that we were lucky to get in. That she had had no idea how bad it was, how unhappy we were. And finally, in 1984, she screamed down the phone 'I couldn't get you out of there – I couldn't get you back!'

'Were we in Care then?' I asked her.

'Never – you were never in Care.'

'How come you couldn't get us out then?'

'You won't be happy till you've destroyed me, will you? Why can't you forget the past? Why do you have to keep going on and on about it? Why does it matter?'

I think Billie found childcare very difficult, and used every opportunity to escape it. Several weeks before Tanya's birth at the end of October 1945, she sent me to my Grandmother – her mother's – while she went for several weeks to the Home for Unmarried Mothers in Welwyn Garden City, where Tanya was born. I don't know how or why she went there, but the letters she wrote to my father from there every day, reveal that it was some kind of institution, and that she was in no hurry to collect me.

2

Arrival at Reedham

September 1949

'YOU can't wear your own clothes in here – you've got to
put them on. Look - they all have your number on. You
are number 17. Go on, put them on now'.

On the bed which is now mine, lies a pile of clothes which
are not new and do not belong to me. A pair of navy blue
lock knit knickers, elasticated waist and legs, a small pocket
at the top of the right leg. Inside, against the small of the
back, a thick pad of labels has built up, each with a different
label in marking ink. More recently, a wide, white tape
label has been stitched over the smaller ones, on which has
been written the number 64. The six has then been changed
to an eight, then the 84 crossed out and 17 written next to
it. Over the years these knickers have been laundered
hundreds of times, the navy has faded, the fabric is soft and
quite thin in places. The gusset is slightly stained. The
waistband is overstitched in different threads, where the
elastic has been replaced many, many times (later I learned
how to do this: unpick a small part of the waistband hem,
draw out the slack and broken elastic, secure new elastic
on safety pin, use pin as bobbin to thread through, re-sew
hem). These knickers are folded and have been placed with
a white vest and a pair of socks on the end of my bed. I am
now Number 17. These are now my knickers. Reluctantly

I put them on, and then the rest of the clothes. My own clothes are gone.

People worry about my hair. They gather around me in groups, discussing it.

'You can't keep those plaits you know, they're not allowed in here.'

I'm a big girl of five. The feeling that I am unacceptable in some way is uncomfortable, but I've never had my hair cut, so it is hard to imagine how I could be parted from the plaits. Even as I sit in this classroom, watching a girl on a high chair, a white sheet tied around her neck, having her hair cut, it doesn't seem possible. It is my hair, how can somebody else – a complete stranger - cut it off? The complete stranger is a woman who wears her own hair in an all round sausage curl, which starts behind one ear, dips to her hairline, goes all the way round the back and ends up behind the other ear. All this is captured in a hair net, except for another, separate sausage curl at the front, which remains free, and wobbles. About six of us sit at classroom desks, waiting our turn. The girl next to me asks if I will cry when my hair is cut, but I don't reply. I still don't see how it can happen.

'Let's have those plaits next.'

It is over very quickly. She just has time to say:

'What beautiful hair you have – shame to cut it off.'

And my two plaits are on the floor. I get the standard, straight all round Children's Home haircut. Fortunately, I cannot see my reflection in the mirror very well, and anyway, now I look like all the other girls.

Reedham Orphanage was an imposing grey edifice atop a high hill, visible for miles around. It was founded in 1858 by Dr Andrew Reed, a non-Conformist Minister and serial founder of philanthropic institutions. By the time he built The Asylum for Fatherless Children, Reed already had The London Orphan Asylum and The Infant Orphan Asylum on his CV, and he went on to create The Asylum for Idiots and The Royal Hospital for Incurables. Given that he died in 1862, only four years after Reedham opened, he appears to have had a serious Asylum founding habit. After his death in 1862, the Asylum's name was changed to Reedham Orphanage in his honour, and the surrounding area became known by that name too.

Tanya and I had arrived wearing identical navy jumpers, each with a row of little white birds across the chest, and black and white checked skirts Billie had made from an old skirt of her own. Our shoes were different though, Tanya had black patent shoes, I had my beloved red lace ups with the squishy soles. My hair was – for the moment at least - in plaits, Tanya's straight, dark hair was short, with a fringe.

A jolly young woman with dark curly hair took us down a long corridor with red and black chequered tiles, into a huge bathroom, where three baths were arranged lengthways down the centre of the room. She bathed us together, and I showed her the trick with the wet flannel that my Uncle Frank had taught me when he looked after us, and she thought it was really good. She wrapped a towel around me, lifted me out and dried me, then did the same for Tanya. She was friendly and sensible, and I thought she would look after us, but I never saw her again, because she worked in the Infants section and, at nearly five and a half, I was in the Juniors.

Then I had to say goodbye to Tanya, which I did not want to do. I knew we would not be living at home with Billie any more, but never thought I would lose Tanya again as well. I was taken far away, along endless red and black corridors, to the Junior Dormitory, which was so big I could not even see the other end. The row of beds down each side stretched into the distance, getting smaller and smaller, all the beds exactly the same: narrow iron bedsteads painted black, red blankets on top tucked in with hospital corners, white pillow slip, white sheet folded down and tucked in. All the sheets showed exactly the same amount of white across the top. Each bed had a wooden cabinet by it, which, I was soon to learn, was where you had to put your clothes after you had folded them, and which also served as a bedside table.

I felt anxious at the thought of sleeping in that big room in a bed without Tanya. Ever since she had been too big for the cot, she and I had shared a bed at home, sleeping end to end. Except when she had been sent to Hertfordshire and I'd been sent to Essex, and never knew when I would see her again. When we were finally reunited, I had believed it would be forever. I explained to someone that I usually slept in a bed with my sister.

'Well you can't do that here!'

My bed had a rubber sheet under the bottom sheet, which at Reedham was called a 'mattress'. I felt humiliated - I had not wet the bed since I was a baby. I lay alone and awake for ages, longing for Tanya. During the night, the sheet became dislodged and I lay on the cold rubber. After the second night I did not move around too much, and eventually the 'mattress' disappeared.

In Miss Edie's Junior Class I was one of the tallest, so I sat at the back. I could not see the writing on the blackboard, was sent to the Sanatorium to have my eyes tested, declared short-sighted and soon issued with National Health pink-rimmed wire glasses. Thus my appearance changed very quickly. I soon forgot about the plaits, and the glasses helped me to see better. The real distress came from the sudden difference in the way people reacted to me. I had been a charming, golden haired, rosy-cheeked child, loved by the whole world, whose every smile was returned. Suddenly I was a snotty nosed, four eyed kid, one of dozens, dressed in ill fitting, secondhand clothes. Suddenly, I was nothing.

Reedham staff will have seen a vain, self-righteous prig, a little madam with a middle class accent who deserved to be taken down a peg or two. Certainly, I suffered for my accent and very soon acquired the approximately cockney accent of everyone else: Estuary English. I retreated into myself, became a sloppily dressed kid with dirty fingernails, a runny nose and permanently scabbed knees.

We all had numbers. Tanya was number 23. Your number was often used instead of your name, and the corridors would ring with 'Number 17 you're wanted'. Your number was also sewn inside all your clothes, which were issued once (blouses or dresses) or twice (vest, knickers and socks) a week. It was stamped on the instep of your shoes; after the number of the previous owner had been XXXXed out. We rarely got new shoes or clothes, but as we grew, they were passed on. Once I saw one of the infant boys in one of our own navy jumpers with the little white birds, and felt outrage. Didn't they know it was a girl's jumper?

I did not know how or when I would see Tanya again. When I asked, I was told she was in the Infants, but where was that? It took ages before I found out where she was and discovered a way of seeing her.

Although only 18 months younger than me, at three and a half she was an Infant, and in a separate wing. If you had a brother on the Boys Side or a younger sibling in the Infants, you were not actually forbidden to talk to them, but you were not encouraged either. The only scheduled times for us to meet were once a month on Visiting Days, and I would never have seen her except by accident or unless I made an effort.

The window to the Infants Playroom looked out over the Girls Playground, but was very high up. I would climb along the front of the building and peer over the huge stone windowsill in the hope of glimpsing her. This began as fun, because I saw others doing it. It was like rock climbing. The Victorian, grey stone building had lots of ledges and plinths for footholds, and if I started on the steps outside the front door of the Girls Side, and worked my way sideways using all the hand and footholds, I could get around the corner until finally I was hanging on the broad stone windowsill of the Infants Playroom. Now all I had to do was haul myself up on my hands, so my arms were straight by my side and my head just high enough to see in the window. Sometimes she was in there, playing or eating, and sometimes the room was empty.

Once I just knocked on the Infants door and asked if I could see my sister and they let me in to play with her and the other Infants for a while. I could not go in myself, I had to knock because the door handle on the infants door was very high up - almost at the ceiling - so no child could reach it. Somebody said this was to stop them running away.

Having succeeded once, I tried again from time to time. Sometimes they let me in, sometimes they didn't. When I saw her, my first and strongest feeling was love and joy, joined swiftly by a longing for home and our mother. Tanya embodied home and everything we had lost. She was as familiar as my mother, part of her, part of us. I remembered seeing her again when Billie and I collected her from Hertfordshire, her round face beaming down at me, her chubby legs at my eye level, when Billie brought the daffodils and we all went home together after being apart for so long. Seeing her brought on feelings of our family reuniting, the hope of things becoming normal again. Mending.

3

In the Shed and Visiting Day

SOON after we arrived at Reedham, I started to think about hurting a baby, someone smaller and weaker than myself. I imagined a smaller, weaker person who was frightened of me, and it gave me a funny feeling: cold, powerful, in control.

I got excited by the idea of being a wicked stepmother, or bad fairy, and seeing the sleeping baby princess and smacking her, cutting her, hurting her. Killing her. I was ashamed of these thoughts and they did not dominate my mental landscape. They were just there, in the hinterland, the badlands of my five-year-old mind.

Generally, we ignored the Infants, they were small. Smaller than we were. The only people in the entire school who were. As one of the youngest Juniors, I was at the base of the hierarchical structure, with the entire weight of the older Juniors, Seniors, Prefects, Mistresses and Matron pressing down upon me. While I sat shivering in the dark shed one rainy playtime, the Infants came out to play. I felt like a big girl, because I was in the Juniors, and Tanya came and sat next to me on the bench, rainy light slanting in from the two open sides of the shed.

'You're not my sister.' I said. This was the worst and most cruel thing I could think of. She cried, of course she cried, and I let her cry for a few minutes. Then I said

'Of course you are my sister really.'

Tanya was the only person in the world over whom I had any power. I only did this a few times and apologised for it a few years later. She said she didn't mind, because she knew I didn't mean it and had only cried so that I would stop saying it.

The very first Visiting Day after we arrived at Reedham was the first Saturday of October 1949. Everybody had to put on hats and coats and get ready. Like all the others, I wore a navy coat over my uniform, and a maroon beret with the Reedham badge on it, which had to be displayed at the front. We lined up by the door of Nightingale Dormitory and Miss Dean inspected us, adjusted our berets, made us re-tie our shoelaces and stand up straight. When she was satisfied, we all marched along the corridor to wait in the Front Hall – and there was Tanya! So we both believed that this was the visit: we were allowed to play together for the afternoon. We were so emotional about this, that we were reprimanded.

'Calm down you two, you're getting over-excited, just sit quietly and wait.'

We were not sure what we were waiting for, but various adults walked through the front door, in ones and twos, and each elicited a cry of recognition from one of the waiting children. Usually followed by hugging and laughter, but not always. Some of the little boys, dressed in maroon blazers and Reedham ties, shook hands with their mothers instead. There was a new atmosphere of holiday, of Saturday afternoon, of love and family. Tanya and I were part of this, happy just to be together, till someone said:

'Hello you two.'

It was Billie, our own Mother.

We burst into tears, we ran to her, we clung to her, and inhaled the perfume of home. It all made sense now. We were wearing hats and coats because she had come to take us home.

She seemed very pleased to see us too, although she did not

cry, but she was visibly shocked by our appearance. My haircut and glasses upset her dreadfully.

'Penny, why are you wearing glasses? And where are your plaits? Where has all your lovely long hair gone – how could you let them do that to you?'

I did not know the answer to this, so I said nothing. Or maybe I told her they did not ask permission, they just did it. She told me that I should have said:

'Mummy doesn't want my hair cut, thank you.'

She was very confident that if I would only speak up, the staff would listen and do as I asked. She explained that it was only my failure to make myself clear which resulted in these misunderstandings.

She gave a hand to each of us and we stepped outside on to the drive.

'Now then, where shall we go this afternoon?'

We laughed at her joke, because of course we know where we are going.

'We're going home with you Mummy.'

'No, not today darlings, this is just Visiting Day. Today we can go out together until 6 o'clock. That's when we have to be back. I think it would be nice to go to a tea shop.'

This was a blow, but we were three and five years old, we lived in the moment. We never knew what would happen next anyway. Billie was here now, and we were all walking hand-in-hand down the long drive away from Reedham. We were going out to a Tea Shop. Six o'clock was hours away.

In the Tea Shop we had toast and jam and cake. Billie drank tea, which she liked strong, without sugar. We could choose between milk and orange squash. We both chose orange squash and told her all about Reedham. She explained again, that if we only spoke up more, the staff would listen.

'Just tell them, darling. Next time, say: 'Mummy does not want me to have my hair cut.' And you must also ask them what happened to all the nice clothes I sent with you. That gymslip is far too big for you, and it has food stains down the front. And what's Tanya wearing, for heaven's sake?'

Tanya beams at us both, jam all round her mouth.

'Tell them you want your own clothes back, they can't let you go out looking like that.'

'Everybody has to wear the same, Mummy. We all have to wear gymslips.'

I could tell she was ashamed of our appearance. Tanya was just wearing a second hand dress and cardigan, short beige socks and brown lace up shoes. She was wearing her own coat, though. But I was in the grey shirt, navy gymslip, grey knee socks and black lace up shoes in which I was destined to spend most of my childhood.

It was a wonderful afternoon. Billie told us all the family news, who was getting married, who was expecting a baby. Now that she didn't have to worry about looking after us, she had stopped serving breakfasts after 7.30am and started work as a secretary in London. She told us all about the office, and the funny things her boss said. We all told jokes and laughed, we adored her, she was more fun than anyone else in the world.

We walked back up the drive to the front door, and it was time to say goodbye. Mummy was going home on her own, and we had to go back to this – this – place. We clung to her, we began to wail:

'Don't go Mummy. Let us come home with you. Take us with you. Don't go.'

'I have to go now, darlings. But I will write you a letter and I will see you again next Visiting Day. Don't cry.'

She unpeeled our arms from around her. The front hall was full of children saying goodbye to their mothers, some sobbing and begging to be taken home.

After the first few Visiting Days, I stopped crying and pleading, although Tanya, who had just had her fourth birthday, continued a little longer. As soon as we said goodbye to Billie, we had to say goodbye to each other as well, and it came to me that all this crying and pleading was useless and even undignified. I began to feel that I was degrading myself by begging, especially as it proved completely useless.

However, until I was about eight, I still cried myself to sleep for the first few nights at the beginning of term, but quietly. Further down the dormitory I would hear other smothered sobs. It was like this at the start of every term, and after two or three nights, most of the crying stopped. From the dormitory, I could hear trains rumbling close, then rumbling away into the distance, towards London I imagined. Every time I heard one, I thought 'My Mum might be on that train', even on days when I knew she couldn't possibly. I didn't know where she was, so she might have been on that train, mightn't she? And she might be on the next one. So the sound of a train was always friendly, because it just might be a link with her.

We became used to Visiting Day, and learned what to expect. We knew that parents were allowed to visit us once a month for half a day. It was always 2-6pm on the first Saturday in the month. Waiting for Billie, we sat on the radiator in Class 4, gazing out of the window. My bum bones fitted into the radiator grooves, the separating part sat comfortably up my arse. Tanya on my left, we sat right up against the window, our feet on the pipe, watching the front drive. The others had all gone now, a few were five or ten minutes late, but our mother was always late, usually about 20 minutes. We knew that.

In front of the window was a strip of green lawn, striped by the lawnmower (*children are not allowed on the grass at any time*) then a wide gravel path (*do not kick the gravel*) then a high hedge, taller than any person. Tall, but thin and therefore semi-transparent. People walking up the drive could be glimpsed through the hedge before they turned left and emerged into full view. They flickered along, heralding their height, their colours and the size of their group. So we stared at this hedge. 'Here she comes!'

We never developed the insurance which saves you from feeling let down. So every time there was a bright flicker - a red coat for example - with flesh coloured stockings and high heels - we said 'Here she comes!' to each other even though we knew she did not own a red coat. She might have bought one. She might have borrowed one. When the figure emerges and is revealed as an older, fatter woman, we are not at all dismayed, because she would be the next one. Or the next.

She always came eventually, and we were always ecstatic to see her. She was the prettiest and most elegant of all the mothers. Her clothes were bright and fashionable, her handbag always matched her high-heeled shoes, and her lipstick was always bright. And she was always so delighted to see us.

4

Reedham Starts the Day

'COME along girls, it's ten to seven'

Miss Henderson is on duty this morning. She is strict and Scottish with a huge fat bosom and skinny legs. I'm as scared of her as I am of Matron. Miss Henderson marches down the dormitory in her high-heeled brogues, shaking the shoulders of anyone still in bed. I jump up quickly before she has the chance to notice me. As she passes my bed, her eyes register that I'm already up and scrambling into my vest and knickers. Somebody is whispering down the end.

'Shut up!' shouts Miss Henderson. 'No talking. Get your vests and knickers on and strip your beds, double quick.'

She swivels round quickly to face my end of the room and I stand transfixed, terrified.

'Penny Wardman, dreaming as usual. Don't just stand there, get that bed stripped.'

'I've got to put my shoes and socks on first Miss.'

'Don't answer me back, strip that bed.'

I start folding each blanket up in the required pattern and laying it over the end of the bed, finishing with the top sheet folded on top of them. The wooden floor is quite rough in places, and we are always getting splinters. That's why I always put my shoes on first. I try to remember to walk carefully.

'Get a move on!' Miss Henderson shouts to the dormitory

in general, as 36 girls in white vests, navy knickers, grey knee socks and black lace up shoes, strip their beds, sliding expertly on the polished wooden floor as they dart around, folding quickly. As soon as my bed is done, I get my socks and shoes on and stand at the end of my bed. Luckily, I'm not the last, Laura Bell has lost one of her socks and Enid Wood is still stripping her bed slowly, as though still asleep. We all stand in silence, waiting for them.

'When Number 36 is *quite* ready, we can lead off.'

Laura Bell's normally white and greasy face is red.

'I can't find my other sock, Miss.'

'You haven't looked properly. Turn your cabinet out. Go on, get everything out. The rest of you, lead off.'

Those whose beds are on the far side go first, in single file, followed by those with beds in the middle, then those on the near side and finally, the three at the end. We go past the cupboards, past Miss Henderson's room, then turn right for the toilets and washroom.

Laura Bell stays behind, miserably emptying her cabinet and going through everything again.

The washroom is circular, with small round white washbasins set into a black slate counter all around the walls. Some of the wash places face out of the window, but the glass is opaque so there's no view. A small, double wooden shelf runs round the room at our eye level above the basins; the bottom shelf has holes at intervals for toothbrushes. On the outside of this shelf, above each basin, numbers are painted in white. Number seventeen is next to the first window. Underneath the shelf, my flannel hangs on its hook. Except for Susan Partridge, who has a tube of Punch and Judy toothpaste (banana flavour) from home, we each have a standard issue round blue tin of Gibbs Three Castles toothpaste. I open mine, run my toothbrush under the tap, then rub it round on the cake of toothpaste to make a nice pink foam.

In the centre of the room is a circular wooden structure with a mirror in the top and hooks to hang our towels on. The mirror, which is about nine inches deep, runs all the way round the top, and slants downwards towards us. We all turn round to watch ourselves cleaning our teeth in the mirror. This infuriates Miss Henderson.

'How many times do I have to tell you lot, get away from that mirror. It is not necessary to watch yourself cleaning your teeth. Turn round and bend over the basin. And you Number 17, you're no exception to the rule.'

That is one of her favourite expressions 'no exception to the rule.' I turn round, rinse my teeth, then remove my flannel dried stiff, from its hook. It has a loop in one corner, and a tape with 17 on in faded marking ink, and it has dried in a long thin diamond shape. I put the black rubber plug in my basin, watch the old, broken chain settle around it and push the tap, bracing myself with one leg back to exert enough pressure. All around the circle, girls are doing the same, creating a Busby Berkeley effect, if you imagined looking down from the ceiling. The problem is there is only enough water pressure to run two or three taps at a time, and we somehow have to negotiate who will go first without talking to each other. A trickle of water wets and softens my flannel. The soap is green: it has been cut into cakes with a cheese wire from bars about 15 inches long. In the morning, we only wash our face neck and ears. Miss Henderson usually inspects everybody before they leave the wash-room, but this morning she's got Laura Bell and her lost sock to think about, so she puts us on our honour. This is another of her favourite expressions.

'You girls are on your honour to wash properly because I haven't got time to inspect you this morning. Get back to the dormitory now and get dressed.'

The toilets are on the right before you get to the washroom. They are in the same room: three white pans, set into one mahogany bench. There had not been a free one before, so after I have washed, I slip on to the mahogany bench and slide around till I'm over one of the pans. I thought Miss Henderson had gone back to see to Laura Bell, but suddenly she is standing above me, fuming.

'I saw you Penny Wardman, going to the toilet after you've washed. How many times have I got to tell you, you wash after the toilet, not before, you dirty little tyke. Go and wash all over again and be quick about it.'

She stands and watches as I get off the toilet and pull my knickers up. Her lips are pursed, and her orange lipstick has made pleats round her mouth.

'Wipe yourself for goodness sake.'

She's after me this morning. It's usually Laura or me. I tear a few pieces of Izal from the toilet roll.

'Only two pieces of toilet paper, you're not at home now.'

She grabs the paper, removes the surplus pieces, screws them up and throws them in the other toilet pan. Then she hands the remaining two back to me, watches briefly while I wipe myself with them, says 'Now go back and wash again!' and marches out. It's Laura's turn now.

We make our beds up: hospital corners, sheet turned down and tucked in neatly. We stand by our beds until everybody is ready and the beds have been inspected. Miss Henderson gives the order to go downstairs. We clatter in our big black shoes down the huge staircase, which spirals widely down from the Tower (out of bounds) down to the hall outside the Staff Room, along the red and black corridor to the Girls Playroom and a few minutes of free time till the first whistle goes and it's time to line up in the Playroom, ready to march into the Dining Hall for breakfast.

5

Holidays

Summer 1952

TANYA and I are in the British Museum Tea Shop, having tea with the nice man we have just met. He is quite short for a grown up, with neatly combed dark hair and a light grey suit. He's really friendly and generous. The waitress brings a pot of tea for three and the nice man asks her to bring scones, jam and a plate of cakes.

'You'd like that, wouldn't you girls?'

'Yes, please!' we reply in unison.

We met the nice man in the Egyptian Mummy section, which is our favourite. We always go to see Ginger first. He is from Egypt and it says on the label he died over 5,000 years ago. He lies in a big glass case, in the centre of the room, curled up on his left side, like a baby. He might even be sucking his bony thumb. He fascinates us: he is yellowy brown, skin shrivelled over bone, yet recognisably human, with a few tufts of curly gingery hair. This is what we will look like one day. This is what our Dad might look like now.

That's the other reason we love Ginger. He arrived at the British Museum in 1901, and we know, because Billie has told us, that as a boy, our father also spent ages at this very glass case, staring at Ginger.

Then we walk slowly around the brightly day-lit room, with

its windows in the high ceiling, where the Mummies stand tall around the perimeter. A few have been opened, but we read on the typed labels that exposing them to light and air causes them to decay, and for this reason, the Museum no longer opens the painted cases, shaped like human bodies. We are discussing this when the nice man comes up to us.

'Hello girls, are you here on your own?'

'Yes' I reply. I always answer for both of us, because I'm the eldest. I am eight and Tanya is six and a half.

'It's nearly tea time, you must be hungry – would you like to go to the Tea Shop?'

He wants to know our names, how old we are, where we live, where we go to school, all the normal questions that adults ask, but unlike most adults, he really seems interested in the answers. He leans forward as I speak, his dark eyes wide open, fixed upon me. He wants to hear about our parents, and our family. I start chattering away, until the arrival of the scones and cakes shuts me up. There is a meringue on the plate and I want it.

So does Tanya.

'You can have it if I can have that.' she says, pointing to the chocolate cup cake.

'Alright' I reply, but the nice man says

'Why not have a meringue each'?

He calls the waitress again, and asks her for another meringue. He encourages us to eat all we want, which turns out to be quite a lot.

Once we are replete, sitting back on our chairs, buzzing with sugar, he asks again if we are on our own.

'Yes, Mummy is at work, so...'

Tanya kicks me hard under the table, and says

'Our Mummy is waiting for us downstairs – don't you remember Penny, she said she would leave work early and meet us downstairs?'

She kicks me again. Suddenly I understand. I am so used to Tanya going along with whatever I say and do, that on the rare occasions she takes the lead, I am shocked. But I am beginning to realise that in many ways she is far more sensible than I am. She has remembered what I have forgotten, that we should not talk to strangers, however nice they are.

I jump up with a loud and theatrical cry:

'Good Heavens Tanya, we'll be late! Mummy will be waiting for us down by the front entrance. Come on!'

Tanya jumps up too, I grab her hand, gabble:

'Thank you very much for the tea' and we leg it down the wide stone stairs as fast as we can go. We don't stop running till we reach Holborn Tube station.

When Billie got home we told her all about our slap up tea and our clever escape. She was highly amused.

'Why on earth did you run away like that? That was very rude, you know.'

She said that if he had a nice accent and was wearing a good suit, there can't have been much wrong with him. She explained that if someone treated to you a meal, you were expected to make polite conversation with them, not to run away as soon as you'd eaten. She thought we were very funny, and a bit silly to make such a drama out of it.

There were three holidays a year from Reedham: three weeks each for Christmas and Easter, and six glorious long weeks in the Summer. The excitement began to build about a week before going home day. There were special, seasonal songs and chants for these times:

No more school, no more stick
No more stinking arithmetic
No more Latin, no more French
No more sitting on the old school bench

In groups of five or six, arms around each other's shoulders, we stamped with our big, black lace-up shoes around the playground like a hysterical chorus line, inventing new and childishly obscene variations, getting ourselves in the mood.

Tanya and I were always in the London Bridge Party. A staff member would accompany between ten and twenty children on the train from Reedham station to London Bridge. The journey was only about half an hour, and parents or guardians would be there to meet us. When I was about ten, Billie said we could find our own way, and sent the money for our tube fares, so that she did not have to take time off work. Now, instead of getting out at London Bridge with all the others, and waiting for Billie, Tanya and I stayed on the train to Charing Cross, from where we could take the Bakerloo line to Kilburn. We would lug our suitcases down the steps from the British Railway station to Villiers Street, along to the tube station, buy our tickets and – being careful to catch the Stanmore train – arrive at Kilburn Station. From there, it was a long walk up Shoot Up Hill to our house, 22 Minster Road, but we knew the way, and were always so happy to be coming home we hardly felt tired. We found the back door key under the mat, let ourselves in and immediately raided the kitchen.

It was a huge house. We had the basement flat, and the garden, and all the upstairs rooms were let, I think there were seven in all. Billie served breakfasts in our dining room downstairs until about 8.00am, when she would dash off to work all day as a secretary in the West End. She only ever worked as a Personal Secretary, which meant working for one man. This was the most prestigious kind of secretarial job. Those lower down the ranks worked for two or three men, and those in the Typing Pool or on Reception, were lower still. Bosses were men and secretaries were girls, regardless of the age of either. When Billie was about 36, and applied for a new job at Matthew Hall, a US engineering firm, she took ten years off her age. She may or may not have mentioned that she had two children. For the rest of her working life, she was ten years older than she claimed.

Billie had shorthand and typing, and spoke several

languages. She also looked the part. She always had a trim figure and dressed well, and she earned a very good salary. She recounted to us once a conversation with Uncle Frank, who had urged her to apply for a particular job. He said:

"You could earn as much as £15 per week!"

To his consternation, she replied

"But I already earn more than that now."

When we were home for the holidays, we would help with serving breakfasts, and then we were free for the whole day. There were usually a few tasks and errands to do while she was at work, but we had a cleaner, so it was nothing more than a bit of shopping or ironing. We went through everything in her wardrobe and dressing table, becoming expert at replacing things exactly as we found them. We dressed up, conducted cooking experiments in the kitchen, listened to the BBC Home Service and read a lot of books. We took long walks down to Kilburn High Road, looking at the shops, or took the 16 bus to Selfridges – we could spend whole days there – just looking, just breathing it all in. About once a week Billie suggested a museum, leaving written instructions on which museum and how to get there, and a ten shilling note for fares and lunch.

Holiday weekends were when we visited family – but only Billie's family. Granddad Wardman, of whom Billie was very fond, had died suddenly two days before Christmas in 1949, and I don't think we saw Lizzie – our paternal grandmother - ever again after we moved to Kilburn in the early 50s. Visits were usually on a Sunday. We would take a tube, then a train to some suburb or other to have lunch with an aunt, uncle and cousins. All the cousins were female and friendly, and all seemed impossibly privileged. They lived at home, in their own houses, all the time, and took it for granted that they could talk to their parents any time, as if it were the most natural thing in the world. Perhaps our cousins visited us in London sometimes, I don't remember it. And although most of our uncles and aunts lived very near Reedham, apart from one

Visiting Day when Aunt Marie came, not once did any of them visit us there.

We would arrive on their doorsteps with our Reedham blazers and haircuts - me with pink National Health glasses - and our Reedham accents. Uncle Frank's wife Siobhan was the only one who actually mentioned this, she commented on it a lot, terrified that her own little girls would start speaking like us. We had not been aware of the change in our accents. Like all children, we learned to speak like those around us, and at Reedham, self-protection speeded up the process.

Soon after we arrived, a big girl grabbed my arm and hissed:

'You think you're everybody, don't you?'

I didn't know what to say. I didn't understand, and didn't reply, I just stared up at her terrifying, sweaty face.

'Miss la di lah, talking all posh, think you're better than everyone else, don't you?'

She yanked my arm up behind my back.

'Stuck up little madam – say you're sorry. Go on, say 'Sorry Miss'

'Sorry Miss'

So, very early, we learned two different accents, two different vocabularies, and that neither was acceptable in the other world.

Everyone was always happy to see Billie, she was very popular in her family. Tanya and I were welcomed for her sake, but I think we appeared a bit rough and wild to the genteel van Tinterens. They probably thought we didn't know how to behave. And they were right, we didn't.

6

Festival Day

THE high point of the Reedham year was Festival Day, held annually on a Saturday in June. According to the staff, the big deal about Festival Day was the attendance of The Lord Mayor of London, wearing his ceremonial robes and chain. Much of Reedham's income came from charitable donations, and the donors were entitled to visit the school and make sure we were all well behaved and grateful. Accordingly, every year, we all lined up along the front drive, standing to attention in our special new clothes, and the Lord Mayor, with his wife The Lady Mayoress, and several unidentified middle aged people, would walk slowly past, inspecting us as if we were troops. Matron and Mr Akehurst the Headmaster, in his academic gown, simpered in their wake. Shortly afterwards, the Lord Mayor and his entourage took their places on a raised platform erected in the Boys Playground and sat back to watch the orphans perform.

The main events were a display of Gymnastics by the boys and Skipping by the girls, but often there were other turns. On our first Festival Day – June 1950 - the Infants performed Nursery Rhymes, and I played opposite Tanya in the starring roles of that compelling drama *Polly put the Kettle On*.

I was Polly and Tanya was Suki. We wore mob caps, long skirts and aprons, and as the Infants stood in a circle singing, I walked to centre stage with a small, black kettle, and hung it on a hook on a tripod of three sticks above a very realistic fire of red and orange tissue paper, torn into flame-like strips. Then I walked back, re-joined the circle and we began the second verse:

'Suki take it off again.'

Tanya walked over to the tripod, removed the kettle and walked back to the circle, bringing this brief domestic drama to a triumphant close.

Hazel Rushworth was the Farmer's Wife, and the Three Blind Mice had tails fixed to their brown costumes by snap fasteners, so all Hazel had to do with her cardboard knife was pretend to cut, and with the other hand, and at the same time, pull the tails off. It required more action than my part, but my costume was better. We had all been well rehearsed, and enjoyed it enormously, but acting was our only artistic input. We were given clothes to wear, told what to say and do and we obeyed.

For us, the Lord Mayor's presence was nowhere near the best thing about Festival Day. It barely registered. The best and most important thing was that our mothers could come, but there were other treats: Festival Day food was much better, and we had new dresses to wear with white socks and sandals. There seemed to be flowers everywhere, and the Girls' Washroom on Festival Day mornings smelt like a florist's – our crazed and stained old washbasins filled with lilac, roses, lilies and carnations. Women we didn't know were busy arranging them in vases, and sometimes they would let us help them, till someone called our number or the whistle went.

There was also the novelty of unscheduled encounters. On Festival Day 1951, I saw a boy with fair hair called Oliver Hockey in the Girls' Playground. I told Billie he was my boyfriend, a bit foolhardy, since I had not yet informed Oliver of his new status. To demonstrate to Billie the strength of our affections, I ran up to him and threw my arms around his neck, crying:

'Oh Oliver!' in passionate tones.

'Gerroff!' said Oliver, who slipped out from under my embrace and ran for it.

Billie chortled:

'I don't think he knows he's your boyfriend, Penny.'

I went all red. It felt as though everyone had seen and I went hot with embarrassment for months afterwards, whenever I thought of it.

On another Festival Day in the early fifties, a group of girls ran up to me, shouting

'Here she is! This is Number 17!'

In their wake, two young women visitors, dressed as all women were on such a day, in pretty, full skirted, cotton dresses with matching accessories. They both wore little half hats - the latest thing - a crescent shape, which sat on the smooth back of the hair, allowing freedom to the curls all around. They both wore gloves, and of course, their handbags matched their shoes. I say 'of course' because matching shoes and handbag was as fundamental in those days as carrying a clean hankie.

'Are you Number 17?' asked one.

'Yes.'

'Here's sixpence, it's a rotten number!' she said, putting the small silver coin in my hand, and without another word, she and her friend stalked off on their high heels.

Birthdays were not marked in any way. Some people got a card and perhaps a parcel from home, and that was it – no presents, no cake, no *Happy Birthday to You* or celebration of any kind. Apart from Visiting Days and holidays, Festival Day was the best thing we had in the early fifties, and we all looked forward to it.

7

New York

May 1952

'NUMBER 17 - you're wanted'

'Who wants me?'

'Matron – you've got to go to Matron's Office.'

Matron sits at her desk, a typed letter in front of her. It looks like one of my Mother's letters.

'It seems your Mother has gone to New York. Did you know about this?'

'No Matron.'

Actually, Billie had mentioned that she was going to visit her eldest sister Tina in New York some time soon, but perhaps Matron won't like it if I had known and not told her. I can tell by the way she says 'New York' that there is something about this news of which Matron disapproves.

'This means she will not be able to visit you on Saturday, and she has arranged for your Aunt...' she peers down at the letter 'er...Marie, your Aunt Marie, to visit you and Tanya instead.'

'Yes Matron. Thank you Matron.'

'Where did she get the money from, that's what I want to know?'

'Don't know, Matron.'

'And pull your socks up girl. Tidy yourself up for goodness sake.'

'Yes Matron. Thank you Matron.'

'Go on - off you go then!'

On Saturday Auntie Marie and Uncle Dick arrive – in a car! I cannot remember being in a car before, and we sit carefully in it, awestruck, while Uncle Dick and Auntie Marie, sitting in the front, talk facing away from us. When required to speak, we address the backs of their heads. Auntie Marie talks most of the time, and asks few questions, so it is a comfortable day. She tells us she has made lots of delicious things for tea: sandwiches, fairy cakes and sausage rolls. They drive us back to their family home in Wallington, where we play with our cousins Susan, Frances and baby Judith in their neat bedrooms.

Visits to our cousins give us glimpses of authentic family life. Because they are my relatives, I have the feeling that if we had been lucky enough to live at home, this is what our lives would have been like. Should have been like.

Auntie Tina, Billie's eldest sister, moved to New York in 1940, and Marie, the second child, the family beauty, became the eldest in Tina's absence. She had married Dick Koenig in 1937, the only one of the eight van Tinteren siblings to have a formal white wedding. It seems to Tanya and me that Auntie Marie does everything perfectly. She is beautiful, and she's had a proper wedding to a man who is still alive. She even has photographs of this wedding displayed in her home, her lovely home, which is pin neat and full of imaginative touches, which express her femininity. She wears pretty, frilled aprons and is full of hints and recipes.

Everything in her home is a wonder and a model of its type. Auntie Marie tells us the continuing story of her house and how they live in it. Why she decided to have the kitchen redecorated, the colours she had considered, the decision she finally took. She explains the philosophy of her artfully haphazard china. You see it is in six colours, each one of which tones perfectly with all the others: orange, deep red, yellow, deep green, lime green and black. And look! You just pick up a cup, chosen at random, then a saucer, and maybe they will match but probably they won't, so you'd have a lime green cup and a deep green saucer and I'd have a deep red cup and a lime green saucer and the whole table has a quirky, haphazard quality which is very 1950s. The word for this is Contemporary.

She shows us her linen cupboard, how and where she keeps the table linen - this tablecloth and its matching napkins, goes with the contemporary china - bed linen here, towels there. This is how a proper house - which you, Penny and Tanya are not lucky enough to have - is organised. The girls put their dirty linen in here, and Auntie Marie puts it in the washing machine (they have a washing machine!) dries it on the line, irons it here, airs it on the clothes horse here and then folds it neatly in the linen cupboard.

They live in an impressive semi-detached house in Wallington, Surrey and give their cast off clothes to Tanya and me. Susan and Frances are allowed to live at home with their Mummy and Daddy, and although nobody ever tells Tanya and me that we are not good enough, not loved enough to live at home all the time, we feel it and we know it, simply because of the difference in the way they - and all our cousins - are treated. Susan and Frances do not wear glasses and can wear their own clothes all the time except when at school. They are indulged, their preferences considered. They can talk at mealtimes and do not have to eat all their food if they don't like it. They have a choice of two parents and can talk to either whenever they like. They have two toothbrushes each, one for the morning and one for the evening, which is correct oral hygiene. The bedcovers on their twin beds have tastefully contrasting frills and matching curtains and in their bathroom is a cork covered linen basket, which can also be used as a seat.

In all these ways, Tanya and I know that we are worth less.

Next time we saw Billie was the Summer Holidays, and she

told us all about her trip to New York. She brought us each a square powder compact, inlaid with Mother-of-Pearl and a child's size tartan umbrella. The umbrellas had transparent plastic handles in the shape of a dog's head. She also brought more of Sally and Ronnie's cast off clothes. Previously, cast-offs had arrived in parcels from New York, along with American sweets called candy, and novelties such as a bar of soap which floated, so you didn't lose it in the bath. The clothes were very interesting, but rarely suitable for anything we ever did. I remember a two-piece outfit, white with navy spots. The top half was like a bra, which you tied behind your back, and the bottom half was a very short wrap around skirt. I tried it on and looked in the mirror. It transformed me into a privileged American girl, off to spend a day on the beach. But it was a skirt, not a swimming costume, and there were no occasions in my life when I could wear it.

She had sailed on the Holland America Line, had stayed with Auntie Tina and Uncle Lou in their Manhattan apartment, and even had a temporary job in an office in the Empire State Building. Then she had stayed with them in their house on Fire Island, where she drank cocktails and got sunburned. For weeks, New York was all she talked of. And all that summer, when not taking out our compacts and powdering our noses, Tanya and I longed for rain, so we could parade about under our special, tartan umbrellas.

8

Mr & Mrs Garcia

1952

I don't remember the announcement itself, there may not even have been one, but one summer Saturday, several Reedham children – including Tanya and me - spent the day with "some nice people". We were dressed in our Sunday best: sprigged cotton dresses with half sashes and peter pan collars, white socks, sandals, maroon Reedham blazers. and berets.

There was the usual lecture to be on our best behaviour, to express our gratitude, to say please and thank you and not to disgrace Reedham's fine reputation, blah, blah, and then we marched to the Front Hall to wait. Tanya and I were delighted to learn that we would be going together, with the same "nice people". They turned out to be Mr. and Mrs. Garcia in a red car.

We sat in the back and they asked if we would like to see their home? What could we say? Yes, please was the only possible answer. We stopped at a shop for some groceries and when we arrived at their home, I offered to carry the groceries in. Their flat was post-war and modern, and up a few flights of steps, and somehow I dropped the bag and broke some of the eggs. Mrs. Garcia was so nice about it, said it didn't matter, but I could not stop apologizing, I knew that eggs were still on the ration. The flat was small and neat, and everything seemed very new. Mrs. Garcia was young and pretty, with dark curly hair. Mr. Garcia was short and a bit fat, with a red face and wavy ginger hair, but he was so kind and anxious to please, I did not allow myself to think of him as ugly. But he was, really.

We had tea and cake, and they asked us all about ourselves. They were surprised to hear that, although our father was dead, we were not homeless orphans, but had a mother, and a house already. They did not probe too deeply.

We had such a jolly afternoon with them in their sunny little flat, chatting away, helping set the blue flecked Formica table for high tea, all sitting down together at the table just like a real family in a poster or a book. We would have been about 7 and 9, and despite our accents, the Garcias must have seen two charming, chatty, middle class girls, anxious to please. We had no idea why we were there, but we were having a splendid time with unlimited food and lots of cake. But more important than that - unlimited attention. They really seemed to enjoy our company, and over 50 years later, that happy afternoon is with me still.

They drove us back to Reedham and said they hoped we would be able to come out with them again – perhaps to the pictures or the Zoo – would we like that? Oh, we would, we would! Mrs. Garcia may even have kissed us goodbye, although I don't actually remember it. I do remember that all the sweets they gave us were confiscated as soon as they departed.

Next Visiting Day, Billie told us that a letter had been forwarded to her by Reedham, from some people in Croydon called Garcia.

"Do you know these people?"

Tanya and I answered enthusiastically, yes we did they were very kind, we had been to their flat and had tea, and they were really nice and wanted to take us out again.

Billie seemed mildly amused and slightly indignant.

"They were asking if they could adopt you! I don't know

where they got the idea that you were available for adoption. Reedham has obviously misled these people entirely. I wrote back and said my daughters already had a mother, thank you."

Even if we had not heard the disdain in her voice, we knew Billie well enough to understand what she meant by "these people." The Garcias lived in Croydon and their address had probably revealed to Billie that theirs was a Council flat.

We never saw the Garcias again, but I enjoyed the idea that we were wanted enough to be offered a place as part of a real family, even though, obviously, we could not accept.

9

Littlehampton

About 1953

THE first year of the Littlehampton outing nobody knew what
to expect. Towards the end of Tea Time one June day in about
1953, Mr Bristow banged his cane on a table in the Dining Hall,
and announced that we would all be going on an outing to
Littlehampton. Every single one of us. He said it was
organised by the Guild of the Nineteen Lubricators, and came
out with the usual stuff about how lucky we were and how
grateful we should be. It sounded quite good, but you never
knew. Those Lubricators sounded very odd, and Reedham
often expected you to get excited about the direst things.

But once we had experienced the perfection of it, the very
name of the place made our hearts leap. When another visit to
Littlehampton was announced the following year, the
excitement was almost unbearable. Those of us who had been
the first time, described the day to recent arrivals with relish,
concentrating on the Fish and Chips, the unlimited Fun Fair
rides, but most of all, being able to ask for anything and getting
it. If anything, the second year was better than the first,
because the excitement began earlier. By the time
Littlehampton Day dawned, we were all very well behaved
coiled springs. Well behaved because the threat of not going
to Littlehampton had a magical effect.

Immediately after breakfast, we were lined up and marched

to the front drive, where several coaches were parked. Rules were relaxed, nobody could have stopped us from talking and anyway, the Uncles were there. That's what they asked us to call them, and they wanted us to talk to them! Apart from Visiting Day, we rarely had the chance to talk to an adult. Adults would say things to us, and we had to answer their questions, but weeks would often go by without an actual conversation with an adult. The Uncles did not know our numbers, they asked our names! They had names like Uncle Reggie and Uncle Charlie. They wore pinstriped business suits and we had one or two in each coach. As we set off, we each got a programme for the day - a proper printed booklet, explaining everything that was to happen on the outing. These had been printed, just for today, just for us. There were several different attractions at Littlehampton, all listed in the programme and we could choose which ones we liked. There was the Boating Lake, the Mini-Golf and the Miniature Railway, but what we all really wanted was the Fun Fair and the Big Dipper. All you had to do was ask an Uncle for one of the free tickets he had in his pocket. These tickets had also been specially printed, with 'Guild of the XIX Lubricators' in swirly writing, and the date. You took them up to any funfair ride and they were accepted. As soon as you got off the ride, you just ran up to an Uncle, asked for another ticket, and with a smile and a pat on the head he would produce another – sometimes three or four. The Uncles were easy to spot because even in the 1950s, nobody else wore pin striped suits in a fun fair. And they loved talking to us, listening to us, giving us free rides, holding our hands.

We had lunch in a special restaurant, with white tablecloths, paper napkins and salt and pepper on the table. We were allowed to sit where we wanted, and to talk. We had already seen the menu, because it was printed in the programme.

'Have you seen what we're having for dinner?'

'It says 'lunch' not dinner.'

'Yes, but we're having it at half past twelve, so it's dinner, must be.'

'Look, Fish and Chips, Jelly and Ice Cream.'

Like people in institutions and on restricted diets everywhere, we talked of food a lot. 'What is your favourite meal?' was a popular starting point for reminiscence. We were children and gastronomically conservative, so there really was only one answer:

'Fish and Chips, Jelly and Ice Cream.'

There were probably the usual worthy speeches before or after we ate, expressing humility and gratitude, but I don't think the Uncles kept us there for long. They knew we were desperate to get back to the funfair. So, full of our favourite lunch, we dashed straight back on the Big Dipper.

The Uncles also had different coloured tickets to buy rock, with 'Littlehampton' all through it, and candyfloss – all you had to do was ask. They never said 'You've just had one' they just smiled and doled out the tickets.

I was holding Uncle Reggie's big, warm hand, after three goes on the Big Dipper, and he had just bought about six of us a Candy Floss.

'Maybe you've had enough of the Funfair now, wouldn't you like to go on something else? Perhaps the Boating Lake, or the Miniature Railway?'

Enough of the Funfair? We hadn't been on the Waltzer or the Dodgems yet, or the Helter Skelter. The others all said:

'Please Uncle, can we stay at the Funfair – please?'

And because he was an Uncle, a Lubricator and bound on this special day to give us anything we wanted, he started handing out more free ride Funfair tickets. To do this he had to relinquish my hand. I missed it. I said:

'Can I go on the Miniature Railway with you Uncle Reggie?'

'Of course you can!'

The others ran off with their tickets, and I slipped my Candy

Floss sticky hand back into his dry and slightly rough one.

We had to wait a few minutes for the next train, and I held his hand all the time.

'How old are you, Penny?'

He remembered my name!

'I'm nine. Why do you take us all out?'

'We enjoy it – did you come last year?'

'Yes, it was really good, we all talked about it for ages afterwards. It was the best day of my life. Everyone said that. Why are you Lubricators?'

'We are all Oil men, we work in the City of London and we earn lots of money, so we like to share it around with children like you.'

'Why are you nineteen – I mean why do you have nineteen of you?'

'That's how many we were when we started our club, which is called a Guild, because we are in the City, and that's the City's name for a club. And oil is used for lubrication, so we called ourselves 'The Guild of the Nineteen Lubricators''.

While I was absorbing this, he asked:

'What happened to your Mummy and Daddy, Penny?'

'My Daddy's dead.'

'And your Mummy?'

'She lives in London.'

We climbed into the miniature train carriage. Uncle Reggie was a bit fat, so it was better that I sat on his lap. He smelt of wonderful things, cigars and Christmas, like my own uncles, but richer, somehow.

When the train lurched forward, I put my arm around his neck to steady myself so I wouldn't fall out. I was so full of sensation, I didn't even notice where we went on that little train. His big thighs were a substance beneath me, his big face close up and smiling. I couldn't remember being this close to a man before. The bristles on his skin where he had shaved were coming through all different colours: ginger, white, brown and black. He had grey hairs growing in his ears, and black hair in his nose. He did not have much hair on his head though, it was bald and shiny. His sharp, white collar cut into his red neck, and the shoulder of his jacket was sprinkled with dandruff.

His arm was around me, around my waist. I had not realised I had a waist before that. Just a small movement of my head and it was resting on his shoulder. When the train stopped, he stood up with me in his arms, and set me down on the ground.

Other children ran up to claim his hand.

Later there was High Tea, with sandwiches, cake and more Jelly and Ice Cream. Then we piled into the coaches to go back to Reedham. High on sugar, we giggled, screamed, threw ourselves at the Uncles. Well I did. On the way back, Uncle Reggie was in another coach, but I managed to slip into the seat next to Uncle Charlie. Uncle Charlie was more wiry. When the coach turned a corner, I leant against him and could feel his muscles.

When we arrived back at Reedham, there was yet another treat. We had to line up outside the Dining Hall to be given money. When we filed in, there was an Uncle, sitting at one of the tables, handing out vivid plastic purses, which closed with a bright, brass zip. One each.

'Thank you Uncle.'

The Guild of the Nineteen Lubricators stood around beaming. Inside each purse were four, bright, new threepenny bits, shiny and fresh from the Royal Mint with the new Queen's head and this year's date. We all thanked the Uncles again and waved goodbye. I kissed a few of them, they didn't seem to mind. As soon as they left, we all had to line up outside Matron's office. She had the Pocket Money Ledger out in front of her. We each handed in our four three penny bits, totalling one shilling, but we were allowed to keep the purses.

10

Born To Be Queen

The Coronation of Queen Elizabeth II: June 2nd 1953

I used to say 'I'm lucky having the same birthday as the Queen' without ever actually seeing where the luck came in. I said it because someone had once said it to me, and Reedham worshipped royalty, often in quite bizarre ways. In 1954, the summer after the Coronation, we were told that the Queen's train would be passing through Reedham station, and we would be allowed to stand on the platform and wave. If we were lucky, the Queen would stop the train, get out and greet us. The staff were tremendously excited about it, and so were some of the children. One of the pretty blonde girls - I think it was Angela Kindersley - was dressed up for the occasion, but precisely as what, nobody seemed sure. She wore a white gown made from a sheet or a tablecloth, and a crown or halo of silver paper. And she held what might have been a wand. Or a sceptre.

The train was due at about 2pm on a summer's day, so we were granted the afternoon off school. As soon as dinner was finished, we put on our maroon blazers and berets, making sure the school badge was in front, and set off in a crocodile down the back road. Maroon and gold were the school colours, and the school badge was in the shape of a shield, with the motto 'Charity Makes All One.' As a child, I never understood that motto, but I think I do now. I think it means that charity makes us all equal, and if I am right, I have never heard a more demonstrably untrue statement. Charity only emphasises difference and inequality, and those in a position to be charitable wouldn't want it any other way.

We had to stand on the platform as if for a group photograph, tallest at the back. Some kind of rostrum had been erected for Angela Kindersley to stand on, and a few older girls surrounded her, in the manner of handmaidens. We were there for some time, squinting down the sunlit railway track for the first glimpse of the Royal Train. I imagined it would be significantly larger than a normal train, and gold, like the coach. No doubt the interior would be lined in some costly, regal fabric - purple velvet most likely - and the Queen would be wearing one of her famous ceremonial outfits for the occasion. Perhaps the robes, with the imperial crown and sceptre. Or maybe nothing elaborate at all, just an ordinary ball gown and a simple tiara. The train would slow sedately to a halt, and she would alight with a lady in waiting and a courtier or two and shake hands with everybody. Well, with the staff, at least. And possibly, Angela Kindersley. I doubted that she would shake hands with all of us, and realised I would probably not get the chance to tell her that she and I shared a birthday.

While we were still waiting for the royal train, a normal train sped through the station and some of the children waved and cheered. The staff looked confused, briefly, and then joined in the cheering as the train disappeared.

'Come on you lot, back up the hill!'

What? Was that it? Apparently so. A normal train and it didn't stop. It didn't even slow down. Nobody had even glimpsed the Queen. Well, that's what they said at first. Later on, people started to remember that - in fact - they *had* seen her. She was frowning - apparently confused by Angela Kindersley. Understandable, really. What was that child doing several feet in the air on a suburban railway platform, mid-afternoon, dressed either as an angel, or an empress or the Statue of Liberty? But had they really seen the Queen, or had they just imagined it? After all, she was always frowning. In all the pictures we ever saw she was frowning, she had frowned throughout the Coronation, apart from the smiling and waving from the coach and on the balcony afterwards. Still, several girls got quite a bit of mileage out of saying that they had seen her and she had gone like this:

(mime of frown and wave) - no, no she went like this

(mime of mouth open, frown and hand frozen in the air) - no she didn't...

What was she wearing?

A blue dress and hat.

And gloves. And a crown.

She was wearing a simple, white evening dress, with long white gloves....

No she wasn't, she had a blue outfit, an assembly, and diamond ear rings and brooch and a white handbag and matching shoes.

What's an assembly?

It's French, it means a matching outfit.

Nobody had really seen her, of course. She probably wasn't even on the train. And if she was - so what? Still, it was an afternoon off school.

On the Reedham notepaper there was the Royal Coat of Arms, because the Queen was our Patron. This was explained to us solemnly from time to time, as if it were important news with which we should be impressed. I tried it on Billie during the holidays.

'The Queen is our Patron you know. At Reedham.'

'Really, dear?'

'What does it mean, being a Patron?'

'It means she lets them use her coat of arms on the notepaper, and things like that. It's like By Appointment. It impresses people, so they donate money.'

I still didn't get it really. Were there really people in the world who would look at the royal coat of arms on a letter and say to themselves:

'Oh look, the Queen is the Patron of this school, I really must send them some money right away.'

What I did know was that Billie was not keen on royalty, for the same reasons that she was not keen on Empire Day, Winston Churchill and God. In fact, everything we were taught at Reedham was ideologically suspect as far as she was concerned, but that didn't ever make her consider taking us away. She just told us that the people who cared for us and taught us were stupid. Well, we knew that.

Despite her place of honour on our notepaper, the Queen did not visit Reedham once during the 10 years I was there, and as far as I know she never did. Although sometimes letters of support or greeting were read out in church, usually on Festival Day, signed by a Lady in Waiting 'Her Majesty has commanded me to write...' I don't think she ever really knew that Reedham existed. As I grew older I realised that these apparently spontaneous missives were in fact replies to letters which Matron or the Committee had written, informing Her Majesty that the Reedham Festival Day would be held again this year, sending Loyal Greetings and humbly reminding her that she was a Patron of the School. Back would come the letter which the Lady in Waiting had been commanded to write and it would be read out to the awestruck congregation, as if the Queen had thought of it all by herself.

The build up to Coronation Day started in February 1952 when the King died. Mr Bristow announced it at breakfast. The staff looked stricken, and some of the older girls were in tears. A girl slightly older than me sat on the playroom bench and sobbed.

'He was a good King.'

I was almost eight and terribly impressed. That girl obviously knew a lot about Kings, because she was able to judge a good King from a bad one. I myself had no idea what kind of a king he had been, but tried the same remark out myself later that day with great success. A small group of prefects was standing in the corridor outside the playroom, talking quietly and dabbing their eyes. In my head I sang my tearjerker hymn, a verse from 'Oh God Our Help in Ages Past' which always made me cry in Church. It reminded me of my Father, of whom I often tried to dream, and whose death at the age of 30 meant I had to be in this place, instead of living a normal life at home.

Time, like an ever rolling stream
Bears all its sons away
They fly forgotten as a dream
Dies at the opening day.

Once my tears ducts were flowing, I sidled up to them and sobbed 'He was a good King.' This got them all going again. One of them put her arm round me and I joined in their delicious, lachrymose orgy. In those days, I would do anything to get in with the prefects.

Teachers put newspaper cuttings on classroom walls; first special souvenir editions of the Funeral with the Three Queens in black crepe veils; then a portrait of the new, young Queen, still dressed in mourning for her father, with such a heavy weight of responsibility on her shoulders. But, unwillingly and selflessly, she was taking on this difficult task, doing her duty. Being Monarch was a very difficult job, everybody said, '...and I wouldn't want to do it.' We all parroted this stuff to each other, as if we knew what we were talking about. Was I really the only one who thought that actually it was a very nice job: elegant clothes, servants, travelling, meeting people and shaking their hands? And the attention! The adulation! I would have done it. I was *dying* to do it. I had the right birthday. If she was so unwilling, she had only to say the word.

We told each other what a horrible job it was. 'You have to

shake hundreds of people's hands every day. That's why she wears the white gloves, to protect her hands. Under those gloves her hands are all bruised.'

'And she has to talk to complete strangers.'

'And she has to eat all the food that's put in front of her and pretend she likes it even when she doesn't.'

'And she has to watch people dancing and singing for hours on end, and she has to clap, even if she doesn't really like it.'

But I thought it sounded wonderful. We had to eat everything that was put in front of us at Reedham anyway, and pretend to like people and things when we didn't really. If she hated the job so much, why didn't she ask someone else to do it? Someone who would appreciate it and put her heart and soul into it. Someone who could smile like anything. Why didn't she ask me?

Coronation Day was to be June 2nd 1953 and everyone wanted red white and blue everything. Woolworth's sold all kinds of patriotic fancy goods, including Union Jack flags in all sizes, but what I longed for - what we all longed for - was red white and blue hair ribbon. At 3d a yard - from Woolworths - of course, it was more expensive than single coloured ribbon, but I thought it immensely glamorous. That summer, anything which combined those three colours in that order - with the white in the middle - gave me a thrill.

One tea time, just before the great day itself, we each found a Coronation mug by our plate. Mr Bristow informed us that Her Majesty the Queen had decreed that every child in the country should have such a mug, and that even orphaned children such as ourselves were not to be left out. He hoped we realised how lucky we were, and as well as the usual 'For what we are about to receive, may the Lord make us truly thankful.' he said a special grace, offering up our thanks to God and Her Majesty for our Coronation mugs. We all thought she had gone out and bought them especially for us. Out of her own money.

Coronation Day was a public holiday, so we had no school. It was also cool and quite rainy, which was a surprise really; a hint that the Universe was perhaps, indifferent to the great event. In the morning we visited all the Coronation displays in all the other dormitories, including those round the boys side - usually *extremely* out of bounds. It was an unsupervised tour too, and far more fascinating than their displays, which were very similar to ours, was simply seeing how the boys lived. The first thing you noticed was the smell. Boot polish, soap and Dettol. Everything about the boys' side was uncannily familiar, as if our own rooms had been subtly changed, as in a nightmare. The same, only different. There was more of everything, so the dormitories were longer and held more beds, the washrooms had more basins, and the toilets had more toilets. And urinals! They took some explaining! Girls who had brothers set us straight. It was interesting and yet depressing. Boys were terrifying, smelly and cruel, and all their clothes were grey.

After dinner, we watched it all on television, the whole school arrayed around the one, nine inch set in the Dining Room. It was quite impressive, but went on for ages. I was looking forward to the anointing, because apparently, the Archbishop of Canterbury was going to pour oil on her dress, and I wondered how she could put up with that. Then Richard Dimbleby explained that the anointing would take place under a canopy. Did that mean she had to take her dress off? In front of the Archbishop of Canterbury? I didn't - I couldn't - ask any of the mistresses about this, but I did ask what happened when the Queen wanted to go to the lavatory. We already knew that the Coronation ceremony would take all day, and that the poor, new Queen would be exhausted at the end of it.

'Miss, if the Coronation takes all day, what happens when the Queen wants to go to the lavatory?'

'Oh they make a lavatory available to her wherever she is, don't you worry.'

That answer raised even more questions in my mind.

Richard Dimbleby announced more great news. Edmund Hillary had conquered Everest, the highest mountain in the world. 'Conquered' meant he had climbed to the top of it, all by himself. How prescient and patriotic of him to achieve this on the very day of the Coronation!

There was some kind of special Coronation tea I think. Fairy cakes with red, white and blue icing; sausage rolls, jelly and custard, that kind of thing. Tanya and I took our Coronation mugs home at the end of term, and kept them for a year or two before they broke. We still have the Queen though.

11

A Very Dirty Thing

1953

ONCE I did a very dirty thing. I was about nine years old and playing down the bank with Irene Harvey and Carol Bowler, when I wanted to go to the lavatory. It was a long way up the bank, across the playground, through by the shed and round on the right to the girls lavs, so I ducked behind a tree, out of sight of my friends, and did a wee.

The next day, as we lined up in the Girls Playroom to march into the Dining Hall for breakfast, Miss Henderson said she had an announcement to make. Yesterday had been her day off, and as she came up the front drive, she had seen one of the girls doing a very dirty thing. A very disgusting thing, and she was going to shame that girl in front of the whole school. We were all intrigued.

'Number 17 - I saw you yesterday afternoon, in full view of the front drive, pull down your knickers and relieve yourself. Have you no control? How dare you expose yourself like that? You are a disgrace. Since you cannot control yourself, you will wear a nappy from now on, and you will stand up in the Dining Room so that everyone can see.'

I felt hot with fear and embarrassment. I knew that what I had done was not wrong. Billie always said if you were outside and a long way from the lavatory, you should hide behind a tree, make sure nobody was looking, and pee on the ground. All I had done wrong was not to make sure I couldn't be seen. But the people who ran our lives had different ideas of right and wrong from the rest of the world. There was no point in trying to reason with them, it simply attracted violence and worse punishment.

She had the nappy ready, and two huge pins. In fact, it was a piece of old roller towel, with stripes, and the pins were the kind which people used to secure the front of kilts.

'Come up here girl!'

I walked to the front of the playroom, the blood racing round my head made a singing noise as it rushed past my ears.

'Stand up on the form!'

I stood up on the built in bench that ran all round the playroom, and Miss Henderson lifted my skirt, pulled down my navy lock knit knickers and slapped each of my calves swiftly to indicate that I should lift my legs and remove my knickers completely. She made me hold the skirt of my gymslip up, while she pinned the 'nappy' each side. It hung down well below my hemline. 'Now get back to your place.'

We marched silently in single file around the two sides of the rectangular corridor which took us to the Dining Hall, and waited outside. When she gave the command 'Lead on!' we assembled ourselves in neat lines outside the forms on which we sat at table, waiting for the boys. We could hear the shuffling and rumbling of the boys, waiting outside their door at the back of the hall, for Mr Bristow to give them the command to enter the Dining Hall. My back was towards this door, so I knew the boys would all see the nappy hanging down.

Although we maintained a strict silence from assembly for meals until dismissal from them, and there had been no chance of anyone speaking to me, I sensed strong sympathy from the other girls around me. The boys would be a different story, and although none of them would dare utter a sound throughout the meal, news of my nappy would be all over the school by bedtime. The boys assembled behind their forms, and Mr Bristow shouted that he was waiting for perfect silence. It sounded perfectly silent to me, and after a few seconds he commanded

'You may sit.'

There was a great shuffling and scraping as we all climbed over the forms and sat down on them. The prefect at each table took the enamel jugs of tea and started down the table, pouring tea into the thick, white mugs without handles. I looked over to the Boys Side for evidence that anyone had noticed my shame, and saw Miss Henderson approach Mr Bristow and start talking to him, every now and then looking in my direction. The singing began in my ears again. Mr Bristow looked at me, and nodded slowly as he listened. She smiled at him, pleased to have his approval, and walked over towards me.

'Get up on the form, you can eat your tea up there, where everyone can see you.'

There was a sharp intake of breath from my friend Enid.

'Number 38, do you want to stand up on the bench with her?'

Poor Enid went red and looked down at her plate.

'Go on, up on the form, pick up your tea.'

My legs were shaking, but I managed it. I stood up on high, looking out over the heads of about two hundred children. Everyone could see the nappy. The hand holding the mug was shaking 'Drink your tea' commanded Miss Henderson 'And you can still eat from there - pick up your bread.' I bent down to pick up the bread from my plate. At least I didn't have to worry about whether anyone had noticed any more. I did worry about whether the thing would stay up or not, but that wasn't my problem, I hadn't put it on. From my vantage point, I saw Miss Henderson approach Mr Bristow again. This time he looked dubious as she spoke. He frowned, she persuaded, he looked unsure, she persisted, he shrugged, raised his eyebrows and nodded. She looked triumphant. He picked up the ladle he kept on the side of the stage and banged it on the end table 'Attention Everyone!'

Although we ate without speaking, two hundred children eating still makes a noise. Everyone stopped eating, put their mugs down and looked at Mr Bristow.

'You may be wondering why one of the girls - number 17 - is standing up on the form, wearing a nappy. Miss Henderson would like the whole school to know it is because - because she is in disgrace, and she will be made to stand on the form, wearing a nappy, for a whole week. Carry on.' The noise of eating resumed, and there was the slight buzz of someone talking.

'Silence!' roared Mr Bristow. He rarely had to do that, and never more than once.

I could not think of anything further Miss Henderson could do to me now. The ringing in my ears stopped and I was no longer afraid. Of course they were all looking at me, but I knew I hadn't done anything really wrong. A new idea was developing - why was Miss Henderson so anxious to disgrace me? And then another question - why did I not feel disgraced?

I was facing the stage, which was normally folded down so that the staff could come in from the kitchen with the meals. The maroon curtains with the gold stripe along the bottom were drawn back with huge gold tassels, and on the far kitchen wall the familiar words WASTE NOT - SPARE NOT in letters 18 inches high. I had been gazing at a version of this view since I first came to Reedham in 1949, at the age of five, but had never seen it from so high up before. I looked behind me at the gallery, the balcony with the huge clock looked unfamiliarly near and intimate, like seeing a famous person close up. I looked at the names on the Tyler Prize for Maths, noticing the different shades of gold, except during the war years, when they were all the same colour. Perhaps they couldn't get the lettering done during the war, and had to have them all done at the same time when it was over.

I looked down at the girls' heads. Only one hairstyle was permitted; interesting how it looked so different on each individual. A side parting - some people were allowed a choice of sides - the longer side held back with a hairgrip and/or a slide. Although forbidden to speak, most heads were not bent over their plates, they were busy communicating with each other in other ways. Silent mouthing was the favourite, and I remain a good lip reader to this day. Miming was popular, especially for passing unwanted food and nudges, kicks and belches were used to attract attention. Some girls could pass notes to the Boys Side during meal times, but I never worked out how they did it.

Standing above it all, it came to me that all this was far more important to poor Miss Henderson than it was to me. It was unfair, it was humiliating, it was vindictive and stupid, but it was not about me at all, it was about her. I imagined her puffing up the drive yesterday, having seen my nine-year-old bottom, planning her revenge. These moments of epiphany were becoming more frequent as I got older and realised that most of the adults who controlled my life were inadequate and stupid.

The nappy disappeared overnight and was never mentioned again. I think Mr Bristow didn't like it, and had a word with Matron. I never heard one word of teasing from any of the boys about it. They could be brutal, and as a famously ugly and weird girl, I was one of their favourites for abuse, but the nappy punishment must have been too much, even for them.

12

Letters Home

ONCE a week we wrote letters home. Each Friday, after tea, we sat in Class Three with our writing pads. Mostly these were bought in Woolworths on Saturdays, and the best one to have was Basildon Bond, with plain pages and one heavily ruled sheet in the front. You tore this sheet off, and inserted it under the first page, so you could see through it to write in straight lines, without any guidelines appearing on the letter itself. Somehow, I never achieved a Basildon Bond pad, and usually wrote my letter on a bit of torn off, lined exercise book.

We were only allowed to write home, and just in case we had ideas about writing to any unauthorised person, somebody else addressed and stamped the envelopes after we had handed them in. I tried to explain this to my Uncle Frank, one holiday, when we were visiting him and Auntie Siobhan in about 1952. We sat in the back seat of his car and he asked why I had not replied to his letter.

'I enclosed a pre-paid envelope for you – there was no need for a stamp – all you had to do was pop your letter in it and post it.'

'We don't have the envelopes.' was the best explanation I could find.

'What's the difficulty? Didn't you find the envelope enclosed?'

'Yes'

I had indeed received it some weeks earlier, enclosed in a letter from my Uncle, inviting me to reply using the envelope. I was eight years old and had no idea what to do with it, no idea who to ask, so I just kept it in my locker, with the letter and my other prized possessions: a really big piece of chalk and my collection of silver paper.

'Those envelopes are not free you know. I have to pay for them. I suppose you've lost the envelope now.'

I replied, untruthfully, that I had lost it. It was simpler than explaining my difficulty. I looked out of the car window at the boring countryside while my Uncle droned on about ingratitude, waste of money and other adult topics.

One of the mistresses sat at the teachers' desk and when we had finished our letter, we gave it to her. The mistress would hand it back and tell you to re-write it if there was anything it in she did not like. You were not allowed to say 'I hate it here, please let me come home.' for example. The safest thing was to send the standard letter, so most of us wrote:

Reedham School,
Purley,
Surrey.
Dear Mummy,
I hope you are well and happy.
Please will you send me a parcel.
Love from
Penny

That was the letter, same thing every week, which you sent to your Parent or Guardian, and when you had written it you could go and play.

After breakfast each morning, we would lead off in single file from the Dining Room and re-assemble in the Girls Playroom, standing in lines according to the table at which we sat. This is when announcements were made and letters given out. The mistress would call your name out and you would go to the front and collect your letter, which had already been opened and read by Matron. Occasionally, Matron would call you to her office to discuss your correspondence.

In about 1957, Billie had been dating a man she met at the office, called Mr Chowan and he had written to Tanya and to me, enclosing a large bar of chocolate each. Although there was no question of us being allowed to have the chocolate - we were simply given the still fragrant envelope in which it had come, with the note inside it saying he hoped we enjoyed it – we were expected to write and thank him. Matron called us to her office and said this week we should write two letters: one to Mr Chowan thanking him for the chocolate. I wanted to say we didn't even get the chocolate, but that would have been cheeky. Instead, I explained that on the previous Visiting Day, Mummy had asked us not to reply to Mr Chowan if he wrote to us. I think she had discovered he was married or something, but I had the idea it was best not to mention that to Matron.

Matron gave us a funny look. Matron was always giving us funny looks. She didn't like our family much, especially me. I thought she might have been reading my mind about writing to thank someone for chocolate we hadn't had. Or maybe she felt guilty, having eaten our chocolate. Well, she would hardly have thrown it away.

Later, I realised it was probably because of what was in *her* mind, not mine. Billie and Matron were two very different women, who cordially loathed and despised each other. Billie thought Matron was jumped up working class, badly educated and with unpleasant Christian and patriotic values. Matron thought Billie had delusions of grandeur and was far too attractive and well-dressed for a widow. She can't have approved of the Men Friends, either. Maybe she thought that if Tanya and I encouraged Mr Chowan, by writing thank you letters, he might marry Billie and she would thus be rid of us.

The rules were no sweets except from the Tuck Shop on Tuesdays, or what you bought on Saturday afternoons in Woolworths. Anything else was confiscated. While Matron could hardly tell us off for receiving unsolicited chocolate from someone who did not know those rules, nor force us to write to someone when our own Mother had requested that we didn't, I could see she felt wrong footed somehow.

'Very well then, I suppose if your Mother says so, you had better not reply. Get back to the playroom now.'

13

The Back Road, the Corridor, the Tower

REEDHAM Orphanage was designed to house 300 children, and shaped like a capital 'E' with the three arms going back into the hillside. There were three high towers, the Main Tower was at the front of the middle arm with classrooms on either side, and at the junctions of the two outer arms, two slightly smaller towers arose: the Girls' Tower and the Boys' Tower. The playrooms, washrooms, bathrooms and utilities were all on the outer arms. Between the building and the steep hillside, ran the Back Road, an important artery, which connected all the utilities such as the scullery, the Furnace and the Drying Room with outbuildings, all on the other side of the Back Road, hard against the hillside.

The Drying Room hummed with heat. As you entered, you were faced with wall to floor black iron, and a row of waist high handles, almost too hot to touch. Pull one of these towards you and a section of the wall, about 12 inches wide, rattled out on rails, revealing horizontal metal rods. On these rods, floor to ceiling, hung laundry: sheets, towels, boys' striped pyjamas, vests, girls' navy knickers, all dried so hard they could stand up independently.

After swimming, we hung our costumes to dry on these rails, and usually had to heave on several of the tall, thin drawers to find a space. Sometimes we just pulled them all out and back anyway, just to feel the rattle of the metal wheels on their rails, and the power of moving all that heavy iron so smoothly and easily. Without the railway propelling each drawer, we could never hope to shift weight of this magnitude. The hard echo of the Drying Room was tempered by its phenomenal heat – it was right next door to the Furnace, which heated the whole building. When we returned a few hours later, we had usually forgotten behind which of the identical black rectangles our costumes lay, and had to pull them all out again in turn.

The two rectangles which formed the inside of the letter 'E' were lined with square, glass covered corridors, floors quarry-tiled in the red and black chequered design which permeated my childhood. These rectangles formed the heart of The Girls' Side and the Boys' Side, respectively, and they each enclosed a small, weedy and unkempt plot, known as the Square. Most of the time we saw this through opaque glass, so the general impression was of light and green, the high, glass ceilings making everything bright.

Starting from outside the Girls' Playroom, you walked down the first long arm of the Girls corridor, past the other door to the Infants Playroom on your right and a long, high wall, against which we played complicated ball games. There was a store-room - always locked - on your left, then the glass wall between the corridor and the square started on the right. All the rooms on the right were built out into this square. The Boot Room, where our shoes were stored in numbered pigeonholes, was next on the right after the Infants, a little further on the left was the Girls' Washroom, with all our pinafores on numbered hooks. Incongruously, this room formed the background to some of my most romantic imaginary encounters.

The Washroom was echoing empty, the red floor wet with recent activity, the thick white basins wedged together, propping each other up, their taps weeping. The Princess removed her spectacles to wash her face and began to cry. Her whimpers bounced around the stony surfaces, amplifying her distress, until the Washroom was filled with her tears. A handsome Prince stood at the door and, in a gentle, masculine voice, enquired

'Princess, why do you weep?'

'Oh, they are cruel to me, *cruel* I tell you. I have been stolen from my own true parents, and made to live in this horrible dungeon, forced to live off gristle and wear these dismal rags.'

'Let me take you away from all this and restore you to your birthright, for surely you should one day be a Queen.'

The Princess gazed into the mirror, and the Prince could see that without her glasses she was truly beautiful!

'Why Princess, without your glasses you are - truly beautiful!

If only your golden tresses were unshorn...'

As you turned right, the Scullery was on the corner, and the door to the Kitchen first on the left. There was a glass-panelled door into the Square, then the corridor took you all the way down to the Dining Room door, at the end, on the left. Ahead, off the main corridor, was a smaller corridor to Matrons Office and the Front Hall. Turn right again and you passed another door into the square, on the right, and the door to Matron's Secretary's Office on the left. From then on, it was classrooms all the way along the left hand side, except for the Science Lab on the right, which was built out into the square. Outside the Science Lab, grew several grape vines, which produced bunches of small, sour but perfectly edible grapes. Towards the end of the Summer Term, those of us tall enough would jump up and grab the grapes. We discovered that the vine leaves too were edible. The grapes would have tasted much better if we had waited till September, but by the start of Autumn Term, they had all been harvested.

Then the glass ended and you were under the dormitories. Last on the left was the door to the Girls' Stairs, which spiralled high up past Nightingale, the Junior Dorm on the first floor, past Fry, the Senior Dorm on the second, and all the way up to the Girls' Tower.

The stairs up past Fry Dorm, on the third floor, were darker than the lower ones and far more shiny, being so rarely used. We would go up there sometimes and climb over the banister, put our feet in the spaces between the balusters and lean right out over the stairwell – a 60 foot drop. Just writing those words now makes me go cold. That building, and therefore that staircase, dated from 1858, so the banister was almost a hundred years old when I started swinging on it. I would pull on it quite vigorously, feel the wobble and creak, as I leant out daringly over the stairwell, holding on with just one hand...

Usually the Tower was locked, but occasionally it was opened and we were allowed up there to look for dressing up clothes. The Tower was really high up, and consisted of a narrow, steep and winding wooden staircase, slippery with lack of use, then a massive iron key opened a small door, into one square room with a window on all four sides. There was a huge view of sky and green fields from every window, and yet because it was a small room, with only one entrance, it felt private. That mixture of spacious bright light and cosy privacy made The Tower one of my favourite rooms, although I can't have been in there more than half a dozen times in my entire life. The first time was in June 1950, when Tanya and I were fitted for our Festival Day costumes for *Polly Put the Kettle On*.

The Tower also stored clothes out of season. Twice a year, a mistress would climb the shiny stairs, unlock the Tower door and either dump the summer dresses and collect the winter coats, or dump the winter coats and collect the summer dresses.

In the Tower lay evidence of happier times. Before the war, Reedham had been a real school, where education had taken place, where girls had played sport seriously, plays had been staged and much care and thought had gone into the costumes.

I especially remember an 18th century style yellow satin dress with big white panniers on the side, and sashes, which tied in a bow at the waist. There were shoes from the beginning of the 20th century, black and brown winkle pickers with buttoned instep straps. There were thick black cotton stockings, not new, but rolled up neatly in small piles, ready to wear again. Tennis racquets, lacrosse sticks with leather handles coming adrift, and broken string nets, white curly wigs, frock coats, cricket pads, croquet mallets, wooden croquet balls and metal hoops, leather suitcases, wicker baskets full of dressing up clothes, and costumes from every century, all probably made in the sewing rooms here at Reedham.

These were all relics of olden times when, it seemed to me, Reedham had been run intelligently, and girls had worked hard and had fun. Whenever I hear the story of Rapunzel – I see her leaning out of the Girls' Tower at Reedham, wearing the yellow satin dress with the white panniers.

Back at the foot of the Girls' Stairs, you turned left into the final arm of the corridor. The Junior Classroom, overlooking the Girls' Playground was first on the left, and then it was straight back to the Girls' Playroom where you started. If you ran down this last bit, a few yards before you got to the Playroom, there was a good slidey bit on the tiles, right by the wall leading up to the Playroom door, where generations of girls had whizzed down the corridor and used sheer momentum to skate the last bit, grabbing the black downpipe outside the door as a brake.

For most of my early years, this was my whole world. The fabric of that building will remain with me forever, and perversely, I loved it. I loved the light, the high ceilings, the symmetry and scale of it. The oak parquet floors in the Dining Room, the waxed oak tables at which we ate, the whitish grey exterior, the wide and wobbly staircase over which we hung. I love it still.

14

Buttering

FOOD was always locked up. Rationing finally ceased in 1956, and when we went into the Bread Room for Buttering on Sundays, the cake was stored in wooden, slatted cupboards, secured with a padlock. The only reason the bread was unlocked now was because Matron had been unable to devise a way of us buttering it while it was padlocked.

There was a rota for buttering. It was only done by girls over 12, and only on Sundays. Your turn came up every few weeks, and if Church was in the morning, you did it in the afternoon, and vice versa. Three of us, sitting up on high stools, perhaps two dozen loaves of sliced bread neatly stacked in the corner of the counter. The bread was made in the kitchens, by Cookie I think. A large, smiling man in white clothes whose legs were of different lengths. You would catch glimpses of him through the open scullery door sometimes, or see him disappear into the kitchen, his longer leg trailing behind him.

First we took our pinnies from their numbered hooks in the girls washroom, then we walked through the kitchen and turned left into the fragrant Bread Room. As the name indicates, the whole purpose of this room was the slicing, buttering and storage of bread and cake. One of the kitchen staff would bring the 'butter' which was actually margarine and butter cut into cubes, in aluminium baking dishes. To make it spread as thinly as possible and go further, it had usually been warmed a bit in the oven.

Buttering was one of the best jobs. You were sitting down - in private and unsupervised - with contemporaries - perfect for a good, long chat. All those loaves took three of us about an hour and a half. And of course, we managed to eat a fair amount of bread and butter during that time. That fresh, home made bread was the very best food we ever got at Reedham: a moist, dense texture and crisp chewy crusts, sliced about half an inch thick to cut down the amount of rationed butter and margarine. We all liked it, but took it for granted. Most of my time there, the bread was white, but in the last couple of years, Cookie started making a few brown loaves every week too.

He must have baked the bread on Saturday night, or maybe early Sunday morning, because it was always fresh and sometimes still warm. You picked up a sliced loaf by holding it underneath with one hand, steadying the top with the other, and placing it in front of you. Three tins of fat had to spread all those loaves, so we needed to go easy and not spread too thickly. Except for the crusts you were going to eat yourself. The crusts were definitely the best bits, and I always chose the very thickest. It was easy to see which was the butter and which the marge, because the marge was bright yellow, the butter a paler colour. We would take a whole cube of butter and spread it on our chosen crust, concealing the crime by standing the loaf with the missing crust at the bottom.

Some of the locked up cake was already sliced. Some slices were slightly thinner than the gaps between slats in the wood, so we inserted our slim fingers from underneath and manipulated a slice until it was aligned with a gap and persuaded it gently out underneath. Chocolate cake was my favourite, but Cookie also made Fruit Cake, Ginger and Coconut. If he ever knew we were stealing cake, he never let on.

15

Billie's Food

THE style of English Tea Time Cookery which Mrs Lawson taught us in Domestic Science at Reedham was a novelty to Billie, and Tanya and I would impress her immensely by making biscuits and cakes at home

We were allowed to take our Christmas cakes home, and Billie was very proud of them. I don't recall her ever making a cake from scratch herself, although in later years, she usually had a packet of Green's Sponge Mixture in the cupboard. From this she would make Apple Cake, Pineapple Cake or Plum Cake, by pouring the mixture over the fruit and baking it, and these fruit puddings were the nearest Billie ever got to conventional English cookery.

Reedham food was entirely different from home food. Although Billie had been born in England, both her parents were Dutch, and had travelled a bit. Billie had travelled even more. She had learned to cook from her Mother of course, and later she spent a year at finishing school in Germany. Later still, she worked in Paris, as a Bluebell Girl at *Le Pigalle* and a dancer at the *Moulin Rouge*, spent holidays in Switzerland, and had been touring Italy with the troupe when WW2 broke out.

At home, we had bread for breakfast, but it was often rye bread, pumpernickel or crispbread. Any cheese or cold meat we had in the larder went on the table, as well as butter, jam, honey and anything left over from previous meals. Tanya and

I loved everything Billie gave us, but we were aware that other families did not eat like this. Billie told us that this style of eating was typically Dutch.

We never had a Sunday Roast, like English families. Billie said roasting was an inefficient way of cooking meat, and she saw no reason to eat a particular meal on a particular day. She cooked whatever was fresh or cheap in the shops or at Berwick St. Market. She taught us how to gut and clean fish, and how to make stock from the bones, then to double wrap them and put them straight out in the dustbin.

She made soused herring with pickling spices; liver, bacon and mashed potatoes; pork chops and cabbage; chicken wings braised with celery; rich and glutinous oxtail stew with red kidney beans. This last was my favourite, we loved sucking the meat from the crevices of the tailbone. Billie always said it was fine to pick up bones and suck them when at home, but

'...you mustn't do it when you're out!'

We knew this remark so well, we joined in the chorus.

She also had a few favourite meals she could cook from the store cupboard: frankfurters and sauerkraut from a jar or tin, served with boiled potatoes and German mustard. Tinned Hungarian goulash, in a bright red paprika sauce, served with rice. Whatever we cooked, we usually made enough for more than one meal, and the dish would appear at each meal until it was gone – we never threw food away unless it was bad.

When milk went sour, we made cream cheese. We waited till it went solid, placed a clean piece of linen inside a bowl and poured the milk in. Then we put the bowl in the sink, tied the cloth with string and hung it over the tap to drip. Usually we did this last thing at night, and in the morning – voila! We emptied the whey down the sink, scraped the cream cheese off the cloth, added a little salt and had fresh cheese for breakfast.

We often cooked with Billie, either helping her, or simply standing watching as she explained what she was doing. She would make a *roux* with 'a walnut of butter' and a tablespoon of cornflour, stirring all the time so it didn't get lumpy, then gradually adding milk, and stock or cheese or whatever. *Roux* (or a 'white sauce' as English people called it) could become cheese sauce for cauliflower; parsley sauce for fish; or form the basis for a *blanquette de veau*. Or you could use it to thicken a fish or meat stock, to start a winter soup.

Another Chapel Market bargain was a huge, old boiling fowl, which Billie got very cheaply, because it was old, and hadn't been drawn or cleaned.

'This is a good opportunity to show you girls how to do it!'

Fortunately, the butcher had beheaded it, but she made us watch her chop its feet off and make a long slit behind its legs to open it up. We pretended to be repelled, but it was interesting. She put her whole hand in the cavity, and found something unexpected.

'Look, it was a hen, and here are all her eggs, waiting!'

Sure enough, a row of bright yolks lay inside the bird, graded – like a necklace - for size. The nearest was normal size, then they got smaller, the smallest being the size of a pea. All three of us found this fascinating. Billie gathered all the little yolks together in a bowl.

'We'll make mayonnaise with those.'

She drew all the innards from the chicken, showing us the heart, liver and stomach and setting them aside as well. Then she gave it a good wash, put it in the largest saucepan, covered it with water, put in a chopped onion and a bay leaf and set it on a low flame.

'No good roasting such an old bird, she'll be tough as old boots. What she needs is a long, slow simmer. She's what they call an old boiler.'

'Just like you!'

'Well, thank you *very* much!'

Later she added celery and carrots to the chicken, and left

it to cook overnight. We got several meals from the meat, then soup, with the giblets added, and finally one of us was set the task of picking the bones for the last of the meat to make a risotto. Once cleaned, the bones went to make more stock for the risotto.

Mayonnaise was magic. We knew it should ideally be made with olive oil, but the only place you could buy that in the fifties was in tiny, expensive bottles from the chemist, so we used Mazola, which Billie said was the next best thing. First she would beat the egg yolk in a bowl till the yellow turned a little paler, then one of us would start to add the oil, literally, drop by drop. This was impossible from the bottle, we had first to decant the oil into a small jug, and hold it at precisely the angle to allow drop – after – drop – after – drop to fall in the bowl, as Billie continued beating, and we watched for the magic to start. Gradually, the yolks grew thick and glossy with the oil, then we could add the drops of oil faster and faster, and eventually pour a thin stream of it. Only when the emulsion was complete would we add salt and a little cider vinegar.

On Saturdays, Billie would go to the market late in the day, looking for bargains. Once she came home with a whole wooden box of tomatoes, and we had endless tomato salad, real tomato soup and fresh bolognaise sauce with spaghetti. Spaghetti came in long parcels, wrapped in blue paper, which we carried home from the Delicatessen under our arms, like baguettes, so they didn't snap.

Another day she came home from the market with a bundle of newspaper under her arm. With evident glee, she thumped it down on the kitchen table.

'Wait till you see what I've got – and so cheap!' We crowded round, inquisitive. 'Let me take my coat off first, girls – darling, hang it up for me. Now I need a knife.'

She cut the string, opened the paper. The blood blossomed red on the paper. It was a head. With eyes, ears and a mouth.

The ears had hairs. The eyes had eyelashes, straight and white. The mouth had teeth. We ran screaming. She called out:

'I'm going to make a beautiful pigs head brawn! It's delicious, you will love it. And so cheap ! This will feed us for a week.'

The cooking smells lured us back to the kitchen. We watched the process with fascinated disgust. She made a crock of brawn in the blue and white striped Cornish ware dish, and tried to persuade us to try it, but we refused. She had to eat it all herself.

Of course, after the holidays, when we went back to Reedham, she had to eat every meal by herself.

16

Rations, Wild Food and Domestic Science

'IT'S no good children, you're eating too much. You will have to eat less, because the Rations won't run to it!'

Matron stood by the stage, at the top of the Dining Hall, one morning in the early fifties, and made this puzzling announcement just as we were about to start breakfast. Puzzling because we didn't control how much we ate – Matron did. We had very little scope to eat more. It is true we all helped ourselves to bread and butter from the two plates on each table, but once it was all gone – as it usually was – there wasn't any more.

She gave the prefects the order to start serving, and the clatter of thick white crockery filled the Hall. The long oak trestle tables seated six children each side. These tables were sticky with old polish, and while waiting for the prefect to pour tea into your handle-less mug, you could get small but satisfying rolls of black gunge, by scraping with a fingernail in the built up areas. It was risky, mind. More than once, I got my head slapped suddenly from behind for this flagrant vandalism.

We sat on benches, known as 'forms'. The boys' tables on one side of the Hall, the girls' on the other, with two prefects at the end of each table. Rattling down the central aisle came the trolleys from the kitchen, wheeled by weary kitchen staff in green overalls. Between the Kitchen and the Dining Hall, was the stage, about four foot high, with the central part folded down, creating a passage to the kitchen. The Kitchen staff would park a trolley at the end of each table, and from these – when the order came – the prefects would serve the meal.

At Breakfast and Tea, each trolley bore a large, white enamel jug of tea – milk and sugar already added - and plates of buttered bread. On Sundays there was a boiled egg each, but for my first few years at Reedham, weekday breakfast was simply tea, bread and butter. Food rationing began to ease in 1954, and different food began to appear at breakfast time. Once a week there was bacon and dipped bread. The bacon was thickly sliced, very fatty and salty, and arrived in an aluminium dish, swimming in about an inch of fat. Also on the trolley was a plate of dry bread, and we each got a piece of bacon and a slice of bread soaked in bacon grease. The idea may have started as fried bread, and lost something in the execution, but it was filling and delicious.

The mid-day meal was called Dinner; the prefects doled it out and we had to eat everything on our plates. It was the main meal of the day, and the same every week. On Sunday, roast meat, roast potatoes, cabbage and gravy followed by jam sponge and custard. I liked all this, except the fat and gristle on the meat. Sometimes you could get away with leaving this, but usually you were forced to eat it. I often managed, covertly, to swap my unwanted meat for cabbage, which – inexplicably – some people didn't like. Monday was Shepherd's Pie, Tuesday was Meat, Greens and (boiled) Potatoes, (Stones, Leather and Seaweed), and Wednesday was Mince. Thursday was the only day when you might get a surprise, perhaps Liver and Bacon, but usually it was Macaroni Cheese.

Friday was my favourite – Fish! It was always cod. In those days, cod was a huge fish, and the aluminium pans held fish of a size you no longer see. It was served with big, soft haricot beans, mashed potatoes and brown sauce, and the giant flakes of cod yielded great big glutinous bones. Saturday was Stones, Leather and Seaweed again. Mostly, I quite liked Reedham food, there was only one thing I truly dreaded: milk puddings. The prefect would serve it up, then walk along the table plonking a spoonful of red jam – splat – in the centre of each dish. I came to tolerate rice pudding and eventually I could eat semolina without having to imagine it was something else. But I never was able to eat tapioca pudding (frog's spawn) without crying, which meant not only having to force down the evil, slimy lumps, but also getting hit on the back of the head.

'Or I'll give you something to cry about!'

The evening meal was called Tea, and for this we once again had tea and buttered bread, but also something extra: a spoonful of jam on the side of our plate to go with the bread, or a slice of spam, fish paste or Marmite, scraped on the side of each plate with a knife. In later years we got 'salad' : lettuce, tomatoes, cucumber and salad cream.

I was never hungry, but never full either, and would never pass up the opportunity of more to eat. In Summer, there was plenty of wild food, and we would run down the bank and into the Meadow to find it. In March and April we ate 'bread and butter' and by June we found hips on wild rose bushes.

'Look, you can eat rose hips, but don't swallow the hairy pips – spit them out!'

'I peel off the juicy bit first, look. If you planted them, they would grow into another rose bush.'

'Let's get some bread and butter now.'

'Bread and butter?'

'That's what you call hawthorn leaves – didn't you know that?'

'Do they taste like bread and butter, then?'

'Yes, just like lovely fresh, crusty, bread with nice thick butter – I *don't* think!'

'Is this them?'

'Yes, go on, take the small leaves – mind the prickles – yum,

yum, bread and butter, all we need now is strawberry jam!'

Later from the hawthorn tree, we ate the bright red haws which came after May blossom. Sorrel was called 'vinegar leaves,' and had a pleasing, sour taste. When we returned after the Summer holidays, we pulled up the Queen Anne's Lace, which had grown huge in the weeks we were away. You had to pull carefully, to preserve the long, white root intact. This root could reach the size of a small carrot, which we would run under the tap in the girls' washroom, and eat. It was extremely fibrous, and tasted like parsnip, only stronger. You could go on chewing it for hours.

The best feast of Autumn, though, was beech nuts. At the top of the Drive grew a magnificent beech tree, and soon after term started, the first husks began to fall. To the uninitiated, they looked pretty, like small, hairy wooden flowers, but not like anything you could eat. The husks split open, each revealing four, brown, triangular nuts, which were easily peeled, delicious and – if you were patient and peeled enough of them - remarkably filling.

I don't know if the Staff we aware that we ate wild food. They certainly never warned us against it, or advised on poisonous plants. Knowledge was passed down the generations of girls, and somehow we all knew what deadly nightshade looked like, and which other berries and leaves were poison, without any adult guidance.

In about 1952, Billie became concerned about our diet, and bought some vitamin supplements called Supervite: the orange transparent ones were cod liver oil, the black, metal tasting ones were minerals. She sent the capsules to Matron, asking if we could please have one of each every day, after meals. Matron summoned us both.

'What have you been telling your Mother about the food here?'

'I don't know, Matron'

'What do you mean? You must have said something. She

82

has instructed me to issue you with –' she opened her drawer, and took out two boxes of Supervite.

'These! What did you tell her?'

'Nothing Matron'

'There is nothing wrong with the food here. Our budget is tight, I don't deny it, and just because rationing is gradually coming to an end, it doesn't mean I can suddenly obtain everything we want. But you get a healthy, balanced diet, don't you?'

'Yes Matron'

'I suppose your Mother thinks she could feed you better! You can go to Sanitorium every day - Sister Hutchinson can dispense them.'

The Domestic Science Room was on the Back Road, not part of the main building and probably not contemporary with it. One side of this large rectangular room was against the steep hillside, but the other side was nearly all windows, and awash with light. It was simply a huge kitchen, with several sinks, each with a wooden draining board, about six ovens, and many cupboards containing mixing bowls, saucepans and baking trays. In the centre of the windowless wall, was a blackboard, and ranged down half the room were half a dozen well scrubbed deal tables, where we sat at wooden stools to write notes and recipes in our Domestic Science Exercise Books.

Almost everything in this room was pre-war, and relentlessly maintained. One thing a Reedham girl learned properly was housework and cleaning. In the Juniors we had one afternoon a week of Domestic Science, usually called DS, and whole lessons were devoted to subjects like 'Care of the Draining Board', 'Scrubbing a Deal Table' and 'Cleaning an Oven.' When we became Seniors, we spent a whole day in the DS room, which allowed for long projects like making and icing a fruit cake. We started on our Christmas cakes soon after the beginning of each Autumn Term. The mixing and baking took up the morning, and in the afternoon, breathing the heavenly massed aroma of a dozen fruit cakes baking, we licked out the bowls and copied Mrs Lawson's Christmas Cake recipe into our grease spotted exercise books.

I enjoyed all this, but we did the same lessons every year. Autumn was Bottling Fruit, and Care and Use of a Kilner Jar. January was Seville Orange Marmalade. That whole day was 20% of our secondary educational time. It was rarely said explicitly to us, but it was a clear indication of the career paths we were expected to take.

Mrs Lawson would bring her own ironing in from home for us to do. I remember getting a pile of ironing which included one of her bras, and feeling that this was far more intimate than I wanted to be with her. She would also take the opportunity to bake and ice cakes for her own family in the course of the lesson. She would use Reedham ingredients to make a cake for herself, as a demonstration model. In the Summer of 1958, while icing yet another cake, I was delighted to find I had some icing left over. It was about egg size, and I planned to eat it, but Mrs Lawson was short of icing to decorate her own cake and asked if she could have it.

I said, 'No, sorry, I want it.'

'But look, I need just that amount for my daughter's birthday cake – please!'

I put my hand over my icing egg, looked her straight in the eye and said.

'Sorry, Mrs Lawson.'

She could have simply ordered me to give it to her, but by this time I was taller than she was. She went away muttering that I was mean, and I did feel a small dart of guilt. But we both knew that her daughter had a far more privileged life than we did. We got few sweets or treats, and I was not going to relinquish my icing for some suburban girl who lived at home with her parents and had her own bedroom.

17

Jane Austen's Heroines

AT the bottom of the girls' staircase, Emma Woodhouse said to us:

'Lets go into the cupboard under the stairs and make a den.'

No, of course her name wasn't really Emma Woodhouse. I have given all the girls who sexually abused me the names of Jane Austen heroines, but they know who they are. I don't feel any animosity towards these girls; they were still only children too and had obviously been abused themselves. I'm recording it because it seems to me an inevitable consequence of herding together all the children who cannot be brought up at home under one roof, in the charge of a very few, badly qualified staff and a system which relies on older children to care for and discipline the younger ones. It wasn't the fault of us children. We all had scars, even if only the trauma of separation from home. None of us had access to an adult with whom we could talk. Bullying and sexual abuse is endemic in these circumstances. To children like Tanya and me, who had been treated very gently at home and had never even been hit, Reedham was a brutal shock. Until I was about 11, I gave off the signals of someone not streetwise enough to defend herself, I exuded the pheromones of victimhood.

I was with two or three other seven years olds and we loved dens. A den could be anywhere - any secret place where staff wouldn't see us. Usually they were under one of the trees behind the church, but under the stairs sounded OK. Even more attractive was the invitation from an older girl - Emma must have been at least 14 - practically a grown up and far more intimidating. A grown up had responsibility - technically at least. They were supposed to look after you. Big girls were noisy and wild; huge black shoes clattering with blakeys, thundering down corridors, thick red legs above short grey socks, they reeked of sweat and anger. Most of the time they ignored us, except to tell us off, send us on errands or order us to make them laugh.

Occasionally I had to perform for them. Somebody had taught me the Guy Mitchell song 'She wears red feathers and a hooli hooli skirt...' One day in the playroom I was singing it and a big girl noticed.

'You've got to do the actions too.' she said.

I froze. What actions? She grabbed my wrist and planted one of my hands on my hip, the other behind my head.

'Now wriggle your hips!' She demonstrated. I copied.

'Now do that while you're singing.'

So I did, and she called a few other big girls to watch. It was a stupid dance, and I performed it with wooden embarrassment. The big girls were hysterical. I smiled uncertainly, not sure what was funny but flattered to be the centre of their attention. And after that, every now and then someone would come for me. I would be reading, playing a good game, or more likely, staring into space and dreaming.

'Number 17, you're wanted'

and I had to go and stand in front of big girls and do the song and dance. Very soon, resentment, shame and boredom reduced my movements to twitches.

'Wiggle your hips more - come on!'

'You've got to be more sexy - look, like this.'

They demonstrated, I copied. But the joke of making a skinny English seven year old in glasses act like a seductive

South American woman depended on my innocence and anxiety to please. My expression became blank and bored. Their laughter subsided.

'Come on - put some sex appeal into it!'

I was no longer embarrassed, but they were. I had to do this dismal dance because there were about six of them and they were twice my age and size. I had no choice. But I wasn't going to be childish like them and find it amusing. Quite rightly, they interpreted my expression as one of superiority, slapped me a few times, called me a snob and that was the end of Carmen Miranda.

The cupboard under the stairs was quite big - it was used for storing cleaning materials. It had a light inside and was big enough for us all - sitting squashed up together around Emma. She sat on a big tin of polish and said we had to practice kissing for when we were older. She turned the light out - you were meant to do it in the dark apparently - and gave us each a long kiss, mouths firmly closed. Then she told us that we also had to rub each others' bosoms, to make them grow. Hers were already quite big. They made pointy shapes underneath her cardigan, even though she didn't wear a bra yet. She said she had got them big by rubbing them every day, and that is what we should do. She would show us how. One by one, she put her hot, dry hands up underneath our vests and rubbed the flat of her palm over our tiny nipples. Did we feel anything? We giggled and shook our heads. Well, keep doing it every day, and you will. Now you must rub mine. She pulled her blouse up out of her skirt waistband, and we took it in turns to rub her breasts with the flat of our palms. They were smaller and firmer than my Mum's breasts. She smiled and said it was nice.

'When you're married, your husband will do that to you. And other things.'

Emma was friendly and kind. She was slightly apart from the other older girls, and never in the audience for Carmen

Miranda. If anyone asked me if I wanted to go in the den with Emma, I said yes. It was friendly and I enjoyed it.

From quite an early age, I was the focus of sexual attention from other, older people. Emma left after about two terms, but she was the first of many. Perhaps I gave out attention-seeking signals. I think a lot of us, unwittingly did that. Reedham children had very little personal interaction with adults; unless we were in disgrace, when we were summoned to Matron's Office to be told off. Answering back was foolhardy, so although it was attention, it wasn't really interaction. But sexual predators always have time for you. Like heat seeking missiles, they home in on children hungry for attention and affection. We were disregarded children in uniform ugly clothes, not only starved of personal attention from older people, but also of course, of their protection.

Marianne Dashwood was about 13. Not a prefect, but five years older than me. I knew who she was - we little ones knew the names of all the older girls - but she had never spoken to me and as far as I knew, she didn't even know I existed. I liked being eight, because I remembered standing outside a baker's shop when I was small, just before we went to Reedham. Tanya was in her push-chair and we were waiting outside for Billie. I saw some big girls in school uniform, talking and laughing confidently, just like grown ups. When Billie came out of the bakers, I asked her.

'How old are those girls?'

'Oh I think they must be about eight.'

'Will I be a big girl like that?'

'Yes, darling, you will one day.'

It took ages, but I got there and it was a wonderful age - you could feel yourself growing, learning new words, new skills, gaining new insights. But at Reedham, there were several layers of powerful older girls between eight and the grown ups. 13 year olds like Marianne had even more power than prefects, because they had absolutely no responsibility.

Technically, they could not give you orders, but they did, and if you disobeyed and they reported you to a prefect or a mistress, you'd be in trouble anyway, because

'She's older than you, and anyway, she will be a prefect soon. You should respect your elders and do as you're told.'

Despite being a big girl of eight, I was sending out the signals Marianne was looking for. Like all bullies and abusers, she must herself have first been a victim. Once she had been vulnerable and submissive, desperate for attention. Now she wanted to relive that frightening time, but this time - *this time* - she would get the powerful starring role. She would direct the action. Instinctively, she knew I was the right one.

In the corridor, outside the girls' washroom, nobody else around, she said

'Number 17, I want you in the Boot Room.'

The Boot Room was a few yards down, on the other side of the corridor. Without a word and shaking slightly, I went in. The room was a one storey, rectangular hut, built out into the central square. The two long sides consisted of numbered wooden pigeonholes for shoes, with a narrow window along the top. At the end, a larger window with a radiator beneath. The central feature of the room was a long, narrow wooden table, the top covered in a silver metal of some kind - for some reason I believed it to be zinc - moulded and folded under the two inch rim - with sharp edges and corners to catch your clothes and flesh. It always reeked of boot polish.

Marianne was not kind and chatty like Emma, and wasted no time with pleasantries. She had various tortures she wanted to try out. One was standing on one leg. She made me do this for ages and I was not allowed to hold on to anything, to wobble or move a muscle. She leaned against the table and I stood a few inches away, while she watched me closely. All the time she was talking, saying you stand still, I don't want you moving a muscle because if you do you're going to get it, I don't even want to see you breathe. She was very strict about it, and did not hit me unless I moved, but the minute I did, she slapped me round the head.

Of course that made me wobble and put my leg down, and if I was lucky, change legs. Sometimes she noticed, and I had to use the same aching leg as before, but sometimes she didn't. At first I tried very hard not to wobble, but soon I realised that she would wait until I did, and that I would get hit anyway, so I might as well wobble sooner and get it over with. After a few wobbles, Marianne Dashwood moved on to the next torture.

For this I had to lie on my back, across the narrow table. My head hanging over the edge, my arms spread out and holding the sharp underneath edge of the metal table. The table was about 18 inches wide, so I was only supported as far as my hips and I had to hold my legs out horizontally, in line with my body.

And then she sat astride my legs. She was not much taller than me, but she was certainly heavier. She bounced up and down and I could feel her pelvic bones on my shins. This was her favourite endurance test, the one she did most frequently. She smelt of the sweat that seeped into her cardigan armpits and was held captive by her beefy arms. She smelt of the menarche, of wild teenage girl, of hatred, fear and insanity. Her mass jiggled on my legs and my stomach muscles strained to hold her. For this torture she told me to close my eyes and imagine myself in various situations. Situations which I could not imagine: fiery pits, snakes, evil demons. That kind of thing. She would get more and more worked up, jiggling on my tiring legs:

'You are a maiden in distress, and I have come to rescue you, I am riding on my horse to rescue you from the fire, which is now scratching your face...'

At this point, to assist my imagination, she would helpfully claw at my cheeks.

'And here I come now, on my noble steed, to rescue you out of the fiery pit and carry you off to safety. Keep your eyes closed. Now I've got to kiss you.'

And her mouldy bread breath came down on my face. I screwed up my mouth, as if I believed you had to pucker up as much as possible. Glad I had to keep my eyes closed. She lay down on top of me, forcing the air from my lungs, and kissed me hard and bonily. I didn't know about French kissing, and fortunately, neither did she, so both our mouths remained clamped.

She experimented - tried out other tortures - improvised. They always involved discomfort and endurance for me, and sadistic monologues from her. But these two were the favourites, the ones she relished, the ones she returned to again and again.

She would come looking for me. I would be playing and she would just appear.

'Number 17 I want you.'

And I would have to follow her - always to the Boot Room, the torture room, to the smell of shoe polish and her endocrine glands. I hated her of course, and feared her intensely. I didn't like the pain much either. But the worst thing, in the end was the boredom of it, the waste of time, the sound of other girls running around outside, playing and having fun, while I was stuck in the Boot Room doing Marianne Dashwood's tortures.

I met Marianne Dashwood recently and would not have recognised her. A sad, dumpy, sixtyish woman wearing a floral frock. It was at a Reedham reunion and although each of us was aware of the other's presence, neither of us made an approach. But towards the end of the day, we were both in the ladies, washing our hands at adjacent sinks. I spoke first.

'Hello Marianne. I don't suppose you remember me.'

'I'm not sure - what's your name again?'

She turned her back to me, drying her hands on the roller towel.

'Penny Wardman. I certainly remember you, Marianne.'

She was shaking. Drying her hands over and over, so she wouldn't have to turn and face me.

'It's such a long time ago. Hard to remember every single person.'

'That's true. But some people do stick in your mind. Do you remember the Boot Room?'

She stopped drying her hands and stood sideways on, facing the sink, looking in the mirror. The door was behind me and I had her cornered. Trying to conceal her shaking, she scrambled about in her handbag, found a hairbrush and started to punish her reddened scalp. I knew that she knew. And she knew that I knew that she knew. She was still shaking.

And I felt so sorry for her. Living well is famously the best revenge. I could see the kind of life she'd had, just by looking at her, and it was evident to us both that mine had been happier and more fulfilling. So I just said that I remembered everything very well, and left.

This wasn't the first time something like this happened at a Reedham reunion. A few years previously, I had met Anne Elliott, and after the reunion about eight of us went for a drink. Anne definitely remembered me, and we talked about our lives since Reedham and about the reasons we had been sent there in the first place. I asked her:

'Anne, were you ever sexually abused as a child?'

'Yes, that's why I was sent to Reedham in fact.'

'I thought so.'

'Did I do it to you, too?'

'Yes, don't you remember - you must remember!'

'Actually I don't. But I'm not saying I don't believe you, because I did that kind of thing. I know I did. I just don't remember any of it. Blocked it all out.'

Anne started summoning me when I was about 11. She was about 15 I suppose, a prefect and a big girl in every sense: thick legs, dark hair swept back in a big wave on either side of her sweaty brown face. She favoured classrooms, usually the Infants, but sometimes Class 3. It's amazing now to realise that the classrooms were never locked and never checked. Murder could have been committed and not been discovered for hours. I had to lie down on the floor in front of the piano, and she would lie on top of me. She didn't say very much, except that I should imagine she was a man. After that she wriggled her pubic bone on mine, grinding my sacrum and coccyx into the wooden floor, and grunting. Avoiding my eyes all the time. When she had finished she said 'Get up. You can go now.'

After Anne Elliot left, the sexual abuse stopped. The tremendous growth spurt I experienced between 12 and 13 triggered several changes in my life. I no longer looked like a victim, so I no longer behaved like one, and nobody else tried it on with me – not at Reedham, anyway.

18

I Nearly Killed Jenny

THE summer holidays were the ones we longed for, there was time to relish the feeling of being free citizens. I remember walking down a London street in my own pink and white dress, thinking 'Nobody can tell that I am not a normal girl who lives at home and wears her own clothes.' In fact, the pink and white dress had been passed down from my cousins Susan and Frances, but it was very pretty and almost new, with cap sleeves, a fitted bodice, gathered skirt, and a broad sash attached, which tied at the back, and I loved the feeling of pulling it tight at the waist. The design was dear little bunches of flowers on a background of pink and white stripes. This seemed to me an adventurous mixture of design styles – flowers *and* stripes. Instead of Reedham grey knee socks, I had white ankle socks, which normal girls wore every day. I thought

'My cousins must feel like this all the time.'

Susan, Frances and Judy were the daughters of my mother's elder sister Marie and her husband Dick Koenig. Their perfect home in Wallington, Surrey seemed to reproach us for our rambling, Victorian house in London, where all the upper floors were let out, and we lived in the basement, which while spacious, was inevitably dark. The rooms were odd shapes, the floors cold stone. We did have a delicious garden, full of roses and apple trees, but it was overgrown and untidy. We loved it of course, and we loved our big house, but Marie and

Dick in Wallington had a neat lawn and well behaved flowers. It never occurred to us - and probably never to them either - that our house was worth far more than theirs. In the 1950s things like that did not matter in the way they do now - priorities were very different - we were fatherless, in Care and way down the social scale.

Billie's brother Walter, his wife Colette and our cousins Katherine and Joëlle lived in Sutton, Surrey. Their house was famous for being small - everybody mentioned it, but to us it was the most friendly and relaxed of all the van Tinteren houses, except Grandmother's. It was just as neat and tidy as Wallington, perhaps even more so, but they seemed actually to like us, and did not seem concerned about our accents or our clothes. Colette was French, and they would all switch from one language to another - often mid-sentence - which fascinated us. If she ever told the girls off, Colette would do so in French, so we never heard her say anything unpleasant. She was very elegant, made all her own clothes, and the children's - even their winter coats. Walter made a lot of their furniture, and became quite worked up if you called him a carpenter

'I'm a joiner - a carpenter just does the rough stuff - I'm a craftsman'

And he was too. He made their oak dining table, several chairs, with woven rush seats, and a few other pieces. We were full of admiration.

But the van Tinterens we saw most of were Frank and Siobhan. They lived in Berkshire, far enough away to merit our staying a week or two. Siobhan was much younger than Frank, and lots of fun. She loved children and had wonderful ideas for keeping us amused.

'Let's put on a puppet show - we can make our own puppets out of papier maché!'

And we did. Under Siobhan's guidance we tore newspaper into postage stamp sized pieces of paper - a whole bucketful. Then we soaked it in water, and Siobhan went to the village shop for something called size and some plasticine for modelling the heads. The wet paper was applied, piece by overlapping piece, layer upon layer, over the plasticine heads, which Siobhan had told us to make with nice long necks so we could insert our middle fingers and wiggle the heads. It took ages, but we loved doing it, seeing our puppets taking shape, talking about the clothes we'd make for them, the dialogue we'd give them. I think Frank made a proscenium of some sort. Overnight Siobhan impaled the plasticine heads on pencils and in the morning we rushed down to see if the papier maché was dry enough to paint. It wasn't, it took two or three days, and in the meantime we made costumes. I can't remember the play and the only character I remember is a witch, with a hooked nose, a black dress and black pointed witchy hat. And white curly hair. This was Siobhan's brainwave, and she knew exactly where to get the hair.

Siobhan always had at least one poodle. Apparently, when they decided to marry, Frank said no dogs, and she agreed. But she persuaded, he relented and she got Tilly, a small, white poodle - and it was Tilly who provided the witch's frizzy hair.

Each family explained itself - ran a documentary for us - as soon as we walked in the door. Penny and Tanya, this is how we interpret the nuclear family and this is how we live. Marie explained how she ran her household smoothly, Walter and Colette showed us the furniture and clothes that they made. Frank and Siobhan told us of their simple, country life. Whatever they actually said, this is what we heard:

'We eat wholemeal bread, which Frank makes, but we have white on the breadboard, because you are from London and know no better. We are country people, simple, honest and true. You are from London, from a broken family, from an institution, and do not know how to behave. London is dirty, corrupt and synthetic; the food is manufactured. As fatherless children, you will be grateful for this glimpse of ideal family life, which we have granted you.'

Frank and Siobhan's was a more glamorous version of the

nuclear family than Marie's. They ate brown bread and played musical instruments. Siobhan was younger and laughed a lot. She was always teasing; it was often hard to know if she was serious or not. Her domestic skills were very limited, which she found terribly amusing, and she took pride in the weakness of her tea.

'Everyone complains about it' she would chortle.

Frank had designed and built their Berkshire house himself, and never tired of explaining its layout and features - the fireplace was of natural brick and Siobhan had made a hearthrug. She explained how she had picked out the colours from the curtains: navy, terracotta and beige, and woven the rug in a geometric design, which we all admired against the simple, natural parquet flooring. They were proud of not having wallpaper; instead they painted the walls with something called distemper, which was much cheaper. Simplicity, a carefree unaffected country style - were the keynote - and they put a lot of work into it.

I was always uncomfortable at their table. Frank had a vegetable patch and took pride in growing food for the family. As we sat down, the food was announced:

'The beans are from the garden, and the potatoes, but the tomatoes are shop bought.' You were expected to praise the freshness and taste of the home grown vegetables and to deplore the shop boughtness of the tomatoes. If you forgot, and praised the wrong vegetable, there would be screams of derisive laughter from Siobhan, echoed by the girls.

We sit around the big pine table, Uncle Frank at the head, Auntie Siobhan, Linnet, Jenny, Tanya, Mummy and me. It is teatime and Uncle Frank slices the bread. There are two loaves.

'White or brown?' he asks everyone before he cuts them a slice. I know the right answer, it is brown, so I say

'Brown please.'

The butter is hard – too hard to spread on the soft bread. I have learned at Reedham to scrape the top of hard butter, over and over again, gathering a small roll of soft butter each time. This makes the butter easier to spread. The younger children are fascinated. Auntie Siobhan cries:

'Look at what those girls learn at Reedham – that is very bad table manners. Linnet and Jenny are going to copy now of course! Really Billie, my children copy everything that Penny and Tanya do, and they are learning some appalling habits.'

And then she is suddenly smiling. Is she serious? I cannot be sure. I wait. My Mother speaks:

'Yes, you shouldn't really scrape the butter like that, dear – it *is* bad manners.' She takes a triangle of the butter and starts at the corner of her slice of bread. She manages to spread the edges of the slice quite well, but makes holes when she gets to the middle.

'Butter's rather hard Siobhan,' says my Mother.

'Rubbish, you townies are feeble, that's the trouble, you can spread it if you try.' She giggles.

Easter 1954

We are all in their kitchen, and Siobhan is about to change one-year-old Jenny's nappy. She has just laid the baby on the long, wooden table in preparation, when the door-bell rings. Billie goes to answer the door, and calls:

'Someone wants to speak to you, Siobhan – can you come?'

'Here, Penny, you know how to change a nappy, don't you?'

Although I have never had responsibility for any child, I have been shown how to change Jenny's nappy a few times in recent days. I have even had a go at it myself, so I know how to do it.

'Yes, OK I know what to do.'

'Don't let her roll off the table, now.'

Tanya has gone with Billie and Siobhan, who are in the front garden with the visitor, but two-year-old Linnet has stayed in the kitchen. Jenny starts to whimper when her mother leaves the room, so as I remove the dirty nappy, I tell her, in what I hope is a grown-up voice, that Mummy will be back soon. I drop the dirty nappy in the bucket, and clean her bottom with damp cotton wool. Then I turn round to take a clean nappy from the basket, and as I turn back, she rolls over and off the table on to the red quarry-tiled floor. I watch, Linnet watches, as Jenny falls - bang. She lands on her back, and looks startled. She is silent for a few seconds, then her mouth opens wide, she takes a deep breath and yells. Linnet stands watching, thumb in mouth, looking accusingly at me. I have been trusted and I have failed. I have let the baby fall. I panic, pick her up, sit down, cuddle her, but she will not stop crying. I am scared. Why won't she stop? I carefully finish changing her, and she screams all the way through. I might have killed Jenny. Bad orphanage child kills good little baby girl who lives with nice Mummy and Daddy who love her.

I try to give Jenny her bottle, but she is really into the crying now and won't close her mouth around it. Linnet sidles up to me and says she wants it. I hand it to her, but she wants the thing done properly, so I put Jenny in her cot and Linnet on my knee, cradling her and feeding her like a baby, which she enjoys immensely. When Siobhan returns this is what she finds. Jenny is yelling the place down and Linnet is having a bottle just like a baby, something she is supposed to have grown out of months ago.

Siobhan shrieks 'Why is Jenny crying?'

'I dropped her.'

My voice is not coming out properly. I clear my throat and repeat it.

The back of Siobhan's hand goes to her forehead, she takes a few staggering steps backwards, the other hand leaning on the table.

'Oh no!'

Eyes closed, then open, she rushes to pick up her baby and walks her to and fro.

'What did she do to you, poor little thing, did Penny drop you? Oh my baby, my poor little baby!'

Suddenly she sits down opposite me, with Jenny still crying on her lap. Leans forward.

'Tell me exactly what happened.'

There is a singing noise in my ears. My face is hot. Linnet stops sucking and stares.

'She rolled off the table and started to cry.'

'Did she start to cry immediately?'

'No, she was quiet for a minute, then she cried.'

'A minute! Billie, when she says a minute, does she mean sixty seconds or just a moment – you'll have to translate for me.'

'How long exactly was it, Penny?' my Mother asks.

'One or two seconds. She just looked surprised.'

'Oh my God. Concussion. She was unconscious. That's concussion if she didn't cry immediately.'

The singing in my ears has become so loud that I am not able to hear everything properly. My mother puts the kettle on, Siobhan sits rocking Jenny, Linnet climbs off my lap and stands leaning against her mother, staring at me accusingly, tears and snot streaming down her face.

'There, there darling, did you have a nasty bump? Oh my poor baby. Billie, I'm taking her to the doctor, if it's concussion she must be seen straight away.'

'Let's see how she is in the morning – I don't think it's concussion – she just took time to register what had happened.'. says my Mother.

As they drink their tea, they discuss the symptoms of brain damage, concussion and blows to the head. Siobhan says Jenny could be paralysed for life. She says this to Billie, not to me. She cannot even bring herself to look at me.

I am not in my own home and have nowhere to escape. Billie is drinking tea with the Mother of my innocent victim.

All the rooms belonged to the family I have wronged. I go into the children's room and sit on Linnet's little bed. I can still hear Jenny crying. I decide that if she is paralysed or her brain is damaged I will kill myself.

Then they'll be sorry.

19

Eleven Plus

Summer 1955

I really enjoyed the Eleven Plus exam. We had no preparation
for it, beyond being told that it was coming, and that those
who passed would go to Grammar School. This was thrilling.
Every time I thought about it, I was seized with the kind of
glee that makes an eleven year old scream and run around for
no reason apparent to any adult. If I thought of it when not in
the playground, I could not control my face. Cleaning shoes
in the Boot Room, for example, under the eye of a Prefect.

'Number 17 – wipe that smile off your face, or I'll do it for
you.'

I longed for the Eleven Plus because I knew I would pass
and therefore would certainly go to Grammar School. The
Grammar School students (students!) took an early breakfast
before everyone else, and then walked the two and a bit miles
to Purley Grammar every day. Of course, they had to return
to Reedham in the evening, but just imagine the freedom of it!
And I would get a real education at last. Naturally, the prospect
of everyone knowing how clever I was also contributed to the
glee.

How could I have known that Surrey County Council had
lots of children and not enough schools, especially Grammar
Schools? In the 40s and 50s young couples moved out of

London to Surrey, seeing the suburbs as a much better place to bring up children. The number of children who passed the Eleven Plus had to coincide with the number of Grammar School places. How could I have known of the resulting social engineering?

One the morning of the exam, we sat in Class Four, exam papers face down on the desk. With stopwatch in hand, Mrs Evans explained that, when she told us – and not before – we were to turn our papers over and start work. Looking intently at the stopwatch, she said

'Very well, children, you can turn your papers over – *now!*'

It was a specially printed paper, with today's date and even the right time on it. First I wrote my name, then looked at the questions. They were so exciting! The exam was in two sections, English and Arithmetic, and this was the English paper. Instead of the normal, excruciating process, of going through all the questions slowly first, to make sure that everyone knew the answers, this was a rare chance to work everything out for myself. And everyone had to keep quiet. The time flew by, and very soon after I'd finished, Mrs Evans told us to stop writing. Groans from all around the room.

In the afternoon, we sat the Arithmetic exam, which was not particularly difficult, but less enjoyable. I preferred the later questions, the ones involving baths filling at such and such a rate, and how many oranges did each boy have. Although less confident about my success in Arithmetic, I finished the paper in good time and knew I'd done better than most of the others.

A few weeks later, Mrs Evans announced the results. She told us that two pupils, John Kennair and Richard Newcombe would be going to the Grammar School next term. Then she said that Penny Wardman had also passed. In fact, John had come first, Penny second and Richard had come last. However, only two places had been allocated to Reedham, and the decision had been taken to award them to the two boys. Mrs

Evans explained that she had told us this because she wanted me to know that I had in fact done well in the exam. She gave the impression that she was not happy about it.

That information changed my interior landscape forever.

What few people knew then, is that in those days, to compensate for girls' precociousness, eleven plus results were routinely adjusted. Boys were marked up, and girls marked down. I believe I came first. But even coming first was not good enough to get a Reedham girl a Grammar School place.

In May 1957 there was another exam, called the Thirteen Plus, which those of us who had almost passed the Eleven Plus could take, and get another chance at Grammar School.

'*Almost* passed! I *did* pass!' I shouted down the corridor at my imaginary audience. The acoustics were excellent for the young drama queen; my indignant scorn echoed satisfyingly. By now, I knew the system was rigged in favour of the boys. By now, I had stopped trying in class unless I felt like it. What was the point?

On the day of the Thirteen Plus exam, I was in a foul mood, and told everyone I wasn't going to try, because it wasn't worth it. Actually, I did try, but of course, covered myself by telling no one. The next day I had my first period.

I never knew whether I failed the Thirteen Plus or if my place went again to a boy. I told everyone I didn't care.

20

Mrs Lane

Autumn 1955

I regularly told Billie about Reedham's poor educational standards, because I thought it might have more chance of swaying her than telling her we were unhappy. However, it was also true. For some time I had suspected that Reedham education was not as good as at other schools. Recently I'd had confirmation of this, having spent time with other children over the summer holidays. My cousins and contemporaries were further advanced in every subject except Domestic Science, which, mysteriously, other schools did not appear to teach. Instead of learning how to do a boil wash, how to iron a shirt or scrub a deal table, they did subjects like French and Physics, which were simply never mentioned at Reedham. Furthermore, they were all talking about studying for O levels, and it seemed that outside Reedham, everyone was going in for these GCE exams. When I heard my cousins listing the exams they planned to sit, I felt jealous and excluded. I knew I was bright enough to do it, but Reedham lessons always proceeded at the pace of the slowest, and being called intelligent was ambivalent praise.

In my early Reedham years, my hand shot up nearly every time the teacher asked a question, but soon they started saying 'Does anyone - *not* you, Penny Wardman - know the answer?' and I'd be left, exposed, my hand in the air and a foolish, eager grin on my face - while the teacher looked for someone else and my classmates sniggered and made faces. Being intelligent and keen did not make me popular, and as the Eleven Plus had proved, didn't get me very far either. After I didn't get my grammar school place, I stopped putting my hand up.

We had no library at Reedham, but there were sometimes a few old books lying around on the shelves behind the piano in the playroom. These were mainly ancient, battered books from the 1930s - Angela Brazil and other boarding school stories for girls. When I was about nine, I found 'Little Women' by Louisa May Alcott and started reading it, quite slowly. It had lost its dust jacket long ago, and was bound in faded green linen. I kept it in my locker and got it out every playtime. It was about some girls living at home with their mother. Their father was away and they had very little money, but they were happy with each other's company and with just a few, simple pleasures. I loved that book. They had a boy next door, and - best of all - their father came home in the end!

When I got to the end, I felt bereft. I saw from the introduction that this was the first of a series, and after that there was 'Good Wives' and 'Jo's Boys,' which I found fascinating, since it implied that Jo got married and had children. I was desperate to read it.

But I couldn't find it anywhere. The Angela Brazils did not tempt me much; they were all about boarding schools and held no interest for me. Already I knew more than I wanted to about boarding school and anyway you could see that they were nothing like the reality. Angela Brazil's boarding school girls were taught French by mistresses called Mamzelle, they had slap up teas in front of a blazing common room fire and were never hit or had to do the cleaning.

So I started reading Little Women again, a little more quickly this time. When I got to the end, I read it again. And again.

"Christmas won't be Christmas without any presents' grumbled Jo, lying on the hearthrug...'

Soon I knew that first line - and many others - by heart. I read that book nine times, until Billie bought me 'Good Wives' and I moved on. That's when I learned to read fluently and when I learned how a book could be an escape from the unendurable present.

I only read Good Wives twice, then found Boswell's Life of Johnson. It looked interesting, but it was very hard. I recognised many of the words, but couldn't hold the long and complicated sentences in my head long enough to understand them.

Mrs Lane found me on my bed, clutching the book and sobbing. She was a new mistress who had the room outside Fry Dormitory and everybody liked her. She was tall, slim and very nicely spoken. She was the only mistress who was a Mrs, not a Miss. This was because she was a widow. She spoke gently to us, called us by our first names and sometimes sat beside us on our beds and talked to us about all sorts of things. I loved her, and once spent my whole pocket money - 6d - on a blue glass ashtray for her. She had taken us shopping and I couldn't wait to get back to Reedham to give it to her, so I left the crocodile and ran up to give it to her as we walked back. I was so proud and happy. She was very pleased and thanked me several times, but she was distressed that I had spent all my money on her.

I think I knew she was nearby when I couldn't understand 'Boswells Life' and sobbed a bit harder in the hope that she would come and sit on my bed. She did, she came and put her arm round me and I explained that I was crying because I didn't understand my book. She said I shouldn't worry because I had my whole life ahead of me. She said:

'I've got so many books I want to read - lots of Shakespeare I haven't got round to yet. Don't worry, there will be time for everything. This book is far too hard for you - it's even a bit hard for me, actually.' She stayed and talked to me, sitting on my bed, asking me about the books I'd read, what kind of books I enjoyed, just as if we were normal people, not in this place, and she was a friend of mine. It gave me a wonderful feeling of confidence, of opening up, that an adult who was not my mother could be so kind to me, so interested in me. I think she knew I had a slight crush on her.

Less than a week after this, we were very late getting up. Usually the mistress on duty would march briskly into the dormitory and start opening the curtains.

'Come along girls, it's ten to seven.'

On the day we were late, Miss Henderson rushed in and cried:

'It's quarter past seven get up, get up quickly. Everything at the double this morning.'

We did everything as usual, except we didn't line up for anything, just dashed into the washroom and back, clattered downstairs when we were ready, ending up breathless and in the playroom, ready to lead off for breakfast. The following Sunday, as we lined up for church, Matron said she had a very sad announcement to make.

'I have to tell you that Mrs Lane (*pause*) has (*pause*) died. I want you all to pray for her at the service this morning. I also want you to be extra considerate and helpful to Miss Randall and Miss Henderson because there will be so much extra work for them until we can find a replacement for Mrs Lane. Lead on.'

That is all the information Matron gave us, but after church we discovered a little more. Carol White had got up in the night to go to the lavatory and when she passed Mrs Lane's room the door was open, the light was on and Mrs Lane was sitting on the floor in a pool of water. Miss Henderson was in there and when she saw Carol, she pushed the door shut.

It was a shock. I had lost a good friend and was heartbroken. She had been wrong, I told everybody who would listen, she hadn't had plenty of time to read that Shakespeare. She hadn't had any time at all. What had been the matter with her? She had seemed so young and healthy. In an attempt to find out more, I asked Miss Randall what would happen to the blue glass ashtray. Miss Randall said it would be packed up with the rest of Mrs Lane's belongings and sent to her relatives.

Months later, I asked one of the older girls if they knew what had happened to Mrs Lane. 'Oh, didn't you know - she committed suicide.' It seemed that Mrs Lane had turned on her gas fire, but not lit it, and sat down beside it. I don't know how Miss Henderson came to be there, but I guess that the water Carol saw had been thrown over Mrs Lane to try to revive her.

21

The Retiring Room

1955

NEXT to Fry washroom, opposite the toilets, was the Retiring Room. It was supposed to be kept secret from the Juniors, and mostly it was. I knew some Junior girls had crept upstairs and peeped in, and one day in about 1955, I did too. It was dark, there was one small window, but it wasn't an outside window and anyway it was painted over. I turned the light on. There was brown lino on the floor, cream paint on the walls, and just four things in the room.

Against the back wall, on the right was a huge, but shallow butlers sink. On the left wall near the door was a cupboard, painted brown like the rest of the woodwork. Over in the left hand corner, under the painted over window, was a metal dustbin, painted red. On the window sill was a pile of newspapers. That was it.

When I whispered to Enid Wood that I had been in the Retiring Room and there was nothing in there she said

'Yes there is – look in the cupboard – that's where they keep them.'

So next time the coast was clear, I had another look. Inside the cupboard were several brown paper parcels, about the size of a shallow shoe box, with the words 'Southall's – Medium' on a discreet white label. There was something dark in the butlers sink, but I didn't pay much attention. I felt the parcels, they were soft. Someone was coming and I darted out into the Fry toilets.

'What's in the brown paper parcels, anyway?' I asked Enid Wood.

'Towels.' she said authoritatively. 'You'll find out when you're old enough.'

'You're not old enough, are you?' I asked.

'Yes, and I'm going into Fry dorm next term and then I can use the Retiring Room.'

'What for?'

'You'll find out when you're old enough.'

The next term Enid Wood went up into Fry dorm and so – unexpectedly – did Irene Harvey. She was a year younger than me, and yet I was still in Nightingale. I asked her why.

'Because I have to use the Retiring Room.' she said in a matter of fact voice.

I could not confess to someone a year younger than me that I still did not know what the Retiring Room was for, so I went back to Enid Wood. She and Irene Harvey took me into Fry Washroom and started to explain about growing up and having babies and body changes and finally got to the part about menstruation.

'Oh you mean it's for your periods – is that all?' I cried out in disappointment.

They both looked confused and indignant.

'Did you know about it then?'

'Yes, my Mum told me ages ago, so I would be ready when it happened. But what do you do in the Retiring Room?'

'You're not supposed to know about it yet, anyway.' said Irene, dignity affronted by my disdain for their precious secret. They re-gained their superiority by showing me round the Retiring Room, and introducing me to its mysteries.

The butlers sink was to soak your soiled knickers in cold

water, the cupboard held packets of sanitary towels, an exercise book and a pencil attached to the cupboard with a piece of string. Each girl who had started menstruating had her own page, and with the pencil, wrote down the date every time she started a period. Or 'came on' as we usually said, I think the word period was considered a bit graphic. The red dustbin was for soiled S.T.s, after you had wrapped them in newspaper. You shouldn't call them Sanitary Towels, because then people would know. You should call them S.T.s.

'But that's not the worst bit.'

'What do you mean?'

'You'll find out when you're old enough.'

I didn't think it could be much, so decided to wait till I was old enough and went downstairs.

Because I wrote it down in the exercise book and it was at the top of my page every time I made a new entry, I know that I started my first period in May 1957. This was followed by one in September, two in January and every 28 days after that. I had already been moved up to Fry Dorm, and was now a fully paid up member of the Retiring Room Club and on the Rota.

'What's the Rota?'

Inside the cupboard door was a weekly rota: two girls were on duty each week. I asked Enid Wood again.

'What do you have to do?'

'It's the worst bit of all, I'm dreading it. You have to go up to Mr Bristow in the Dining Hall at the end of breakfast and ask to be excused. Then you have to get the old S.T.s from the dustbin in the Retiring Room and take them down the Back Road to the Furnace. And you have to go in and ask Old Tom to open the Furnace door and then you have to throw them in. I'm dreading it.' said Jean, with relish.

'Why?'

'Because all the boys can tell when you're on. They can tell when you've started, because they see you going out of breakfast early and they know where you're going. And when you're on, they can smell it.'

I pretended to believe her but I didn't really. I couldn't tell if someone was wearing a sanitary towel, so how could the boys? And getting out of the Dining Room early for an unsupervised ten minutes when you could talk and run and laugh seemed more of a treat than a chore. If not many girls were on, and there were only half a dozen newspaper parcels, you could stuff them inside your jumpers and not bother to take the metal bucket from inside the red dustbin. Old Tom was friendly enough, his job for years had been to keep the furnace going to heat the whole building, and any frisson he got out of pubescent girls burning their newspaper parcels must have worn off long ago.

Along the Back Road, between the Infants toilets and the kitchen, and next to the Drying Room, was The Furnace, so hot, the door was always open. The huge iron cylinder had a round metal door, just below our head height. Old Tom didn't say much, but he smiled a toothless smile, and opened the Furnace door for us using a special opener with a scorched wooden handle, the Furnace door itself being impossible to touch. Then we would stand there, throwing the parcels one by one into the big, bright fire, watching the newspaper burn off in a quick bright flame, then the S.T.s uncurl and move around, briefly alive, before they became ash, their shape still discernible against the background of burning coals.

22

Knowing Our Place

REEDHAM was a popular target for charity - not all of it as wonderful as the Guild of the Nineteen Lubricators' annual trip to Littlehampton. There were other events, smaller and more local. Despite all the hectoring about which forthcoming event we should be grateful for, all the benefactors merged in my mind into just one - The Rotary Committee. I looked Rotary up in a dictionary once, and concluded - uncertainly - that they conducted their meetings while walking round a circular table. I hated them anyway, because everything that went wrong, everything that was our fault, they would pay for to be put right, and then make sure we knew all about it. And were grateful.

'You girls must stop being so careless. Do you have any idea of how much it costs to repair a window? Now the ball that was thrown has been confiscated, and the girl who did it has been severely punished. When will you learn? (*pause for effect*). From now on, throwing balls of any kind is not allowed in the playground. Where is the money going to come from? The budget is very, very tight, let me tell you. Once again I will have to beg the Rotary Committee to find the money to pay for this broken window, and all because of your carelessness and ingratitude.'

I longed to point out what we all knew, that the Netball pitch was marked out on the playground, and that our PE classes often consisted of a game in the playground. Supposing the playroom window had been broken accidentally during a netball match, instead of during playtime? Were we supposed to defy the sports teacher and refuse to play Netball, because it was suddenly against the rules?

The Rotary Committee also had to stump up for my broken glasses. I was at Reedham for ten years, and wore glasses for all but the first term. I must have broken my glasses four or five times in that whole period. Given that I was a normal, healthy child who ran about, played Netball and Tennis this doesn't seem excessively careless, but all the staff acted as if they were deeply shocked by my wickedness every time it happened. And every time it was the long lecture in Matron's office about my ingratitude and clumsiness, the longsuffering generosity of the Rotary Committee. In retrospect, I recognise that my broken spectacles must have been paid for by the National Health Service, to which my Mother contributed. The Rotary Committee had nothing to do with it. But even if I had known that then, I would not have said anything. I didn't start answering Matron back until I was about thirteen.

At one of the charity parties, there was a show with a compére, and he invited anyone to come up on stage and recite a poem or sing a song. I knew a poem: *Sir Smashem Up'*, I had learned it by heart from a book I found when I was quite young, having picked up the idea that everyone should have a party piece. I loved learning things by heart and relished performing.

My hand was the first to go up. It may even have been the only one to go up. I stood up on the stage and recited the whole thing perfectly. I understood it and was able to recite it as you were meant to do 'with expression'. Everybody clapped at the end and my grin felt the size and shape of a banana. I couldn't get rid of it or tone it down. Full of myself, I swaggered back to my seat, basking in applause and brimming with confidence, and the show carried on. During the next act, Miss Tanner, the Infants' teacher, who was sitting behind me, leaned forward and hissed in my ear:

'Fancy making a fool of yourself like that? Stupid girl!'

Shocked. I was deeply shocked. And puzzled. What was she talking about? I had obviously been a great success - not only did I know it in my heart, but everybody had laughed and clapped a lot. Was she mad? What had I done wrong? What did 'making a fool of oneself' mean, anyway? I had not been foolish, I had been triumphant! I didn't tell anybody about what she said, and although her hatred and anger stayed with me, I did not take it to heart. I was able to keep it slightly at a distance because I knew she was wrong. Eventually I recognised that it was *her* embarrassment, probably tinged with jealousy. Embarrassment that one of the underprivileged children in her care had not known her place. Got above herself. Drawn attention, sought the spotlight. Shone.

One of the staff once told us that we should not get above ourselves because we were all 'destined for the servants' hall' anyway. Most of the staff at Reedham seemed to share this opinion, were anxious that we should know our place and would probably have shared Miss Tanner's embarrassment. But not all of them. Although I thought I had completely lost the 'posh' accent which had attracted the bullies when we first arrived, one day Mr Davies stopped me in the corridor:

'Here, Penny Wardman. You speak nicely, don't you?'

'Er, yes Sir. Thank you Sir.'

'Keep it up, it's very good. Very good, now you keep it up.'

'Yes, Mr Davies. Thank you Sir.'

And he rushed off. In our daily lives we saw few men, and if they addressed us, it was as a group, rarely as an individual. I was so overcome with the attention and the praise that I couldn't keep quiet about it. Some people never learn! As it happened, the few people to whom I boasted to about this were decent enough not to call me a big head or worse. The incident made a huge impression on me, but also made me even more worried about the way I spoke. It was something

I had to think about a lot, because adults, especially Billie, were always commenting on it.

As soon as we arrived home for the holidays:

'Oh I do wish you wouldn't speak in that dreadful Reedham accent.'

By the time I was 14 I was retorting that in that case she shouldn't have sent us there, then, if she didn't want us to pick up the accent. Of course, when we returned to Reedham, we had to drop the cut glass swiftly, and throughout our childhood, Tanya and I were constantly adapting the way we spoke. Wherever we were, it seemed our accents were unacceptable. We were far from knowing our place.

23

Running Away

Summer 1958

I became a Prefect soon after my 14th birthday in May 1958, and it felt wonderful. I was one of the tallest girls, and my height had recently led to an amazing development. One afternoon, playing netball, I discovered that by simply raising my hand and jumping a little off the ground, I could prevent a smaller, tougher girl from scoring a goal. Overnight I became Good at Sport. After years of dithering around at the back, ungainly and with no idea of the rules, suddenly I knew exactly what to do. It didn't matter that I couldn't run for toffee, all I had to do was hang around the goalpost and jump when necessary.

A few of us became Prefects that term, and this gave us access to the Prefects' Recreation Room, known as the Prefects' Rec. It was a large and comfortable sitting room, off the classroom corridor, set out into the square, with light on three sides. There was a gas fire, a piano, easy chairs and a sofa, and we could use this room whenever we had free time. In return for this privilege, we were expected to help the Staff by keeping the younger ones in order in any way we saw fit. There were no restrictions on how we did this, we were expected to discipline and punish them, and to beat them if we wanted.

It was an exhilarating time when I was rapidly losing fear

and respect for everything that had held me in silent terror for most of my childhood. The last Prefect to have sexually abused me had left at the end of 1957 and now I was a Prefect myself, I knew nobody was going to try that on any more. Nor had I any desire to perpetrate it. My contemporaries and I had vowed that when we were Prefects we would break with tradition and not bully the little ones, as we ourselves had been bullied. We had strong feelings about justice and freedom, mainly focussed on the way we were treated, and the way we - once Prefects - were expected to treat the little ones. Some of us had little sisters and could not bear to bully and hurt them in the way that, up till now, Prefects had always bullied and hurt the younger girls as soon as they got the chance.

So we sat in the unaccustomed luxury of the Prefects' Rec. and agreed on a bit of a manifesto. We were going to be a new, and wonderfully magnanimous breed of Prefect, who would stand up to Matron on everyone's behalf. I was the originator of most of this, and where I got these radical ideas from I'm not sure, but I do know that my new and hazy grasp of socialism had some influence. I quickly discovered that I was quite bossy and inexplicably popular.

One day Miss Randall lost her keys. She came into the Prefects' Rec. one evening and asked if any of us had seen them. Poor Miss Randall, bespectacled, round-shouldered, hooked nosed, her skin angry with excema, was probably only about ten years older than us. She was one of the nicest mistresses we'd ever had, which simply meant she often spoke politely to us, using our names rather than our numbers. I think she hoped we would like her for this, see her as the soft cop, when the rest of the force was sadistic and corrupt, but of course we took advantage of her humanity and had our revenge on her for the brutality of her colleagues.

She had a strong Belfast accent, and we pretended not to understand her for as long as we thought we could get away with it. It seemed she'd had her keys in the morning, but by lunchtime they were no longer dangling from her belt. She definitely had them after breakfast when she went up to the Tower to get the summer dresses out. The Tower was out of bounds and meant to be locked, and she definitely remembered locking the door behind her. If she didn't find them before bedtime, she would have to tell Matron, because she could not move freely around the school without them. None of us had seen her keys, and Miss Randall went off for a final search before she walked along the red and black tiled corridor to Matron's Office.

We lined up in the playroom, before marching in to breakfast the next morning. Matron came to address us. She told us that Miss Randall's keys were missing, and this was the chance for the person who had taken them to own up. We all looked blank, some of us shrugged a bit and looked around at each other with raised eyebrows. Matron said that the theft of the keys was very serious as it held keys to internal and external doors, so whoever had taken them could gain access to any room in the building. Until recently, I would actually have shared Matron's concern about this, and felt guilty, despite being innocent. But recently, I'd started to think more about the gaps in Matron's logic. If someone had stolen the keys yesterday morning, *why wasn't anything missing yet?* If it had been me, my tummy would not be rumbling for breakfast now, I'd have raided the Kitchen and Bread Room last night, and treated the whole of Fry and Prefects' Dorm to a midnight feast of such magnificent proportions, that future Reedham girls would speak of it, down the decades, in awestruck tones.

Matron pulled out the usual stops: how lucky we were to be here, the ladies from the Rotary Club Committee had worked so hard to raise money for us to have all the privileges we were now enjoying, things that children before the war could only have dreamed of. 'Believe me, you girls have got it easy these days.' and so on. This was Matron's all-purpose rant, designed to make us feel generally evil, unworthy and guilty. She was very good at it, after telling us how bad we were and how ungrateful for our comfortable and privileged lives, she always followed with the guaranteed tear jerker. She would pause, scan the room for anyone already close to tears, look them in the eye and say in a quiet voice, 'What would your mother say if she knew that you had been so ungrateful and wicked?' I had always been one of the first to cry at these words, but for the first time ever, I remained unmoved by 'What would your mother say?' I was busy thinking. However, there was sufficient sniffling to satisfy Matron, and she moved on. 'Visiting Day will be cancelled until those keys are found. I want you all to go now, before you have any breakfast, and look everywhere for them.'

Whilst Matron was droning on, I was thinking about the summer dresses Miss Randall had brought down from the Tower. Since yesterday morning, they had been lying on the Prefect's bed by the door, and I had been hoping she would give them out soon. The weather was hot and sunny and we were all fed up with our winter uniform of grey flannel shirt, navy gymslip, grey knee length socks and black lace up shoes. The shoes wouldn't change, but we were given beige or grey ankle socks, and the summer dresses were only two years old, in a pretty, sprigged design, red on white. Once a year, on Festival Day, we were issued with white ankle socks - Lord knows what happened to them for the rest of the year. Suddenly I visualised what could have happened - suppose Miss Randall had come down from the Tower, put the keys on the Prefect's bed and flung the pile of dresses on top of them! As soon as Matron dismissed us, I told Irene Harvey and Enid Wood my idea, and we raced up to the dormitory, lifted up the pile of dresses and found the keys. Overjoyed at the certain restoration of Visiting Day, we careered down the wooden staircase, across the lobby to the Staff Room. We barged in without knocking and plonked the huge, heavy bunch of keys on the table in front of Miss Randall.

She was sitting at the table by the window, her elbows on the dark green chenille cover, examining her fingernails.

'Miss Randall, we've found them - guess what - they were under the summer dresses! When you carried the dresses down from the Tower, you must have thrown the keys down on the bed first, then the dresses on top of them!'

Why didn't she look pleased? Her face looked white and strained; red blotches of excema stood out here and there.

'What's the matter, Miss Randall?'

'Don't tell Matron you found them there, please girls. I'll get into terrible trouble.'

She spoke very quietly, picking at a hangnail, not looking at us.

We knew of course that the mistresses were as frightened of Matron as we were, but we rarely got such hard evidence of it. Miss Randall's vulnerability was terrifying. Furthermore, she was asking us to cover up for her by lying, which seemed unfair to us. If the circumstances had been reversed, we knew she would not have covered up for us.

'But we'll lose Visiting Day if we don't tell Matron' said Enid. Miss Randall looked desperate 'Tell her you found them somewhere else' she implored. I despised her for being so scared of Matron that she was prepared to ask us to lie and sacrifice our Visiting Day in order to save herself.

'We can't Miss, someone else will get blamed for it, one of the girls, and that's not fair, because it was your fault Miss. We've got to tell the truth!'

Miss Randall took the hangnail to her teeth and ripped it off.

'You must do what you think best, I suppose. I can't stop you.'

The three of us hurtled down the corridor, not even pausing to slide on the shiny bit, and only slowed down as we got towards Matron's Office. Our hearts bursting with justice, excitement and importance, we knocked and waited for Matron to call 'Come in'. If you didn't wait, she would make you go out and do it again, and to be sure that you did, she usually left a pause of five or six seconds before responding to a knock. We waited, panting, exchanging happy glances, confident of praise. Eventually, she called.

'Come in.'

'Please Matron, we've found the keys. We've given them to Miss Randall. She's got them now, Matron.' She finished writing something and looked up at us, without smiling.

'Where were they?'

'Please Matron, under the summer dresses, on the Prefect's bed. Miss Randall must have put the keys down, then put the dresses on top of them when she brought them down from the Tower yesterday morning.'

'Whose idea was it to look there?'

'Mine Matron. I just thought, well....'

'Thank you Number 17, that's quite enough from you. You seem to have a lot to say for yourself these days, very full of yourself, aren't you? It seems to me that you found those keys mighty quickly young lady. If you knew exactly where to look for them, you must have known where they were hidden. And you knew where they were because you yourself put them there.'

I was horrified. 'No Matron!'

'Don't you contradict me you great lump. And don't think this means you will have Visiting Day now, because it's still cancelled. Get out of my sight!'

'But that's not fair!' we all shouted together.

'I beg your pardon?' said Matron, in a terrifyingly calm tone. I was shaking, I hated her, she was not going to get away with this.

'It's not fair' I repeated, alone this time.

'One more word out of you madam, and it's bread and water for a week. Now shut up and get out.'

We left without another word. Not that anyone was scared of getting bread and water, which was not a bad punishment, but we were incensed at the injustice of it. Matron had simply gone back on her word. The keys had been found, but Visiting Day was still cancelled. Before we could discuss it much, the whistle went for breakfast, and we all ran to the playroom to stand again in the six lines of twelve girls, which corresponded to the tables we sat at once we reached the Dining Hall. Miss Randall said

'You can lead off now' to Irene Baker, who was the first Prefect in the line by the door, and Irene started the march, in single file, to the Dining Hall.

The march to breakfast, the meal itself and the assembly afterwards were all strictly silent, so there was no opportunity to talk properly until we were doing our duties. Between breakfast and the first class of the day, we each had a domestic task to perform, known as our Duty, and this would change every term. That term I had cleaning the bathroom, which was one of the worst duties, simply because it took so long, there were eleven baths in that room - not counting the cubicles at the end, and two sinks, they all had to be cleaned with vim and rinsed out, the taps polished and the whole floor swept and mopped. Although two of us were allocated to it, there was only three quarters of an hour between assembly and the whistle for class, so you couldn't hang about. As I tipped the gritty vim on to the grey cloth and wiped the greasy ring from each bath, I simply decided to run away.

At playtime I told Irene and Enid.

'I'm running away. I'm just going to get on the train and go home. I'm not going to spend all my money on Saturday, I'm not going to spend any of it. If we can't have Visiting Day, then I'm going to see my Mum anyway.'

'Me too' said Irene 'I'll go to Mrs Hodder. She said I can always go there whenever I want, and I know where she lives and everything.'

Irene was a real orphan, with no family, and during the

holidays, she stayed with various foster mothers. Mrs Hodder was a favourite with everyone who went to her.

'I'm running away too.' said Enid.

'Where are you going, then?' asked Irene

'I'll go with you Irene. Can I come to Mrs Hodder with you?'

Planning our escape was thrilling. For some reason it seemed wiser to go on a weekday, so we settled on the following Monday. The longest period in the day when nobody would be looking for us, was after tea and before bedtime. So, the next Monday we set out after tea at about 5.30, in our Reedham clothes, went to Reedham station and caught a train. We split up at London Bridge - I knew exactly where I was going, and Irene and Enid seemed confident about their destination. In 1955, our house at 27 Carleton Road, had been compulsorily purchased by Islington Council, and with the proceeds, Billie had bought another big house 22 Minster Road, NW2, which of course she filled with lodgers. I took the Bakerloo Line to Kilburn and walked to my house, where the door was opened by a very surprised Billie. Once she got over the shock and realised that I was OK and had only run away because I was unhappy, she was actually quite pleased to see me. She rang Matron, told her I was safe and that she would be returning with me next day.

I told Billie I didn't want to go back. I explained the injustice of Visiting Day being cancelled, why Tan and I both hated it, please couldn't we go to a normal school and live at home with her, study for exams and wear our own clothes?

'Would you like to go to Stage School? I could make enquiries about that if you like?'

'Oh yes, Mummy, that would be wonderful – thank you.'

'I've been reading about some of these schools, they teach singing, tap and ballet. How are you getting on at Mrs Parrott's by the way?'

Since I was 11, Tanya and I had attended Mrs Parrott's Ballet Classes every Saturday morning. Mrs Parrott had a large house on the Brighton Road, to which we walked, down the drive and along Old Lodge Lane, clutching our drawstring linen bags, containing pink ballet shoes and the white cotton piqué ballet dresses Billie made for us.

Billie said she would see what she could do, but meanwhile I had to go back.

Next day she took me out to a posh chemist in Cricklewood Broadway and bought me some exquisite, grown up toiletry items, among them a back brush of blue transparent plastic, which I loved. She rang Matron again. Irene and Enid had been picked up at Mrs Hodder's and returned last night. I heard Billie tell Matron that she would prefer it if we were not punished too severely, since we had been protesting at what we perceived to be an injustice. She did not tell me how Matron had replied to this, but it made no difference, because I knew Matron would take no notice, and that our punishment would be particularly harsh. Not simply for running away, which was pretty bad, but for discussing and criticising her regime with other adults, outsiders. We were no better than informers. I didn't care. I'd just spent 24 hours at home with my Mother, and had briefly been cherished. I'd escaped once. I could do it again.

The memory of that 24 hours I spent at home in May 1959 still has an aura of optimism and joy about it. There was our own home, our wild and wonderful garden, our funny little kitchen - it was all there waiting for me. All I had to do was get out and go home, after that the world was full of possibility. I lay in bed, caressing my back brush, longing for home, civilisation and Cricklewood Broadway, plotting my return.

I started hoarding money. Originally, I didn't have a very clear idea of why I was doing it. The possession of cash was strictly forbidden. One Saturday, soon after I ran away, as we walked along the Brighton Road to go shopping, I saw a familiar figure approaching.

A woman in a grey, sleeveless dress with a wide black belt

and full skirt was walking towards Reedham. She wore black high heels, matching handbag, and had dark, curly hair. As she drew nearer, I could see that the grey fabric of her dress was in fact a small black and white pattern. I could see that her lipstick was red and that it was - my Mother!

She was on her way to see Matron about something – possibly about my recent bid for freedom - and had not expected to be allowed to see me. When parents came to the school outside visiting day, there was normally never any question of them sneaking in an unofficial visit - no matter how far they had come, and Billie had no idea she would to meet me. We were overjoyed to see each other. The mistress did not see and the crocodile did not stop, but I stepped aside for a minute. She asked where we were going, and when I said 'Shopping' she produced half a crown, gave me a kiss and I ran to catch up with the crocodile.

In Woolworth's I found Tan and told her. Her dismay at having missed Mummy was tempered by the magnificence of the 1/3d which was now hers. It was like a small lottery win. Each week we would queue up in front of Matron for our pocket money. She kept our records in an exercise book, and had a black cash box in front of her. Pocket money was provided by our parents or guardians, kept by Reedham and doled out by Matron. Theoretically, you could withdraw it as you wished, but in reality if you asked for more than a shilling, you had to say what you planned to spend it on. Threepence was a normal, modest amount - it would buy you quite a few sweets. Sixpence was good, because with that you could buy something from the toiletry or stationery counters.

That Saturday I had set out with sixpence, so already I felt prosperous and expansive. With my share of the half crown, I now had 1/9d - almost two shillings. It was actually too much. Too much excitement. Too much to spend in 20 minutes. Too much to spend in Woolworth's. There was never a question of us being allowed into any other shop. The crocodile would come to a halt outside, forty eight girls in 24 pairs, blocking off the entire shop's frontage to other customers. The mistress would bellow:

'When I blow the whistle, I want you all lined up out here, in your places, ready to go back. OK - in you go.' And we would rush into Woolworth's, our big black shoes clattering on the wooden floors and shaking them like thunder. Residents of Purley were used to us and probably avoided Woolworth's on Saturday afternoons. After about 20 minutes, the whistle would pierce through the store and our shoes would thunder out again.

After I had told Tan every detail of my brief encounter with Mummy, we looked at the half crown, trying to decide what to buy, so as to get some change and divide it up. It was too difficult. It was too much. 'You keep it for me.' said Tanya.

I spent my sixpence, but did not break in to the half crown. We were meant to hand in any unspent pocket money when we got back, but this rarely happened, as we were all experts at spending every last farthing. So I kept the half crown. It was big and silver and had once been in my Mother's purse, then in her hand, now in mine. She had given it to me and I wanted to keep it. After that, I started asking for slightly more pocket money and spending slightly less. There was no real plan yet - not in the front of my brain anyway. I'd ask for 9d and spend 4d - gradually adding a few pennies each time. Now that I knew it was possible, one day soon, I was going to run away again.

This time I was going to go alone, at night, and I would not be wearing Reedham uniform. Some old navy serge skirts from the thirties had recently been discovered in the Sewing Room, and were being issued to girls whose busts were too big for gymslips. This was more of an economy measure than respect for our appearance or maturity, but I'd obtained one and it really didn't look too bad. It was plain navy, knee length and a-line. With a white blouse it might just pass for civvies. As part of our summer kit, we had been issued with sandals - the brown leather, crepe-soled t-bar sandal which most children wore in those days. They were by no means adult shoes, but they were not the dead giveaway that the black clodhoppers were. I decided to wear them without the knee-length, grey socks. Bare legs would look a bit odd, a bit institutional, but it seemed to me there was nothing to identify me with Reedham.

I thought that my best chance of getting away unseen would be when I was next on dormitory duty. Nightingale and Fry dormitories always had a Prefect sleeping in the end bed (the Prefect's bed), by the door, ostensibly in case of emergencies but in fact to keep order. The younger girls tended to go to sleep earlier, so my chances of slipping out unobserved seemed better.

I had my running away clothes, and my money, ready in my locker. It was almost mid-summer, and even after lights out at 8pm the girls were restless in the long daylight. They fidgeted and whispered, and I thought they would never settle.

'Shut up you lot or I'll come and thump you!'

Giggles, and the sound of bare feet scampering out of one bed and into another one. I was not a very strict Prefect, so they were not taking me seriously. Time for a bit of acting.

'Right!' I yelled, 'Anyone out of bed has had it.'

I started down the dormitory, checking heads on pillows, my bare feet squeaking along the polished floor. Sure enough, Valerie Smith's bed was empty. And Cheryl Cook's bed was over-populated. I dragged Valerie out of Cheryl's bed, whacked her hard on the backside and flung her back towards her own bed.

'And you can stop that noise Number 15 or I'll really give you something to cry about.'

Then I threw back Cheryl's covers and whacked her on the backside as well.

'Now shut up and go to sleep all of you. If I hear a peep out of anyone they will be in deep trouble.'

The dormitory was silent with shock, and surprisingly soon

a steady breathing sound established itself, as sleep slipped into every bed but mine.

As soon as I was sure they were all asleep. I went silently to the washroom, changed my clothes and crept downstairs. By stepping on the outside edge of each stair, and not in the creaky middle, I achieved a virtually silent descent.

And then I simply walked out again. Down the drive, my heart pounding, and out of the school gates. It was still light, the evening was warm, there were people walking about, behaving normally. I knew I looked odd, but decided that authority and confidence were my best hope.

I had no plan, but if I went home again I knew what would happen - she would send me back again. Ultimately she would betray me, ultimately she was on Reedham's side, not mine - she wanted me there.

It never occurred to me not to get on the London train. I had a vague idea that if I got on the other platform and went in the opposite direction, I would end up at Tattenham Corner - whatever that was. London was home, it was all I knew, all I wanted.

I had some romantic idea of running away to seek my fortune. That the adults in charge of my destiny did not know what they were doing, did not have my best interests at heart, and that I would have to take things over myself. An idea began to form of finding a real home, with real parents who would immediately see my potential and love me for it. I wanted a proper home with two parents, one of whom would be a father. My room would be ready and waiting for me. They would buy me decent clothes, help me with my homework and send me to University. I needed to find them between Reedham and London Bridge. From the map on the carriage wall, I saw that Norwood Junction was the next stop, after that it was London Bridge. There were houses here - small and dark, but apparently with people living in them.

There had been nobody selling tickets at Reedham and I'd

planned to pay at the other end, but there was nobody there either, so I had a free journey. It was getting dark, and Norwood Junction was a strange place, not like anything I knew. I selected a house, walked up the path, knocked on the door. The man who answered it had no shirt on, just an old fashioned, yellowy white, woollen vest with sleeves, and dirty trousers held up with braces. He had not shaved recently, reminding me of Robert Newton as Long John Silver in Treasure Island.

'I wonder if you have a room for the night' I asked, inspired by all those folk tales where the young traveller trudges for miles through the forest until, footsore, she stumbles on a lonely cottage in the middle of the woods, where…well I was only just 15 and had led a sheltered life! The man looked startled, stepped back and said 'You'd better come in.'

Suddenly I didn't want to. I would like to tell you that it was morality or an instinct for self-preservation, but I don't think it was. It was snobbery. The house was shabby and so was the man. He didn't speak very nicely. I didn't feel he would appreciate me properly and do what was best for me - I was certain he would not send me to university. If he did have a bed for the night, it would not be the nice girl's bedroom I had in mind, with the clean, crisp linen, the dear little desk, the bookshelves and the frilly lampshade.

So I ran.

I selected the next house more carefully, looked for a nice one with a tidy garden. A middle-aged woman invited me in, and I sat at her dining room table with her and her friend, and told them my story. Which was complete bullshit. To their credit, they listened attentively and did not laugh once. It went something like this:

I was an orphan, and had been living with my last remaining relative, an Aunt in Purley, Surrey. Tragically, she had died suddenly last week, leaving me destitute and alone in the world, so I had set out to seek my fortune.

They asked me lots of questions. They asked me if I was hungry and brought me a boiled egg, some bread and butter and a cup of tea. The eggcup was light blue plastic, with ridged rings around it. They seemed to accept my story completely, which was good, because when I was telling it, it had sounded a bit unlikely to me. They said I could stay there and I began to relax. When I had thought of two parents, I'd imagined one of each, but these two middle-aged women had a sort of grim kindness. They seemed to have taken to me and would certainly do until I could scout around for something more suitable.

I was finishing my second cup of tea when there was a knock at the door and in came a police man and woman. They asked if I was Penny Wardman who had run away from Reedham. I went cold inside. I felt disappointed, foolish and angry. The two women who had pretended to befriend me had shopped me. They had telephoned the police from another room. No one at Reedham had yet noticed my absence, but when the police rang Matron, she went round looking for empty beds.

As they drove me back to Reedham, the policewoman, who was very young, asked me why I'd run away.

'Because I hate it there. I want to go home.'

'Well, you must have done something wrong or you wouldn't be there. Why don't you just behave yourself, then they will let you go home?

'I haven't done anything wrong. It won't make any difference if I behave myself, you don't understand. They won't let me out and I've done nothing wrong.'

'If you've done nothing wrong, young lady, then why are you in there? Because your Mother can't manage you, I expect. Look, let me give you some advice. Just keep your head down, do your time and you'll soon be out. The more you run away - the more time you'll have to do.'

She was not local and obviously thought Reedham was

some kind of Young Offenders' Institution. The policeman put her right.

'It's actually just some kind of boarding school for fatherless children' he told her 'It's not somewhere I'd send any child of mine. She's not there because she's done anything wrong - though she has now. You shouldn't go knocking on doors like that - you could end up in trouble.'

'Fatherless children - what exactly does that mean?' asked the policewoman

'My Father is dead, and before you ask, he was married to my Mother.' I folded my arms and stared out of the window. They shut up after that.

It must have been about 11.30pm. Matron was standing at the top of the steps. She thanked the police officers, looked me up and down with disdain and said

'What have you got to say for yourself?'

I stood and stared at her, making my eyes hard. I was never going to speak to her again.

'I see, it's dumb insolence, is it? Well, you are in a lot of trouble, I can tell you.'

She swept ahead of me, past her office, along to the Girls Side. Miss Fortune was waiting at the end of the corridor in her strangely formal navy dressing gown, with the white lace collar of her nightdress neatly arranged outside it. Her carmine lipstick was freshly applied. She was tall and slim, with rather good taste in clothes, but her great fleshy face with its blotchy skin and her strong Yorkshire accent made her a comic figure. Then there was the question of her name. If she really could not, or would not, marry, then why did she not change it?

'Thank you Miss Fortune. Number 17 - I will see you in my office after breakfast tomorrow.'

Miss Fortune escorted me to my bed, waited while I retrieved my nightdress from the washroom and put it on. Then she took away all my clothes.

'Have you got any money left?' she whispered.

Silently, I gave her my money and got into bed. I was not going to talk to any of them, and I was now absolutely determined to get out and next time to get it right. I knew that I could trust nobody, the whole adult world wanted me to keep quiet and to stay in Reedham for as long as possible. I was going to run away again as soon as I could, only this time I would confide in no one. I would ask for nobody's help. I did consider my grandmother, my many aunties and uncles, but I knew the first thing they would do would be to ring Billie. If I explained to them how bad Reedham was, they would say I must tell my Mother all about it. As if I'd never thought of that myself.

But I *had* told her, and she had simply sent me back there. So, I would have to run away again and live independently somehow. Get some kind of job, save enough money so I could get Tanya out too. How could I write to her without them knowing where I was?

I must have slept - it was daylight now - the incredibly early dawn of midsummer. The rest of the dormitory was fast asleep, like two rows of neatly arranged logs. The sunlight was shining directly on to my face, and either that or the birds singing loudly outside, had woken me. I crept out and looked at the landing clock - exactly 4.30. Behind me was the big red tin box which served as a hall table. It was a fire box of some kind, believed to contain a fire blanket and buckets of sand, but it was always padlocked and I'd never seen it used or even opened. On it Miss Fortune had left my clothes, and my money in a neat little pile. I almost laughed out loud. Did she imagine I wouldn't see them there? Did she imagine that, having seen them, I wouldn't be off again? Either she was stupid or she thought I was. Or perhaps she hoped that I would escape again.

In fifteen minutes I was at the bottom of the drive. Reedham station was closed and I had no idea when trains started running. The little row of shops under the bridge were all closed and deserted - the morning was beautiful and silent, except for birdsong. There was nothing to do but to wait for the trains to start running. I stood in the phone box and read all the instructions for calling Fire, Police or Ambulance.

'This telephone box is located in Old Lodge Lane, by Reedham Station, below the Railway Bridge.'

Then I inspected all the shops, memorised all the cigarettes available in the tobacconists, read all the advertisements 'Craven A - for your throat's sake' and the menu in the café window. I went back to the phone box and rang Directory Enquiries, which in those days was a free service. I dialled DIR and asked for the telephone number of Mrs H M Wardman of 22 Minster Road, London NW2 and got the correct answer GLAdstone 7319. Then I looked up everyone I could think of in the telephone book. I didn't dare call Directory Enquiries again in case it was the same woman and she got suspicious.

With terror I suddenly became aware that a man was approaching the telephone box. A policeman. He looked in as he walked past, then, when he got to the bridge, he turned and walked back. I tried to look busy, flicking through the telephone directory. He opened the door.

'What are you doing?'

'Looking up my phone number.'

'Don't you know your own phone number?'

'I've forgotten it.'

'Where do you live?'

'Hampstead.'

'How did you get here from Hampstead that this time of the morning?'

'I walked.'

'You walked here from Hampstead?'

'Yes.'

This time I was taken to Matron's flat - the first and last time

I was ever there. She sat at her dining room table, I stood in front of her while she asked a lot of questions. She was uncharacteristically interested in the answers. I forgot my resolve not to speak to her until it was too late, so then I just answered her to get it over with. She was shocked - or affected to be - by everything I had done, but what made her the most indignant was that I had not paid my train fare to Norwood Junction.

'You say it so casually - as if it were nothing! There was nobody to collect your fare so you just strolled out without paying! Do you realise that is stealing? You could go to prison for that. I have no idea where you will end up young lady, but I do know that you will come to no good. It was lucky for you that the people whose door you knocked on last night were prison officers. They knew immediately that your story was a pack of lies. They knew you'd absconded from somewhere - and that you had no business to be running around, late at night, knocking on doors. You've brought disgrace on yourself, on your Mother and on the whole School. Now, you can sit there until it's time for breakfast, and I want you to think seriously about what you've done, and how you can make amends.'

I sat against the wall, under a pendulum clock, which ticked loudly and struck every quarter hour. Matron got herself a cup of tea and sat, facing me, reading a book. For almost two hours, I sat there, under her eye, until 7.30 when Miss Randall came to escort me to breakfast.

'From now on' said Matron 'You will not be trusted and you will be watched all the time.'

24

Reading by a Senior Girl

Summer and Autumn Term 1958

THE 24 hour surveillance lasted only a day or two - Reedham was too short staffed and badly organised to keep it up. However, the summer holidays were now very close and there didn't seem much point in running away again. The end of term was always a wonderfully euphoric time, especially the end of Summer Term. Six weeks out of Reedham was like forever - autumn and the end of it were so far in the distance. I did hope that Billie would say we would not to have to go back, that we could go to local schools. Apart from telling her, and running away, I did not know how to convey to her that I really did not want to be there. I also hoped that Reedham would not allow me back, and actually made a few feeble enquiries about what you had to do to get expelled. But the summer holidays drifted pleasantly away and - as I did every summer - I simply forgot about Reedham.

'I'd better get your suitcases out - you girls are going back next week.'

Going back. Without much hope, I explained to her once again how much I hated it and how poor the standard of education was. She listened, she sympathised. She sent us back.

The excitement of seeing my friends again kept me

preoccupied and reasonably happy for the first few weeks, and before I could start making fresh escape plans, Billie wrote to say that she had arranged for me to start at the Italia Conti Stage School in Archer Street, London W1 next term. I could leave Reedham in December, and live at home. The only sadness was that she could only afford for me to go, Tanya had to stay at Reedham. All the same, my euphoria was mighty. I walked on air, I was invincible. This must have been hard and lonely for Tanya, but she didn't complain. At least she knew now that escape was possible.

There was a Carol Service in the church on the last Sunday of the Autumn Term, and traditionally two Reedham scholars read a passage from St Matthew. Because outsiders came to the Carol Service, a roneo'd Order of Service was produced, with the words to the hymns, and chapter and verse of the readings, one of which was:

St Luke, Chapter II verses 1-14
Read by a Senior Girl

I had behaved so disgracefully in the past year, that normally there would be no question of my being considered for this honour. However, there was a real problem. I was one of the few senior girls who could read fluently.

In recent years, the number of children at Reedham was declining, and the reason was simple. People were no longer willing to send their children to boarding schools generally, and Reedham, with its reputation for brutality and low educational standards, was suffering from this trend more than most. Parents of existing pupils were removing them once they realised, and increasingly, new girls would depart after a term or two. After a week or two. As a result, there weren't that many girls from which to choose.

Whoever selected the Senior Girl had to decide between someone biddable who would read haltingly, and someone stroppy who would read well. Which was likely to let the school down the least?

Mr Maw informed me that the honour would be mine and offered me the chance to practice reading the passage aloud with him. I was such an arrogant little cow, I told him airily there was no need. He emphasised that this was The Bible, and 17th century English, didn't just trip off the tongue. But I didn't want to go over it slowly with Mr Maw, just as we always did in class, while he explained every word as if you were thick. Tanya and I had been reading Shakespeare aloud with Billie for years; the Bible wasn't difficult. Also, I was beginning to understand my power. I knew they weren't going to trust it to anyone else and I wanted them worried.

So I strolled into the Carol Service with no idea of which passage I'd be reading. Or if I was going to read at all; I had an idea of simply sitting there when the reading was announced, refusing to move, letting Matron and all the rest of them sweat in front of all the people they wanted to impress, while I sat impassive in the front row. Just the thought gave me more euphoria - more adrenaline.

Unfortunately, by making Matron sweat like that, I'd also be denying myself the largest, most attentive audience I'd ever had. I loved reading aloud, and was reluctant to pass up this golden opportunity for showing off.

I was seated on the end of the front pew, so I could slip out easily and approach the lectern. Waiting for the congregation to take their places, I quickly looked up the relevant passage in St Matthew and rehearsed it in my head a couple of times. Matron made the continuity announcements, and then sat in majesty on the podium behind the lectern, on a kind of velvet throne outside the vestry. Before the service started, she had been busy meeting and greeting important middle aged Purley residents, probably the Rotary Committee. I wouldn't know, we were never introduced to any of them and they all looked the same. I was hoping she was worried that I'd stumble over

St Luke. By the time she sat down, I'd read it enough times and knew I could read it aloud perfectly. Heart thumping. All through the service till it came to my bit. Of course it was 'my' bit, I was 15, and everything that happened in the whole world was about me.

'The lesson will be read by a Senior Girl.' announced Matron, giving me her cold, watery stare.

Matron sat down. The congregation rustled and adjusted itself. I did not move. Matron frowned at me and very slightly jerked her head, to indicate that I should arise and approach the lectern, but I did not meet her eyes. The girl next to me nudged me. I think I gave it about 20 or 30 seconds, before I stalked, as only a teenage girl can, slowly and insolently up to the lectern. The big Bible was open at the correct page and the passage marked. I looked up and around at the assembled multitude, only one of whom meant anything to me. Apart from Tanya, everybody in front of me was irrelevant to my real life, which would very soon begin. Soon I would never have to see or think about any of them ever again. I gazed at them all. Matron cleared her throat. Finally, I read the passage, slowly and perfectly.

25

The Pat Glover Agency

Summer 1957

FROM time to time Billie had the idea that we could become child
stars, or models at the very least. In the summer holiday of 1957,
when I was 13 and Tanya 11, she sent us to the Pat Glover
Agency. She wrote down the address for us, and explained that
this place found work for child photographic models, and all
we had to do was go in and introduce ourselves. She thought
we had a good chance of being taken on and getting some
well-paid work, which would undoubtedly lead to a career in
show business.

We were quite excited about this idea. She told us what
clothes to wear, wrote instructions for finding the place, left us
money for our fare, and went to work. It was somewhere in
Soho, we found it, eventually, walked up a narrow and shabby
staircase and knocked on the door. There was a small, untidy
office with one harassed looking woman. She said

'Yes?'

'Is this the Pat Glover Agency?'

'Yes'

'Our Mummy says have you got any work - modelling work?'

She saw two lanky girls in glasses, Tanya's were broken and
mended temporarily with sticking plaster. Although we wore
our best summer dresses, they were last year's and too small

for us. My hair was escaping its plaits. We wore Reedham sandals and short white socks.

'Where is your Mother?'

'At work - she told us to come and see you.'

'Do you have any photographs? What work have you done?'

'Nothing.'

'What is your Mother thinking of? The least she could do is come with you. I don't hire people who just walk in off the street.'

She looked disdainful. We could see she thought we were rubbish and a waste of time, two clueless kids who had walked in off the street; two idiots with no idea how to present themselves, whose mother didn't believe enough in them to accompany them. We were both disappointed. Billie had told us that if this agency took us on and found us work in the theatre, it could be a way out of Reedham and into a new life. But worse than the disappointment, was the embarrassment. We had exposed ourselves, looked stupid, done it wrong, weren't wanted.

When we told Billie what had happened she said it was our fault. We should have been more positive, sold ourselves, said we would get some photographs taken. We should have told the woman about our weekly ballet lessons at Miss Parrot's. We should have left our phone number. But we never wanted to go through that humiliation again.

But that summer is when I first got the idea that there was a way out of Reedham which Billie was prepared to consider. When Billie asked if Tanya and I would like to go on the stage, we both said yes! After that, she began talking about stage school, sending me first, then Tanya and would I like that? Of course I said yes. What Billie did not realise was that I would have said yes to the Siberian salt mines. Anywhere. In the Christmas holidays of 1959/60, when she was spending a lot of money on the equipment I would need for the Italia Conti Stage School, I remember us walking up Fordwych Road, back to Minster Road, arguing. I said I didn't really want to go to stage school, anyway. She was livid. By the time we got to our front door we were really yelling at each other.

'How can you say that? Every time I asked you if you want to go to stage school, you said yes. How can you say now that you don't want to go?'

'It was your idea, not mine, it's stupid.'

The row continued for hours. She said stage school had been my choice, not hers, because she asked me if I wanted it several times and I had enthusiastically agreed, gone to the audition, gone out with her to buy the special clothes and shoes. And now, after she had spent all that money, days before I was due to start, I was saying that I didn't want to go.

It was fear, of course. I knew my way around Reedham by now, and had risen painfully almost to the top of its pile. Now I would have to mix with children who had been brought up at home. They were different from Reedham children, they were polite and confident, knew how to behave and didn't tell people to shut up. I had seen some Conti's girls when I went for the audition, they were graceful and smiling, secure in the world, which they knew loved and esteemed them. The adoration and cherishing they had absorbed since birth glowed on their skin and they had no idea of it. To a lesser extent, it was also about money - I would never be able to afford to dress as well as the others - but I sensed that talent and charm would have seen me through. I may have had talent, it was too early to say, but any charm I had was so laced with Reedham resentment that it became brash and defensive. I knew that amongst these girls - and boys - that was another thing - I would have to speak to boys - I would stand out as something less, something undeserving. I did not know how to behave, how to speak politely and confidently to other people as equals.

So I told Billie I didn't want to go on the stage, I wanted to go to University and be an intellectual. She said don't be stupid, you're too young, you don't have any academic qualifications and university costs far more money than we could afford, so forget about it.

26

A Leaving Outfit

Autumn 1959

WHEN Matron heard that my Mother would be withdrawing me from Reedham and sending me to another school - a stage school - she sent for me immediately. As I walked along the corridor, I reminded myself that this woman now had very little power over me. I knew what to expect from the interview and vowed that whatever she said - *whatever* she said - this time I would not cry. I reminded myself of the emotional hand grenades, she would lob low and suddenly towards the end of an interview. The classic was:

'What would your Mother say?'

She used this one frequently, because it was so simple and so effective. Any child separated from its home and its mother, given a serious talking to and feeling guilty, will have difficulty holding back the tears at the sudden, quiet mention of its Mother. I knew it was a cheap trick, a literal tearjerker, and I wasn't going to fall for it. Soon I would be out of this place, a free person. Just the thought of liberty, the idea of it, was like a bird fluttering joyfully in my chest every time I remembered.

I no longer feared Matron intellectually, I knew her powers of reasoning, like those of all Reedham staff, were limited. Emotionally, however, she was very powerful - she knew how to play on a child's longing for love and home. Reducing us to tears was a satisfactory way to end an interview; as the child stood, gasping with misery, she would subvert that emotion into gratitude for herself and for Reedham.

'You want your Mother to be proud of you don't you? Think how upset she will be when she hears of the terrible things you have done. I want you to write to her on Friday, telling her how sorry you are, and that you will never do anything like this to upset her again. She knows how hard we all work here at Reedham to make sure you get the best of everything. It is a struggle for us all, resources are limited, and we rely on all the children - especially the girls - to pull their weight. The mistresses - myself and all the staff - work long and hard for you, and this is how you repay us. A little gratitude for all we do would be in order, I think. I myself was in this office till midnight last night, working on your behalf to make sure Festival Day runs smoothly. These things don't just happen by themselves you know, they involve a lot of work which you never see. So much of what I do you never get to hear about. Now I want you to go away and think about what I've said.'

So now, barely noticing the switch, we found we were crying for the distress caused personally to Matron. At this point her face would develop a softer look - still serious, but perhaps a slight smile - oh she was very good - and she would gently suggest that you blew your nose. She knew of course that we were not issued with hankies, and that we would not dare use our sleeves in her presence. She would leave you with tears and snot streaming for as long as she could stand it, then produce a tissue from her drawer.

Ever since I was five years old this woman had been able to make me cry whenever she liked. No more. I was *determined* not to.

I knew what it would be about.

'Why is your Mother sending you to Stage School, when you are getting a perfectly good education here?'

'Don't know Matron' was the safest answer. She didn't

really want to know my answer to this question, she wanted to give me hers. It was wisest with Matron not to be too clever, not to use any long words. Not to use any wrong words. Once, she'd asked me to run an errand for her and I'd cheerfully replied 'Righto' before running off to do it. She called me back.

'That is not the correct way for you to address me Penny Wardman, it is far too informal. That is far too casual an expression , one you would use to one of your friends - an equal. You will remember that I am your superior, and speak to me accordingly - do you understand?'

'Yes Matron. Sorry Matron.'

She could not tolerate anything but submission, and I could not be submissive. I was clever and I knew it and I wanted everyone to know it too and to admire me for it. I knew she was going to talk in a disparaging way about my Mother and I knew I couldn't just take that submissively, it was unfair and my Mother was worth ten of her. She was right about one thing, anyway, she and I were definitely not equals. I waited outside her office, full of fear, rebellion, loathing, exultation and adrenaline. I was going to play it cool, at least to start. After all, what could she do to me now?

'Come in Penny.'

The use of my first name! Was this supposed to trick me into over-familiarity? Did she hope I'd reply 'Well, hello there Ida, what can I do for you today?' As if.

'I understand from your Mother that she is taking you away from Reedham at the end of the Autumn Term, even though your education will not yet be finished?'

'Yes Matron.'

'And you are going to go to...' she peered down at the paper in front of her, though I knew she'd learnt the name of the school by heart, and had already rehearsed this distasteful information with the rest of the staff at some length '...the Italia Conti Stage School. Is that right?'

'Yes Matron.'

'And what, pray, are they going to teach you there?'

I could have said 'don't know Matron' but as well as inviting her scorn, it would deny me the chance to let her know what a good time I was going to have, what a rackety, glamorous, show biz life I was going to lead once I was out of there.

'Ballet, Tap, Musical Comedy, Modern Drama, Shakespeare, Singing and Modern Ballet. And Voice Production' I had the Italia Conti prospectus memorised.

'Really - is that all?'

'No Matron, we have three hours classroom teaching every day as well, and I can take my GCEs next year'

'Good Heavens!' This was evidently news to her, and she did not like it. Reedham education was designed to prepare us for domestic service, and, if we were lucky, marriage. From the age of 11 we had spent a whole day on Domestic Science, and I think the boys spent a similar proportion of their time on Woodwork and Gardening. I suppose the roles of housekeeper and handyman gardener in the larger homes of our social betters was envisaged for us, and GCEs would not be of much use, so Reedham had no truck with them.

She had probably been planning to tell me next that I could not expect a very high academic standard at Conti's. Implying that Reedham's dreaming spires were unsurpassed educationally.

'Well, you always had ideas above your station - you and your Mother - always thought you were better than anyone else. So, it's to be GCE exams now is it? The practical all round education we offer here isn't good enough for you, I suppose. It does a girl no good to get too many exams, you know, to be always studying. Men don't want to marry a girl who is too clever. What good does your Mother think these exams are going to be for you?

'Mummy thinks 'O' levels might help me getting a job, if I don't get a job on the stage right away.'

'Well I hope you realise how lucky you are young lady, and make the most of the opportunity you've been given. No other Reedham girls have been allowed to study for these exams, although Mr Maw is keen for some of the brighter boys. Well, your Mother has great ambitions for you, I must say. Just make sure your head doesn't get even more swollen. And don't think you'll be getting a leaving outfit, because you won't. The Committee is at liberty to use its discretion - leaving clothes are not a right, they are a privilege. As you are leaving early, and with your record, I doubt very much if they will allow me to buy you a leaving outfit.'

'Yes Matron.'

She seemed to have run out of steam. The news about the 'O' levels had shaken her. I wondered if she had finished, if she had, I would be able to leave her office without crying, which gave me a pleasurable feeling of control. I did mind about the Leaving Outfit - it was something everyone looked forward to. A few days before the end of term, Matron would take the three or four girls who were leaving to Allders in Croydon and buy them a complete outfit. It was something much discussed as we grew up. The general belief was that you were allowed to choose everything yourself, although there were rumours of Matron putting her foot down over a shocking pink blouse and some two inch heels. The consensus was that Cuban heels were the limit.

These would be your first adult clothes, and almost as significant, almost as thrilling - new clothes. Never worn by anyone else, purchased just for you, with money, from a shop, after having tried them on in the fitting room to make sure they were the right size. And you got everything matching. If you had black shoes, you got a matching black handbag and gloves, but not a black hat, which was too old. You would get your hat to match your coat in that case. Most girls left in the summer term, and white bag, shoes, hat and gloves were what everyone longed for. You got a coat, a skirt, two sets of underwear, two brassieres, one suspender belt and two pairs of nylons. It was like a trousseau - fresh new clothes for a fresh, new adult life.

The Leaving Girls were allowed to wear their outfits to the final Sunday service of term, and before Church, modelled them in the playground for the admiration of the rest of us. It was always fascinating and amazing to see girls who we only knew as children, in scruffy Reedham garments, transformed by clothing into adults, into young women. Young ladies. The breasts and hips, which had looked bulky and unnecessary under a gymslip, now had a purpose.

As if posing for the fashion pages of Woman's Own, they would stand stiffly in a small group, pretending to talk to each other, looking up to admire the school buildings they had seen every day of their lives, looking down to check that their stocking seams were straight. A few girls close to them in age would hover nearby, but most of us kept a distance, stood back to admire the spectacle, carefully memorising every detail for discussion later.

The sensation of the Leaving Outfits of 1958 had been kitten heels. We had never seen them before and were enchanted, because they narrowed like stilettos - for which we all longed - but very sharply, in a heel barely an inch and a half high - and Matron had permitted them! They were adorable. The Leaving Outfits inspired hours of analysis and information exchange. Which outfit was best, which had cost most, that sweet little half hat made entirely of white flowers that Jean Humphries had, Mary Hoopers' legs looked quite nice in Cuban heels, have you ever worn suspenders, do you put your knickers over or under them, why don't we wear liberty bodices any more, did you see Jean take a compact out of her handbag and powder her nose? You get the compact in the handbag when you buy it, no you don't, you just get a mirror, will you wear make up when you're grown up, no fear. Maybe lipstick, but that's all. And then we would each start compiling our own fantasy Leaving Outfits.

Personally, I never thought much about being a bride, as a

girl. I knew I was not the kind of girl anyone would want to marry. But I did think a lot about my Leaving Outfit. Not only did it represent the threshold to adult life, the start of choosing your own clothes, of having them new, from a shop. It also meant – by definition - you were getting out. It was, after all, a Leaving Outfit, and once you had those clothes on you could just walk down the drive and out of there. You would just be a normal young woman, in her own clothes, free to do anything, go anywhere and no one could stop you. A person. That is what a Leaving Outfit meant to me, so I was disappointed to hear I wouldn't be getting one. But not enough to make me cry.

Just before the end of term, as we lined up for our letters after breakfast, Miss Randall announced

'No 17 you'll be going out today, so don't go to your classroom. Get your outdoor clothes on and be outside Matron's Office by 9 o'clock'

'Where am I going, Miss?'

'Leaving Clothes, I think'

Matron and I walked down the drive. Each year there were fewer girls at Reedham, and most of them left in the spring or summer terms. In December 1959 I was the only leaver, so it was just her and me. She explained that the Committee had decided that I must have a Leaving Outfit of some sort. Normally they expected to spend £25 on each girl, and as I had been at Reedham so long - ten years in fact - as a special concession, they were allowing £15 for my outfit. It was peculiar, we were two women out shopping for clothes, walking side by side, talking, and yet she was addressing me as she had always done, as if I were standing, in disgrace, in her office. There was no alteration in her manner, no small talk, no hint of intimacy. On the bus we sat, side by side, staring straight ahead. It was rumoured that she sometimes took the Leaving Girls out to tea afterwards. I didn't think she would take me and I didn't want her to. Although I wanted the tea, I no more wanted to be in her company than she did in mine.

She evidently had a system and we started with the coat. It was charcoal grey, with patch pockets and there was no question of me choosing it. I tried it on and it fitted. It was OK - quite boring in itself, but it was a new, grown up ladies coat. She asked me if I liked it

'Yes Matron.'

She found a plain black skirt, a pale green blouse with a peter pan circular stitched collar and a pair of black court shoes with Cuban heels. By the time she'd bought me a set of underwear (but no bra) there would be no money for a bag, hat or gloves. It didn't take very long and I didn't really choose anything. She knew her way round the store and marched confidently up to each item, held it up and said 'Would you like to try that on?' What could I say? There was a moment with the pale green blouse. She asked me if I liked it. It was the kind of thing women her age and build wore. I knew I would never wear it. I knew my Mother would never wear it. I knew it was a waste of money. But I also knew that Matron and I would never find a blouse on which we agreed, so it might as well be this one.

'Yes Matron. Thank you Matron.'

The actual garments didn't matter. It was my Leaving Outfit. I would be leaving in it and that conferred all the glamour, all the cachet of kitten heels and sweet little half hats. Out of there and free. There have been bad moments in my life since I left Reedham, but I have never been anywhere that bad again. Nowhere else have I been punished around the clock. In those ten years, I paid, in advance, for every bad thing I ever did since.

Matron did not take me to tea, and Mrs Baker, my Mother's cleaning woman was delighted with the pale green blouse.

27

Walter Gilmore

Summer Holidays 1957

EVERYONE at Reedham – even staff – looked forward to the holidays. Especially the long Summer holidays. On the last Visiting Day before the 1957 Summer holidays, Billie brought someone with her – a man called Walter Gilmore. He was tall, deeply tanned and his slightly receding hair was greying at the temples. Twinkly, blue eyes. Cigarette holder. Good clothes. About six foot one. He seemed tremendously sophisticated and prosperous to us, and looked very like the kind of older man featured in newspaper advertisements for Daks trousers at Simpsons. He was disturbingly attractive and Tanya and I were immediately in awe of him.

He took us all out to tea in Purley, and Billie announced that Walter would now be lodging with us permanently. And when we came home for the holidays soon after, there he was, sitting at our table, telling Billie she had mixed the mustard wrongly. Eager to please, I offered to do it. He showed me the correct method, and thenceforth mixing the mustard with Coleman's rich, yellow powder from the bright square tin was my job. Two teaspoons in an eggcup, mixed with just a tiny drop of cold water until it was nice and smooth.

At first, I was delighted with Walter, but Tanya wasn't. There he was, an intruder at our table, ordering us, and our Mother about. She seethed with indignation, but she was only

12, there was nothing she could do. He had the authoritative manner of a man used to dealing with staff, and at first would clap his hands when he wanted something, which puzzled us. He explained to Tanya and me that when he clapped his hands, we should run and see what he wanted. He wanted a glass of water now and told Tanya to go and fetch it for him. Billie was quite cross about this and explained that in England when you wanted a glass of water you got up and fetched it yourself.

Billie had met Walter when he stayed a few days as a lodger at 22 Minster Road. We had not met him before, of course, being safely away at Reedham. He was born Sidney Walter Gluck in Bermondsey in 1903, into an immigrant Jewish family. He was the middle of three boys and his father died soon after the youngest was born, leaving his mother to bring them up alone. In a poor area, their family was among the poorest. As a very young man, he went to Northern Rhodesia, and it transformed his life. He changed his surname to Gilmore and dropped the Sidney. The poor East End kid was suddenly living in golden sunlight, in a world where he was one of the elite. The young Walter Gilmore was only an accounts clerk at first, later he become a Chartered Accountant, but all white people, however humble, had status and a wonderful life. Servants took care of all the drudgery, and when he left the office each evening, it was on to the club for cocktails, tennis, swimming or bridge. He was a charming and popular young man, rather good at tennis, and soon married to his first wife. His Bermondsey accent gave way to patrician tones, he never had a trace of white African twang.

While still married to his first wife, he began an affair with Clare, who eventually became his second wife. We knew that Clare was beautiful, sophisticated and very wealthy, because Walter told Billie and Billie told us. I never saw a photo of her, but always imagined her with a hard face like the Duchess of Windsor, well dressed, thin, and chain smoking. After he divorced her, Walter returned 'home' to London. He stayed a few days with us at Minster Road when he first arrived, then found a room in Baker Street, which he felt was a better area. Some time after that, he and Billie bumped into each other in Baker Street, they started dating and in 1957 he moved back to 22, Minster Road, but this time to the big, best back room.

He had breakfast with all the other lodgers, but he also spent a lot of time and had quite a few meals downstairs with us. There were things about modern English life which needed explaining to him.

He had hired a car, and one rainy night saw a young woman walking without an umbrella. He slowed down, leaned out and offered her a lift. She screamed and ran away, which puzzled and upset him enormously. He couldn't stop going on about it. In Northern Rhodesia, apparently, if you saw a white woman out on a rainy night, offering a lift was the only decent thing to do.

'What about a black woman then?' asked Tanya, innocently.

'They can look after themselves, believe me.' said Walter.

'We don't call them black, darling, we call them Negroes. And a Negro woman is called a Negress.' said Billie, tactfully.

Black people in London upset Walter. He had thought he was returning home to the all white country he'd left in the early twenties. When we all went out together he would make very loud remarks, intended to be overheard.

'He's a long way from home' or

'Good God Billie, there's another one!'

He often referred to black people as natives, and Tanya got into trouble for suggesting that in England, we were the natives - not them.

'The word native has changed its meaning' he said 'Now it means Negroes, not us. You're just a child, you know nothing.'

The worst thing was when he saw a mixed race couple walking together in the street. He really could not bear it. He would stop and stare.

'Look at that Billie - look - a white woman arm in arm with

a Negro - how can she do it? I don't understand it Billie - it's not normal. Disgusting.'

As he stood staring and shouting at them, Tanya and I would shuffle forward, trying to distance ourselves. Billie would tell him it was a free country and people could do what they liked and please would he stop embarrassing us all and upsetting himself.

It was the embarrassment we hated. At the time we didn't consider much the feelings of the people he'd insulted. After all, lots of people agreed with Walter about coloured people, although most kept it to themselves in public. Privately, Billie told us that there was nothing wrong with coloured people, they were just the same as us, but most people were in favour of the Colour Bar, just as most people were in favour of nuclear weapons, and we just had to accept that, although of course, we could and should protest about it. 'But don't tell Walter I said that - it will only cause another argument.'

For a while, we kept quiet, though we always knew he was wrong. Later I started arguing with him, refusing to eat South African fruit and joining marches on the South African Embassy. We had stand up rows and he hit me once or twice. Now, I'm really grateful to him for focussing my ideas, forcing me to confront the issues of race, apartheid, economic sanctions and democracy at such a young age. I began to read the Manchester Guardian and the New Statesman specifically to find arguments against him. He came to embody everything I knew to be wrong.

28

Keeping Him Company

New Year 1958

DURING holidays, Tan and I would help Mummy by serving breakfasts at Minster Road. We watched and waited by the frying pan, tea towel folded ready to take the hot plate, then carry it carefully through to the waiting - invariably male - guests. Early in January 1960, Walter got a bad dose of flu, so while Billie cooked and served breakfasts downstairs, my job was to take a tray up to him.

Because he was now officially her 'boyfriend' and as he was ill, he had other meals in bed too. So twice a day I was sent upstairs to take him his food and 'keep him company.'

'Don't just plonk the tray down and come straight downstairs dear, he's been on his own all day poor chap - stay and chat a bit.' said Billie as she handed me the tray. 'And tell him there's more sausage if he would like some.'

He talked a lot about Rhodesia, and his trips 'home' to London every three years. He and his second wife Clare would sail from Nairobi to Southampton on one of the Cunard liners - often the Queen Mary. 'They treated us like Royalty, you know, and it was one long party. One makes friends very quickly on board, playing deck quoits – can you play quoits? I'll show you one day. We always dressed for dinner, and there would be dancing afterwards, one long party. Just one long party.'

In London they would stay at the Dorchester for about three weeks, shop extravagantly at Harrods, go to night clubs and return home with their booty. Clare was from a wealthy family; she and Walter owned a tobacco farm, and from the twenties until the end of the fifties, Walter had lived the idle, hedonistic existence of a prosperous white farmer in Africa. But he had found her with another man, divorced her immediately and angrily, walking away with comparatively little.

I asked him about the tobacco farm - I knew it was silly, but I imagined low bushes with cigarettes blossoming between glossy green leaves; beaming Africans bending to pluck the white, cylindrical blossoms. He described the plantation, stretching way into the distance. It was much bigger than farms in England and he had hundreds of Negroes working for him. He explained that some of the women were very attractive and once or twice he had been unable to help himself and had made love to them. Of course, he added, if they got pregnant, he had to sack them or his farm would get a bad reputation. Once immorality is condoned, it is impossible to keep discipline - they don't respect you, you see.

I thought perhaps I'd not heard him correctly, what he'd just said seemed so incredible. I repeated it to Billie when I got downstairs.

'Take no notice dear - he's ill. People often say funny things when they've got flu - they get slightly delirious.'

I asked him about it again, but he seemed to regret having confided in me.

'You didn't tell your Mother did you?'

'Yes, I only told her what you said.'

'For God's sake don't tell her - please let us have a few secrets of our own. A man can't help being aroused if a woman gives him the glad eye you know.'

'What's the glad eye?'

'Oh come on, don't pretend you don't know.' And, using

his napkin, did his hilarious eye rolling pastiche of an exotic temptress - just as he'd done at Christmas with Billie's lace scarf as a yashmak. Making me laugh.

'That's the glad eye - what you're doing now. You're very pretty when you smile you know.'

I was flattered and uncomfortable. I loved the attention and the praise and I didn't want to go. He was looking into my eyes and smiling.

'Why don't you read to me?'

One of the ways Billie suggested I keep him company was to read aloud to him. I was good at this and I enjoyed it too. Furthermore, it was good practice for my stage career.

He chose something from the pile of Reader's Digests he kept by the bed, and I started to read. After a bit he put his hand up my jumper, under my bra and on to my left breast. I froze.

'Carry on reading.'

And I did. I carried on reading something about famous golf players, while he fondled my 13 year old breast. I loved him and I hated him. I liked what he was doing and he shouldn't do it. But I didn't know how to stop him. He had sudden and terrible rages which petrified me and permeated the house with anger. If I made him lose his temper I would be in trouble with Mummy. In trouble with both of them.

When I finished the article, he asked for a kiss goodnight. His lips were big and squashy and his moustache prickled.

'Don't say a word to your Mother.'

I didn't say anything to Billie, naturally. Even if I had wanted to - what could I have said? But she knew. In 1969, as she and I drank tea in the kitchen at Maida Vale, I told her. I probably wanted to hurt her and make her jealous of me, but told myself that she had a right to know. I was prepared for an emotional outburst. So I was staggered when, quite calmly, she said:

'Oh I knew about all that, of course.'

'You did? Why didn't you say anything?

'You must remember dear, Walter and I were not married at the time. I didn't want to sleep with him before we were married, because I know he would have looked down on me if I had given in to him. But by letting him play around with you, I thought it would take the pressure off me. I knew there could be nothing serious between you.'

I can't remember how I responded, but I know I didn't say much, just carried on drinking my tea. The enormity of what she had just said did not hit me until I told Tanya about it a few days later.

The reading and fondling went on until his recovery, when it stopped. He tried to revive it once or twice, by announcing that he was having an early night and asking me to come in and read to him, but I pleaded homework. The sexual tension between us never went away, it blended with the other feelings I had about him: intellectual disdain and physical fear.

29

It's My Body

January 1960

I am in the bath at 22 Minster Road, drinking the tea Billie has
just brought me. I want to destroy my looks, so that she will
be hurt. She keeps going on about how I am becoming a young
lady, and how beautiful I am and trying to get me to frizz my
hair up when I want it smooth and buying me horrible brown
and sludge green clothes in what she calls Autumn Colours,
and saying how beautiful I look, when I don't. She comes
home with horrible clothes for me and I have to be grateful.
How would she like someone else to choose her clothes for
her? She brings home these garments for geriatrics, which she
has got in a sale and says I look lovely when I don't. I look like
a stupid child in that fawn v-necked jumper, and the matching
skirt she made to go with it. I am not, *not* going to wear it any
more.

Except that I have nothing else to wear. Standing on the
dusty, dark stairs at Conti's today, waiting for Jill and Julie,
my new best friends, I look down at the stupid skirt. As they
come down stairs, Jill says

'What a peculiar skirt - where did you get it?'

'My Mother made it.'

Why can't I lie? Why do I automatically tell the truth,
regardless of the embarrassment caused to anybody - in this

case, me. Except what lie could I tell? Is there a better excuse for a garment which looks like an out of work teddy bear?

Today was my first day at Conti's and I have worn my best clothes. The fawn jumper is one of her cast offs. The offending skirt is also fawn, made out of a furry blanket kind of fabric, and gathered, so that the waistband can easily be let out as I grow. The gathering makes my hips huge of course, and then over that the fawn jumper stretches. I am all fawn, all forlorn. She has this thing about me and Autumn Colours, because she says my hair is auburn, which it isn't, and I wouldn't want it if it was. Says she always thinks of me in greens, golds and browns. As far as I can see, they are all just different shades of mud. I want to dress completely in black, like a bohemian. The forlorn skirt is mid calf length. My shoes, also fawn - are OK though - because for shoes she has to take me with. However, they are flats.

But what will I wear tomorrow? The other girls wear pencil skirts, small Shetland jumpers in soft pastel colours, and stiletto heels. They all wear the new bouffant hairstyles, which they backcomb eternally in the dressing room, in front of the huge mirror, holding golden Elnett Satin aerosols at arms length, and spraying towards their hair. I am the only one with curly hair. I can do a bouffant, but it takes ages and must be straightened first. Even the promise of rain destroys it. I cannot possibly afford Elnett Satin. I am also the only one with glasses, and I'm the tallest. At Reedham I always looked stupid, but so did everyone else. At Conti's I am suddenly surrounded by sophisticated girls apparently from wealthy homes and I'm frantic to look like them.

When I get home I announce that I *must* have a pair of stilettos.

'Everyone else has them - and I can't wear that horrible brown skirt - I must have a pencil skirt - from a shop. A black pencil skirt from Neatawear.'

'Penny I am not made of money! It's either the brown skirt or your navy school skirt...'

'I'm not wearing *that.*'

'You could try tucking the jumper inside the skirt darling, then your hips wouldn't look so big.'

'Oh you don't understand, you are so stupid, that's such a horrible skirt, why did you have to make it gathered? Anyway, nobody wears tucked in now. I just look so stupid and ugly.'

'No you don't Penny darling. You are a beautiful girl. If you would only brush you hair back from your face so we can see your lovely forehead...'

She comes at me with the hairbrush and I know what she wants to do. She wants to brush it up into a cloud of frizz, like a dandelion clock. She expects me to sit there and smile as she ruins my hair - am I supposed to be grateful or something? Then she'll say what a good figure I've got, and how pretty I look when I don't smarm my hair down. What business is it of hers what my figure is like? She only knows that because she's always making excuses to come into the bathroom when I am trying to have a bath in private.

'The human body is nothing to be ashamed of!' she trills, and she's started walking around naked herself now, to illustrate her point. She has never been modest about her body in front of Tanya and me. When we were little and got in bed with her she used to let us pretend to be babies and suck her nipples - one each side. It makes me feel sick to think about it now and I wish I didn't think about it, wish I didn't remember it.

When she comes into the bathroom, I hug my knees to my chest and say what do you want.

'Let me look at you.' she says.

'No, I don't want you to - it's my body.'

She's always had this joke that since we were born from her, our bodies are hers and she is therefore entitled to inspect them whenever she wants to. Only it isn't really a joke.

'That's my body there - I want to see how you're developing.'

Developing. I hate that word developing. Development.

In the summer holidays of 1957, when Walter Gilmore had arrived in our house, she had inspected my budding breasts. They were very new and were little more than a hard lump behind the nipple. She felt them, and then said I had to go to the doctor.

When we got there, Dr Amster was on holiday and there was a male locum in her place. A locum was a substitute for Dr Amster, and turned out to be an old man of about 40 with grey hair and glasses. He was not clear about exactly what was being asked of him.

'I'd like you to check my daughter's breasts doctor and see if her development is normal.' Billie explained.

He still appeared baffled, so Billie told me to take off all my clothes except my knickers. I really, really didn't want to do this.

'Come on Penny' said Billie 'don't be shy.'

'I don't want to.' I said.

'Now don't be a silly girl, this man is a doctor, come on, off with those clothes.'

I stood, exposed and stupid as my Mother invited the locum to examine my breasts. He felt the hard lumps.

'That's perfectly normal development.' he said 'They will soften and grow very soon.'

'Oh good doctor, I just wanted to be sure that everything was developing normally. She started her periods in January, didn't you, dear?'

'Yes.'

Feeling perhaps that more was expected of him, or maybe because he wanted to, the locum pulled down my knickers.

'Pubic hairs coming along nicely. Nothing to worry about.'

'Oh, thank you doctor.'

After further exchanges of explanations, reassurances and pleasantries, I was told to put my clothes on.

That is why I hate the word developing. And normal. And locum.

Years later, my Auntie Pauline, the youngest of Billie's eight siblings, told me that Billie had done exactly the same with her when she reached puberty, but Pauline had put up more resistance.

'You're not my Mother, you're only my sister, I don't have to do what you say!'

But Billie was 13 years older than Pauline, and my grandparents left the older children to parent the younger ones much of the time. Billie, who would then have been in her mid-twenties, marched Pauline off to the GP for an inspection, to check that she was 'developing normally.' Billie had made Pauline take off *all* her clothes for the doctor.

'I was so full of shame and embarrassment, it really affected me badly. Penny. I wish I'd been around to stop her doing it to you.'

If she comes in this bathroom now and says anything - *anything* - I'm going to kill myself. No, I'm going to make myself really ugly. This is my face, my hair, my body and I can ruin it if I want - then she'll realise. Shave my eyebrows off, cut my skin, cut big lumps from my hair, frizz it up so much that even she can see how revolting it is.

There's no lock on the door because the Bendix is in here and she needs to do the washing. Anyway, she says it's only us girls. She says she can come in any time - and she does.

'I thought you'd like a cup of tea, dear.'

'I don't want tea in the bath, don't you come in here when I'm in the bath. I want a lock on this door - I want some privacy.'

'Don't be silly dear, here's your tea.'

I jump up and grab the towel.

'Stop looking at me.'

'No need to be self conscious Penny. I don't know what you're getting so emotional about. Why does everything have to be a drama with you? The human body is nothing to be ashamed of.'

And that's when I do it. While she's in the kitchen, I shave my eyebrows off with her underarm razor. I cut my arms and my face with scissors, making satisfyingly bloody wounds. I smear her red lipstick all over my face and chest. I frizz up my hair like a dandelion clock. Then I put the clock I bought her for Christmas down the toilet and pee on it.

Great! She's really upset. She doesn't understand. I don't understand it myself.

'It's my body. It's not beautiful, it's ugly. I don't want you looking at it. I don't want to look the way you want me to look. I hate you. And your alarm clock is in the toilet all peed on.'

30

West End Lane

1960

I left Reedham at the end of 1959, and started at the Italia Conti Stage School in January 1960. Tanya had to stay on at Reedham, but Billie and Walter visited her every Sunday. The Reedham Chapel was a normal Church, and its services open to all. Some time in 1959, a few parents began attending services, then waiting outside afterwards to see their children. Matron didn't approve, but there was nothing she could do. We told Billie about this, and she too began to turn up on Sundays, very often with Walter. Tanya thinks this was Walter's influence, he was always insistent on doing the right thing, whatever he deemed that to be. He felt that Billie should visit her children as often as she possibly could, and she must have wanted to impress him with her strong maternal feelings.

Walter Gilmore had many ideas about how and where we should all live. He insisted that Billie buy a television set. We had to say 'lounge' instead of 'sitting room', we had to start using linen table napkins, and never call them 'serviettes'. He considered that Minster Road was not a good enough address, and thought Billie should stop doing Bed and Breakfast, sell the house and buy somewhere in a better area. If she would do so, then he would marry her. So she sold 22 Minster Road in early 1960 and while looking for a home suitable for a man of Walter's status, he moved back to Baker Street and Billie rented a studio flat at 126 West End Lane, West Hampstead. We had very little space, but according to Billie and Walter, it was a far smarter address.

While Tanya was still at Reedham and Billie and I were both out all day, this wasn't too bad, but then Tanya came home for the Easter holidays.

At first, it was great - Tan and I had missed each other badly. Billie was out at work and we had all day to play the sandal game, listen to the Home Service, read Billie's Vogue magazine and examine our spots. And talk.

Billie and I slept on two single beds under the windows overlooking West End Lane. Tanya slept alongside me on a camp bed. We had a separate kitchen and shared a bathroom with the other two flats, but everything else went on in that one room. It was cramped for two, but with three of us, and the camp bed permanently up, space was really tight.

Billie would leave for work each morning

'Now, don't lie in bed all day girls. Get up and have a good tidy round. Make your beds properly - I want to see everything nice and tidy when I get home from work. I've left 10/- on the table - get a pound of tomatoes (don't pay more than 1/6d) a loaf of rye bread and a packet of Daz. We'll have to go to the laundrette tonight. I must dash or I'll be late again'

She runs downstairs; the door slams. So we bound out of bed, skip to the bathroom to wash and clean our teeth. Then we quickly make the beds, straighten up our modest dwelling, whip out the Ewbank and....

Well, of course we don't. We are teenagers. We have all day. We lie in bed, dozing and talking. We make tea and toast, leaving a trail of crumbs and sticky marmalade. We look through Billie's things. The only make up she uses is red lipstick - which looks good on her but is not the height of fashion. As a student at the Italia Conti Stage School, I now have my own cosmetic bag, which contains the following, carefully chosen, iconic items:

1. *Max Factor's Pan Stick - Fair.* Everyone at Conti's has Pan Stick; Fair is the second palest shade (Ivory is the palest) and after detailed consultation with the other girls, trying out their different shades, I set down my carefully saved 7/11d on the glass counter in Selfridges, in return for my own pristine tube. It literally reeks of glamour.

2. *Lentheric Mascara - Black.* Lentheric is known to be the brand used by 'The Profession'. Their stage make up is the industry standard and there are girls in that dressing room who have been on stage and actually used it. You can buy special boxes to put your stage make up in, but everyone knows that professionals only use old cigar boxes. All mascara comes in a little compact style case, with a mirror on the inside lid. The base is divided into two compartments - one with the block of mascara, the other holds a tiny brush. The instructions say to dip the brush in water, rub it in the block of mascara and brush it on your lashes. I've never seen anyone use water - everyone uses spit. You can buy mascara in various colours, but we would never dream of using anything but black.

3. *Coty lipstick - Bermuda Coral.* I loathe this lipstick. What I really want and am saving up for, is Lancome's *Coq de Roche* a delicate, pale orange which everyone at Conti's lusted after. Walter Gilmore bought the Coty for Tanya and me last Christmas and immediately wished he hadn't. He bought it on Billie's advice, and on Christmas morning we dashed off to try it on, still in our dressing gowns. I opened the pure new tube, smelling of womanly sophistication. The metal case was red and gold, I twisted up the sleek, immaculate cylinder, it seemed a shame to spoil it, but I did. Very carefully, I traced my lip line. Of course I had tried lipstick on lots of times, and already owned Outdoor Girl's Skiffle Pink, which was far trendier than Bermuda Coral, but in a push up plastic case. From Woolworths. Coty was expensive - in a swivel case! Billie thought Tanya and I looked charming, but Walter was

worried. He saw what I had already seen in the mirror: my new, glamorous sexy self. He could see I was grown up and beautiful - everyone could see that. If it wasn't for all the hair, and the glasses, and being so tall and having no decent clothes, I could easily be one of those models in Vogue.

'Don't you think it's too grown up for them, Billie?'
'No of course not, lots of girls wear lipstick at this age - for special occasions.'
'Anyway, when I go to Conti's I'll have to wear stage make up and everything.'

After Christmas he got flu and I had to start reading to him in bed.

Tanya and I are sitting at the tiny kitchen table at West End Lane. It is almost 2pm and we are still in our nighties and dressing gowns. The kitchen sink is full of dirty dishes - this morning's breakfast, several mixing bowls, thoroughly scraped out, a badly burnt cake tin. On the table is the remains of the most recent and most ambitious of our cakes. Much of it is burnt, but some seems edible. As soon as I cut into it the aroma penetrates through the pervasive stench of burnt. It is unmistakable. Curry. It is a recipe of our own invention; one of a series testing the veracity and limits of Miss Lawson's universal cake recipe.

The first recipe everyone did with Mrs Lawson was Mock Crab Paste, which involved tomatoes and salad cream. We soon moved on to cakes, and Mrs Lawson impressed upon us that the most important recipe to learn was 'One Egg 3-3-5' - a basic cake recipe which could be endlessly adapted. That is: one egg, three ounces of butter or margarine, three ounces of sugar and five ounces of flour. You start by creaming the butter and sugar together, beating it until it reaches dropping consistency. Then you add the egg, then the flour, spoon by spoon, and a little baking powder, even if you've used self-raising.

As often happens, this morning our first cake has got no further than the dropping consistency stage, when it tastes remarkably like butter icing, only crunchier. We had taken it in turns to taste the mixture until there really wasn't enough to add an egg to, so we started again, vowing to buy more butter and sugar when we went shopping later. Tanya put on quite a few pounds at that time, and the only reason I didn't was because I had about a dozen dance classes every week at Conti's.

Next time we got as far as adding the egg, and discussed which variation to try next. We had already been through all Miss Lawson's suggestions:

1. substitute an ounce of cocoa powder for an ounce of flour to make chocolate cake
2. add an ounce of dried fruit for fruit cake
3. add vanilla essence for vanilla cake (boring!)
4. add the juice and grated rind of a lemon for lemon cake
5. ditto for orange

We had already tried grapefruit, peppermint and (remarkably successful) cream cheese. When we presented Mummy with the remains of these interesting confections on her return from work, she was delighted. While having breakfast at about 10.30, we discussed it. Why had nobody thought of savoury cakes before? We reflected that all recipes had to originate somewhere, after all, the very first cake must have been an experiment. We decide to explore this promising and exciting territory and seek inspiration in the larder.

'I know!' said Tan 'Curry Cake - we can substitute a tablespoon of curry powder for a tablespoon of flour.'

While waiting for the cake we play the sandal game. Ever since we were very little, Tanya and I had a game with bare feet and ribbons. We would take a ribbon each, usually from our hair, and wind it round our feet and ankles, in and out of our toes to make a strappy sandal and then say 'Do you like this one?'

The answer was always yes. We took it in turns to admire each other's sandal and made endless and complicated permutations. This game started when we were very small and carried on well into our teens. It was one of my favourite pastimes, but it was only for home - we never played it at Reedham. Physically we differ in every respect - you would never guess that we shared a set of parents - but our feet are identical. Most people have a second toe longer than their big toe, but we don't. Our toes are small, even and neat. Have you seen Uncle John's feet? They. Are. Huge. What's that smell of burning?

The tiny kitchen is filled with a pungent bluish haze. We turn the blackened cake onto a plate, and as soon as I can touch it I cut - no, *carve* - a chunk and examine it closely, peering over my steamed up glasses.

'Do you want to try it?' I ask Tanya.

'No, not really, I'm full up.'

'So am I.'

'It smells hideous. Let's just throw it away.'

'We can't - what will we tell Mummy we did with the ingredients?'

'Tell her we burnt it.'

'She'll be furious.'

We are overcome with despair. We have spent the morning doing cooking experiments and we have the worrying feeling that time has, once again, slipped away. A bluish cake and curry haze hangs in the air. I cross the hall into our room and check the clock on the mantelpiece.

'Tanya, it's half past two - she'll be home in three hours.'

'Oh God, what shall we do? We've got all this mess to clear up - what shall we do?' She starts to whimper.

'Let's get dressed, I'll go and get the shopping, you start the washing up…'

'I can't - I can't do all this. You made this mess as well as me – please, you've got to help me!'

'I will, when I get back from the shopping'

'Can't we both go shopping?'

'Yes, but it will save time if you make a start while I…'

'We've got plenty of time, we've got three hours Penny.'

'You always say that, you always think you've got lots of time and then you're always late. We've got to start now you stupid little girl. You always want to make a mess but you never want to clean it up, do you? I hate you.'

Tanya starts to whimper again, I start rushing about angrily, trying to conceal the evidence and salvage the day. We usually manage to get the place straight by the time Billie walks in.

31

Poetry, Politics and Ginny

Early Spring 1960

I have a secret. It's about a poem I've written at school called *The Garden*. The secret is that I know it's rubbish and my Mother does not.

Our teacher at Conti's, Miss Matthewson – universally known as Matty - asked us to write a poem, so I wrote something which sounded like the poems I had heard. Something which sounds very like Billie's poems. It's about a garden path, which beckons enticingly, snakes seductively, promising secret bowers and hidden delights. The garden is 'she', and her curves and allure are female.

It's derivative, its rhymes are either cliché or awkward and forced. My Mother loves it and shows it to everyone. It is her idea of what a poem should be. I don't know enough about poetry to explain it myself, but I know this poem is bad.

But I am hooked on her praise. She is so rarely proud of me these days, it is hard to relinquish and tell her the truth. Which is, that at sixteen I don't care much about gardens - never give them a thought. That any poem I wrote from the heart about sexual seduction would feature a young human male, not a female garden path. My deepest feelings are about nuclear weapons, cosmetics and clothes (especially shoes) and boys. I would rather die than write a poem on anything I cared about.

So, my secret is that I recognise bad poetry and my Mother does not. She's not the type to praise it if she didn't think it good. Furthermore, it really is her type of thing. Its subject is universal and unthreatening. It's not complicated, controversial or difficult. It scans and it rhymes. It has a beginning, a middle and an end. And perhaps most importantly - it *sounds* like poetry. It sounds like her serious poetry.

Her best poems are written for fun, about colleagues at the office, and usually produced at Christmas time. They are doggerel, but very funny, and she keeps none of them. The ones she does keep, the ones she insists on reading aloud to us, are always about Nature or Politics. They rhyme and scan, and in order to do so make tortured use of archaic forms like 'twixt' and 'twain'. Despite their meaning being self evident, she always insists on telling us what they are about afterwards. I say to her sometimes:

'Look, if the poem isn't clear, if you need to explain it, then it's not a good poem. And I do understand it, so you don't need to explain it.'

'I know, dear, but I just wanted to be sure you understood it.'

She thinks my garden poem is wonderful, and has put it away somewhere for safekeeping, believing it to be my first important work of literature. I know it's dismal, formulaic stuff, which came quickly and easily from the brain and not the heart. And now I know that my Mother can't tell the difference. In later years, I will pity her for this, but at sixteen I despise her, while continuing to soak up the praise.

Billie's comic poems were really her best work. Within the family, she was tremendously popular, all our cousins adored her, and many declared her their favourite Aunt. She was attractive, well-dressed, witty and amusing, but outside the family, she had few friends. Mostly these were 'girls' she had met at work, but she did not nurture these friendships, so they became one-sided and petered out. For Billie, family was all that mattered. She was the fourth of eight children, and the third girl. Tina and Marie, the two eldest always shared a bedroom, the third child Frank, being a boy, had his own room, and from a very young age, so did Billie. She was always lonely, and longed for the intimacy of a shared bedroom, but after a long wait the next child was another boy, and so were the two after that, so unlike the others, she never shared a bedroom. If they had been poorer, and unable to rent such large houses, she might have felt more included in her own family.

Despite this lonely childhood, she never thought of seeking playmates outside the family. Her parents had arrived in London from Amsterdam in about 1909, and when Billie was born in 1915, they were all still speaking Dutch at home, which must have cut them off from other children. My grandparents had eloped; she was poor and Catholic, he was middle-class and Protestant, and his family disapproved of the match. My Grandmother spoke no English when she arrived, although my Grandfather was fluent, and it was not until the elder children had been at school for a few years that they started speaking English at home.

Something else which set the van Tinterens apart was my Grandfather's liberal politics and rejection of religion. Class and religion had threatened to separate him from the woman he loved, and he wanted nothing further to do with either.

In every family there is something which acts as currency, which acts as a metaphor for what is really going on. If it's football, you can argue about players and goals and break your father's heart by choosing to support a different team. If it's food you can refuse to eat with the family, or what your mother has cooked. You can eat, or not eat, grow fat or thin, argue with or placate your parents with every mouthful. In some families it's money which parents and children use to control each other, to negotiate, to please and to distress. In our family it was politics. Which explains why, for a few months in early

1960 I declared myself a Conservative and broke my mother's Socialist heart.

Ginny Strevens was briefly my best friend at the Italia Conti Stage School, and she was a Tory. Her father was an artist who had become very rich from mass-produced sentimental pictures of children, most of whom looked very like Ginny, with heart shaped faces, big dark-rimmed eyes and a wistful expression. He had gone to live in the US with his new wife, leaving 15 year old Ginny in the care of her two elder sisters, who were models. I spent the weekend at their flat in Hans Crescent, Chelsea once. The models were away in the country. It was a vast, grandly carpeted room, gloomy and swagged. Several beds were pushed against the panelled walls. The only other furniture was a full sized aluminium dustbin, bright and new, in the centre of the room, into which they hurled rubbish, such as laddered stockings and dead flowers.

There did not seem to be a kitchen, and when I asked Ginny about supper she looked bewildered, and explained that they didn't eat much, because they were models. There was a bathroom off the big room, so I had a bath instead. Most of the floor space was taken by a chrome and glass trolley, piled with cosmetics, more than I had ever seen at once before outside a shop. Dozens of lipsticks, eye shadows, mascaras, rouges, all expensive, mostly French, all messy and crushed and smeared and smelling sexual and exquisite. I think we occupied the whole weekend with maquillage. At that time I wore Panstick (Fair) Lentheric Mascara (black) and Lancome's *Coq de Roche* lipstick. On the trolley I found a wonderful mauvy brown called *Olympia*, also by Lancome, which you could only get in Paris, said Ginny. It was the first brown lipstick I had ever seen and I was determined to have some.

I had been flirting with cosmetics for some time. That weekend it got serious, and the relationship was solemnised in that bathroom mirror, with Ginny and the trolley with its glamorous burden as witnesses. I soon found that you could get Olympia at Selfridges, and incorporated brown lipstick into my persona long before Biba and the Cardiac Arrest shades of the seventies.

But there was something else. Ginny and I talked long into the night. As soon as her schooling was over she was going to the States to live with her Dad. Her Mum had died some years ago, her sisters were rarely there, they were living it up with the Chelsea Set - and didn't want her tagging along till she was old enough to go in pubs. She got herself up every morning, took the tube from Knightsbridge to Piccadilly Circus, buying herself a round of toast and a cup of tea on the way in. This was often all she had to eat all day. She was very thin and desperately lonely. She told me all that, and I listened, and I didn't hear a word of it. What I heard was money and freedom. She could do exactly as she liked. She had a charge account at Harrods down the road, and if she needed money, she had simply to ask for it.

At school she was witty and popular, best friends with Julie Samuel, whose Aunt, Christina Foyle, owned the famous bookshop. They had been educated at expensive private schools, while I had no idea how to behave or speak to people. They were confident, neat and groomed, in expensive and fashionable clothes, while I was the tallest in the class, and usually wore my mother's cast offs. Although I was never quite in their clique, they were actually very nice to me, explaining that it was very embarrassing for them when I was rude to the teachers. From them I learnt that it was far cooler to treat the teachers as equals.

I don't remember how my weekend with Ginny came about, but I do remember being thrilled at the prospect. The reality, while fun, gave a glimpse into what lay behind her constant shrieking laughter at school, into her fear and desperation. Afterwards, I still thought she was cool and her life was glamorous, so I struggled against acknowledging what I'd discovered - that she was a sad and lonely little girl who missed her dead mother and absent father terribly.

Ginny was a Conservative for the same reason I was a

Socialist - it was how she'd been brought up. She taught me three new words: plebs (short for plebian), trogs (short for troglodytes) and proles (short for the proletariat). These words described other, lesser, ordinary people, and while they fascinated me, I didn't like them much and didn't use them except at home to upset my mother.

'You're talking about the Working Class, the ordinary people of this country. You may not like it, but anyone who works for a living is working class and that includes me. The class system stinks and you're no better than anyone else and hang your coat up when you come in.'

At that time, I saw nothing peculiar in my Mother's combination of revolutionary socialism, sexual prudery and bitter snobbery. She may have loved humanity in the abstract, but individual members of the human race usually disappointed her. When she left Maida Vale, I helped her pack. She was very concerned about the valuable crystal chandeliers, which she had bought at great expense from Waring and Gillow, and wanted them wrapped carefully. She produced a pile of old newspaper and I sat on the floor wrapping each crystal teardrop in a page of the Daily Worker.

32

The Ritz, Kingsbury

Spring 1960

IN the Ritz Ballroom, Kingsbury I am wearing Billie's black and white sack dress. It is elegant but does nothing for my figure. With my unfashionable hair and square black beatnik spectacles, I do get asked to dance, but I'm an offbeat choice. I have come here with Sandra, who lives locally. Sandra is mainstream - everybody's taste - 5'5", blonde bouffant hair, white sleeveless blouse, very full skirt over net petticoats over hooped petticoat, held tightly in the middle with a wide, white plastic belt. She has perfect white stilettos and American Tan seamless stockings. And she can jive. She is rarely off the floor.

Despite her popularity in the Ritz, at Conti's Sandra is an outsider like me. We go home together on the Bakerloo line, and we get on, but our backgrounds are very different. All we really have in common, apart from being in the same class, is that neither of us fits in with the wealthy, confident middle class girls. Sandra is respectable working class, her parents are shopkeepers, she lives in Honeypot Lane, Kingsbury and has been preparing for the stage all her life. Every Saturday has been devoted to ballet and tap, and finally her adoring parents have scraped up enough money to send her to the longed for stage school. It's expensive, but they think it's worth it because she loves it so much and is such a talented dancer.

179

I have been meeting Sandra and a group of her Stanmore friends on occasional Saturday nights ever since we were new girls together at Conti's in January 1960. I meet them outside Kingsbury tube and we walk to the Ritz, pay our 2/- entrance and go straight to the Ladies Room to re-do our make up and hitch up our petticoats. Then, with skirts and hair bouffant, we sail out together into the Ballroom, and sit along the wall, waiting to be picked off. I enjoy these outings, but never have much luck with suburban boys. I'm the wrong type and I know it. I'm too tall and, worse still, I look brainy.

Once, when I was wearing a pink linen dress, with a dropped waist, a good-looking, dark haired boy asked me to dance. When I stood up, he laughed.

'You're nearly as tall as me!'

I smiled, and tried to follow his jive movements. I really fancied him, couldn't think of the right thing to say, something that didn't sound brainy. But he got in first.

'Are you Ban the Bomb?'

'If you mean am I a member of CND - then yes. I march from Aldermaston every year and will do so until they ban nuclear weapons.'

'Blimey, I thought you looked brainy!'

'You only think that because I'm wearing glasses.'

'No, no, you look the student type. I've been to University myself, you know.'

'Really, whereabouts?'

'University of Life - ha ha!'

After a slow dance I went outside with him - round the back of the Ritz. We snogged up against the wall, he was pushing up against me. I didn't specially like it, but I did fancy him, he was the sort of boy I aspired to – good-looking, confident, mainstream. He asked me to meet him outside the following week, but he stood me up. I'd taken ages to get ready too, borrowed (without permission) Billie's best brown suit, stood on the steps for hours, waiting long after I was certain he wasn't coming, because I didn't know what to do next.

While I stood there, trying not to cry, I realised it must have been him who had stained the pink linen dress. When I was ironing it, Billie had said

'What's that stain on the skirt Penny - it looks like a man's semen.'

'Well it isn't. And if it was, it *would* be a man's, wouldn't it? It wouldn't be a woman's, would it? Stupid Cow!'

'Well, what is it then? I have no idea where you go or what you get up to, anything could happen. I don't know who your friends are, but you've got to tell me Penny, what is that stain?'

'I have no idea - why don't you just leave me alone.' I slam the iron down and glare at her. I am wondering how she knows what it is. To me it looks like an anonymous food stain. I also wonder how it got there. Standing outside the Ritz in my high heels for over 2 hours, thinking abut it, realised that he must somehow have come on my skirt. I didn't even see him get it out. I missed it.

I did once attract a mainstream, suburban boy. Well, a man really. The first time I went to the Ritz, it happened as it was supposed to. I danced with a policeman called Jeff who was 27 and he asked me out to the pictures.

'Who is this man?' demands Billie, suddenly overcome with parental responsibility. She insists that I ask him in to meet her before he takes me out. I can see she's not happy and I know why. It is not because he is 27 and I am still only 15. It is because he is ordinary - ordinary looking with an ordinary job - not even in an office. If he had been good looking and charming, instead of awkward and polite, she'd have simpered and giggled, which would have been embarrassing, so I don't mind really. He's a man and he wants to take me out, he'll do!

At the pictures he immediately starts to snog me, and I don't get a chance to look at the film, which is annoying. He does that kind of kissing where they put their tongue in your mouth, which I do not like. Every time I turn my head away, he takes hold of my chin, turns it towards himself again and latches on. He kisses me with his eyes closed, and with my short-sighted vision, I can see reflections of the film flickering on his shiny eyelids, but not enough to follow the plot. His kisses are long, wet and boring. He takes me home and is already talking about our next date. I don't know how to say no. At my door there is more tiresome snogging. My jaw aches and I can't wait to get inside.

Next week, when he calls round to take me to the pictures again, I don't answer the door. Tan and I are alone in the house, and we hide in the bedroom, trying not to laugh. I feel terribly guilty, because he's a nice, kind man. I don't even mind his lack of conversation, my van Tinteren genes mean I'm happy to talk all the time with him my attentive audience. It's the relentless snogging I can't take.

33

Swiss Cottage Odeon

Easter 1960

I am in the Swiss Cottage Odeon, watching *The Story of Ruth*, but actually thinking about my sister who is driving me mad. She is home from Reedham for the Easter holidays, Billie is out at work and Tanya and I are meant to be tidying the place up. But with just the one room, it's much more cramped than we are used to. Once again, we have slept late, and at two o'clock in the afternoon, her camp bed has not been folded away and she's still in her nightie. I'm fed up with doing it all. So I just walked out. We have recently moved to West End Lane, and are almost next door to West Hampstead tube. I had intended to go to Kilburn and walk along the beloved and familiar Kilburn High Road. But inadvertently I got on a train going in the opposite direction, so got out at Swiss Cottage instead.

It's afternoon and the cinema is almost empty. Someone is sitting at the end of my row. The whole cinema is empty and there he is. I look back at the screen, heart beating. He is standing up, something is about to happen. He is young, with short blonde hair. Good looking. I am very excited and I am also terrified. Surely he won't - he does, he has! Now he is sitting right next to me, on my left. I look straight ahead at the film, seeing nothing, wondering what will happen next.

I have longed for a boyfriend and now I might actually have

one. So far, he has said nothing, but coming to sit right next to me must mean something. It's an approach, isn't it? He has approached me. He is interested in me. He is moving around a bit, getting comfortable, but he hasn't said anything yet. Should I speak first? No, I can't.

He's fidgeting quite a lot, I know he will speak soon, and he does:

'What do you think of that?'

I look. It is the first penis I have ever seen, and it is huge. I know the theory, that penises grow big and stiff, but sticking up out of his trousers it was about six inches long. I had no idea they got that big. I do know that this is not how courtship is supposed to commence, but he is young and very good-looking and I am fascinated.

'Would you like some of this?' he asks. He has an American accent and smells of peppermint. I nod because I cannot speak. I have no free will. He is my longed for boyfriend, and I am so grateful to him for noticing me. My real life is about to begin.

'Come with me' and he grabs my hand, leads me towards the EXIT sign. The penis has disappeared - what has he done with it?

At the EXIT sign he pulls me towards him and kisses me. It's wonderful. A real kiss, a man and a woman, embracing. And I am the woman. I can feel his penis up against me. He is agitated.

'Quick, quick, come with me.'

We are running across the road, towards the bombed church, he is gripping my hand, pulling me along. The churchyard is a bomb site, we are hidden from the road by the remains of a wall. He kisses me again, puts his hand up my skirt and I feel ashamed. I am ashamed because I am wearing Reedham knickers: navy, lock knit, elasticated legs. I am about to have sex for the first time in my life and it will be spoilt by my horrible old underwear.

'I'm sorry about my knickers.'

'What knickers - let me see.'

'They're my old school knickers.'

'School knickers - great - keep them on - I'll go between the elastic.'

I have no idea what he is talking about. How do you go between the elastic? He tells me to lie down on the grass. Going between the elastic means I don't take my knickers off, and the elastic cuts my leg as he performs sexual intercourse on me. It doesn't last long - I had thought it would last longer than that.

It doesn't hurt. It feels like something I always knew, always wanted, meant to be. It feels as if all my life my vagina has been waiting for an erect penis. It also feels incomplete and unsatisfactory in some way. It had started to feel like the beginning of something, but no, apparently this is all there is, a big penis in your vagina, in and out a few times. I'm probably not doing it right. I'm not very attractive, that might be the reason. I'm lucky to have found a boyfriend at all.

And that is how I met my boyfriend Ray Johnson. I give him my phone number and a few days later he actually calls! At West End Lane the three flats shared one phone and it's on the first floor landing. I know it is him as soon as I answer.

'Hampstead 1234'

'Can I speak to Penny?'

'This is Penny speaking - is that Ray?'

'Sure, how many guys have you got?'

'Oh, only you. Well, a few others, but you're the main one.'

I sit down on the hall stairs. Of course I have no other boyfriends, but have an idea it's best to sound in demand.

We arrange to meet at Swiss Cottage tube the following day. I'm early, he's late. As soon as I see him, my heart turns over.

You can tell he is American by the way he dresses, even before he opens his mouth. His fair hair is in a modern jazz cut and his head is slightly too big for his body. He has a wide face, high cheekbones and a beautiful mouth. He is tanned and has perfect white teeth. Underneath his brown-flecked jumper a white tee shirt is visible, and he wears chinos and tennis shoes.

Close up he has green eyes and I cannot take my eyes off him. He's the same height as me.

'Hiya doll.'

He grabs the nape of my neck and starts snogging me there and then. Then he takes me over the road, back to the bombed churchyard and we have sex again. I'm wearing my best knickers this time, but he doesn't notice. Or he doesn't comment.

Afterwards he wants to talk. Wants to know how old I am, where I live, all about my family. We sit on the grass among the graveyard rubble and the weeds and I tell him my life. He is really interested in me and asks me lots of questions. I am in heaven.

Up until now, no male adults had ever paid me this much attention, really listened to me. Walter Gilmore had wanted me to read to him, but apart from that, he does all the talking, he is not interested in listening to Tanya or me.

Ray not only listens, he pays attention. He asks questions. Soon there is nothing he doesn't know.

'When was your last period?'

'Oh, last week I think'

'You *think*! You should *know*. You should always know exactly. What day did it start?'

'Oh, wait - I was at school - it was in tap class so - Thursday. It was Thursday.'

'So, that's 10 days ago?'

'Er - yes.'

'Just as well I pulled out again then. As soon as you've had your period I can come inside you for a couple of days. We'd better do it the other way now.'

The other way? What other way? What had he pulled out

again? I was aroused and embarrassed to hear a man talking so directly about periods, using the right words, sounding involved and authoritative. Talking about my body as if he understood it. But what was this other way?

'What is the other way?'

'I'll show you darling. Stand up and bend over - lean on the wall – look.'

The wall was in fact a big, white tombstone, cracked and mossy, sunk sideways into the earth. Waist height. He led me over to it and placed me in position. Immediately he had my skirt up and my knickers down again. I could feel a hot hardness pushing up against my arse hole.

'No, not there, you've got the wrong place.'

'No I haven't darling - just relax - you'll enjoy this.'

He pushes it right up my arse and I scream. His hand comes over my mouth.

'Shut up baby - do you want the Police to come and find us?'

Despite the big and horrible pain, I do not want the Police to come, so I stop screaming and start weeping instead. One last push and then a hot stinging in my bowels. It was over. Hot stuff was leaking out of my arse and stinging.

'Stop crying baby, you know you loved it. Get a Kleenex and wipe yourself.'

'I haven't got a Kleenex.'

'Well use your hanky then. Look, wipe that spunk away as quick as you can, don't want any of it finding its way up your pussy. You should always carry kleenex. Listen baby, I want to tell you something. When you meet me in future, I want you to go to the bathroom first.'

'What?'

'Go to the bathroom, baby. Empty your bowels before you come and meet me - OK? It's better for me that way.'

We go for a coffee and on the way he explains that he has no money on him - would I mind paying for the coffee? Of course I don't mind. He tells me he is a professional tennis coach and works in the Queens Tennis Club, Regents Park. Perhaps I'd like to go there with him one day and watch him play.

34

Ray Johnson

Early Summer 1960

I told Sandra at the Ritz as we stood around between dances.

'I'm not a virgin any more.'

I could see she was really impressed. She rushed over to tell her friends Carol and Linda and immediately I was surrounded by Kingsbury girls.

'What does it feel like?'

'What's his name?'

'What did he do?'

'Where did you do it?'

'Do you feel different?'

'Tell us all about it'

We are like a flock of birds moving across the sky for no apparent reason, as with one accord and no evident leader, we swoop into the Ladies. The boys watch, uncomprehending, as all the girls down that end of the dance floor swiftly vanish.

In the Ladies, I did not tell the Kingsbury girls exactly how I first met Ray - I said it was a pick up. Picking up someone was quite daring in itself; eventually having sex with him was extremely daring. Picking up someone in the way I had, and going immediately to a graveyard and having sex with him was impossible to tell anyone.

I told them he was American, very good looking and a
professional tennis coach. They wanted to know how it felt,
if it hurt, was I worried about getting pregnant? I loved being
the centre of attention, but didn't want to talk about what they
wanted to hear. I didn't want to talk about the actual sex. So
I came out with pretentious stuff about the mystery of
becoming a woman, informed by years of reading Evelyn
Home's Problem Page in the back of Woman's Own. They had
wanted more detail, but pretended to lap it up anyway.

The Queens Club Regents Park is where rich people play
tennis, and where Ray hopes to pick up some coaching. He
takes me there one day to watch him and his friend John, and
I sit on the bench for an hour as they run about in their tennis
whites. They both look gorgeous in a way English men cannot
manage. Their shorts are shorter, brighter and closer fitting,
and their tennis shoes and special, thick sports socks glow
white against their tanned legs. Most of the other men, the
English men, wear baggy old shorts, discoloured plimsolls,
mingy little grey socks.

John is American too, but he's tall and dark, with a craggy
face. I don't like him much. No, that's not it. I'm scared of
him. Ray has told me that John likes to hurt girls. I am not
sure what he means, but I do not like the way John looks at
me.

'You're lucky you're with me baby - John likes to rape girls.
I don't enjoy that kind of thing myself.'

'How does he rape them?'

'Oh, he takes them back to our place and then he just rapes
them. This girl last week I felt sorry for her, she was so tiny.
He just pushed her back on the bed and got on top of her and
she kinda disappeared, you know. All I could see was John
on top, pumping up and down, I could see he was fucking
something, but I couldn't see what it was. Heard it screaming
though.'

'You were in the room?'

'Sure. We've only got one room. When you come back with us, you won't mind if John's in the room when we make out do you? He'll enjoy it, I can tell you. I bet he wants to join in.'

In those days, it was still widely believed that rape was impossible unless the woman permitted it, and was therefore always the woman's fault - I half believed that myself. Although I was shocked by what he said, I somehow had the impression that the tiny woman obliterated by John was complicit in her own rape. The information disturbed me, but not as much as the suggestion of John being present when Ray and I had sex. We were standing outside the Men's changing room waiting for John to come out.

'Yes, I do mind, actually.'

'*Actually*! I love the way you talk.'

'I love the way you talk, too.'

'No really. You sound so upper class, not just because you're English. You live in Hampstead, you went to boarding school, I bet your old lady's got loads of bread.'

'What?'

'Money. I bet your old lady's loaded.'

'No she isn't. We live in a rented flat. It wasn't that kind of boarding school. We haven't got any money – honestly.'

'Oh come on baby, you always look like a million dollars, your Mom's just sold a great big house. You've got a job, haven't you?

'Only a holiday job till I go back to school in September.'

'Well, at least you're lucky enough to have a job - I've got nothing. I used my last half crown to pay for the court. It's 5/- John and I paid half each and that's all my money gone' He looks at me. Powerful, charismatic, clever.

'Can you help me out, baby?'

'Of course. What do you want me to do?'

'I mean, help me out with some cash. Just till I get some coaching work.'

'I don't understand - how can I help you?'

'Just lend me £2 till next week. Have you got £2?'

'Yes, of course, yes, here you are. Only I need it back next week.'

'Of course, of course, thank you darling. Soon as I get some coaching.'

In the summer holidays of 1960 I worked in Woolworth's Oxford Street, and was taking home almost £5 a week. After lending Ray £2, I still had enough to give Billie 30/- for my keep, and enough for fares and lunches. What I had lent him was all my spending and saving money.

Ray was always short of money. He and John were usually behind with their rent. Once, they were so much in arrears, they simply packed all they could into their tennis bags with their rackets, and strolled out as if going out for a game, and never went back - they had another room already lined up. It was called a Moonlight Flit.

Ray always said he was trying to get work as a tennis coach, and I think he did do that sometimes, but not often. Once, he suddenly had a bright idea about how to get some money.

'We could stand at a bus stop, and you could get talking to a well dressed woman, then you could quickly grab her handbag and run.'

'No, I'm not doing that!'

'Oh, listen it's easy. Choose one of those new, clutch type bags, not one she's got over her arm - you can just grab it and run. You can run, baby, and I'll be waiting for you round the corner. You won't get caught. What's the matter?'

'I'm not doing that - I'm not stealing.'

Ray was a bit startled by this. He was so used to my anxiety to please, my willingness to fall in with anything he wanted, that he became quite agitated, begging, pleading, bullying. He told me I had no idea what it was like to be short of money, coming as I did from a prosperous family and never wanting for anything. I wanted to please him, to do anything he wanted, but I wasn't going to pretend to be someone's friend and then rob them.

When he realised I wouldn't relent, he came up with another plan.

'You get talking to them, we'll pretend to be brother and sister, then I'll grab the bag and run.'

'No, that's worse. I'd be left standing there and she'd say 'Your brother's just run off with my handbag!' Anyway, if we were brother and sister, how come we've got different accents?'

He came up with more scenarios, involving handbags, railways stations, lost tickets, missed trains, him and me as brother and sister, an assortment of sob stories designed to extract cash from the public. He'd start each one with such enthusiasm, spinning a yarn, trying to draw me in by his inventiveness and style. I listened to them all - I enjoyed them. I told myself that these were just make-believe scenarios, like the imaginative tales Tanya and I still occasionally told each other. I knew I would never do any of these things and told myself that neither would Ray.

In another part of my brain I knew that he could, would and probably did do things like this. And probably worse. I remembered how I'd met him. I knew he was a flasher and a con man. And his friend was a rapist. But he talked to me, he listened to me, he spent time with me, he kissed me and made love to me. Since our lodger Mr Mottiwalla had built me a cardboard house, and let me bend his fingers, when I was a tiny girl, no adult male had ever taken such interest or devoted so much time to me, and I loved him.

In the three months that I went out with Ray, I lent him a total of £15. Although I never mentioned how much he owed me and never asked when I was going to get it back, I kept a running total in my head. Mostly it was a pound or two each time, but the last time, the final time, he asked me for £5.

We are in Lyons Corner House at Marble Arch. It is a

Thursday, and as it just happens to be my pay day, I am treating us both to coffee and doughnuts. Ray takes an interest in everything about me, including my work, he wants to hear all about Woolworth's, how many hours I work and do I get extra for overtime. He devotes some time to this topic, takes a great interest in my pay and conditions, because he doesn't want to see me exploited.

'How many days do you work each week?'

'Five. Well, it's meant to be five, but one of them has to be a Saturday because that's the busiest day. But you get a day off in lieu. In the loo, we always say.'

'But you can work that day - right?'

'Yes, I did that last week - worked six days because when I go back to school in September I won't be earning any more after that, so I've got to save up.'

'So does that count as overtime, that extra day?'

'Yes, time and a half - I got almost £7 in my pay packet this week.'

Even as I say this, I realise what's coming next. From his eyes I can see that he knows I know. We both know I am not going to resist, that I am going to give him what he asks for. But both of us can sense a change in me.

'Baby, darling - could you let me have £5? I'm really behind with the rent and that bitch landlady is waiting on the stairs for me every night. I've got some coaching lined up - rich Arab kids from Bayswater - I'm gonna buy you some beautiful jewellery next week. I have seen this fabulous diamond bracelet which would just suit you - do you have any diamonds baby? You would look fabulous in diamonds.'

Slowly I take the big blue note, the bulk of my pay packet, the representation of a week on my feet in stiletto winkle pickers, which hurt by the end of every day, and hand it over. As I do so, I realise that at this moment I am more offended by his promise of jewellery than by his taking more of my money. I realise he knows nothing about me personally. This is part of some kind of 'how to bend any woman to your will' script. In some seduction manual he has read, it says that all women's eyes light up when you mention diamonds, or something. That might be true of American women, but it isn't true of me. I've never been interested in jewellery, but I realise I am quite interested in money. I realise that I am especially interested in the £15 of mine he will shortly have extracted from me, and that I will never see again. It represents about a months wages.

Slowly I hand the important blue bank note, the star of my pay packet - I haven't even had time to put it in my purse - over the table. Instead of discreetly taking his hand as I usually do, and transferring the folded note from my grateful palm to his, I hand it over the formica table top - in full view.

It comes to me that I am paying him off. That this £5 is the price I have to pay for getting rid of him. Everything about him is old fashioned: the neat preppy clothes - I long for shaggy, beatnik Englishmen with black polo necked jumpers and duffle coats. Men who read books, who can teach and tell me things, who will take me on the Aldermaston march and to trad jazz clubs where we can jive. Tennis? Jewellery? These are not cool, they are middle aged, American and boring.

He is sweating. Suddenly he looks old and desperate as he quickly takes the £5 note; almost snatching it from me.

35

Norman Thaddeus Vane

IT is Tuesday March 7th 1961 and I am waiting in the Kenya Coffee House in South Kensington, which is expensive. I have only enough for a cup of Colombian, the cheapest coffee. My return tube fare from West Hampstead was 1/6d, and now all I have in my purse is a threepenny bit and a farthing. You can't get anything in here for threepence farthing - I've already looked. The cheapest thing is a rock cake and that's 6d. Anyway, I'm too excited to eat - Norman will be here in a minute. He lives in Chelsea, so South Ken is his nearest tube station. I love him so much, my stomach contracts every time I think of him.

I went with him to see the first night of his play at the Pembroke Theatre in Croydon last week. I was so proud. It was far better than I had expected - much wittier. The heroine says 'That's the way the cookie crumbles' which is a cliché now really, but also 'That's the way the mop flops' which is far more original, and got a big laugh. At the start the stage lights didn't come on for ages - the Pembroke is a Theatre in the Round - so no curtains. What's supposed to happen is the stage lights go on instead. Only they didn't, everything was quiet, and then the leading actress - Kika someone - Markham I think – said:

'Anyone got a shilling for the meter' and got a tremendous laugh.

Norman took no notice of me during the performance. He

didn't even sit next to me, and I was so disappointed. I sat right at the back, and he sat with Mr Woodward and the producer and some other people at the front. He didn't turn round to look at me once. At the end, they all shouted 'Author – Author!' and he went on stage and bowed all round the audience. I hoped he could see me clapping like mad. I wanted everyone to know I was with him. I wanted him to stride up the aisle, two steps at a time, take my hand and bring me down to the stage to share the applause, but of course, he didn't.

I waited in the foyer and we came back to London together on the train. He told me they were going to keep the line - about the shilling for the meter - in the play. We arranged to meet here at 7 tonight and now it's ten past. I shouldn't have got here early. Anyway, he waited half an hour for me last week, when I got lost. I expect he's forgotten and I feel like crying. Deep down I know he won't come now, yet I cannot help hoping, too. If he's not here by 7.30 I will phone him and ask him if he still likes me. Damn, I've finished the coffee now, I meant to make it last.

If it weren't for the fact that I'm here, where he was before, with me, when he wrote his name in the back of this book, I could believe that none of this ever happened. Underneath his name he wrote:

c/o William Morris Agency
T.V. Administration
1740 Broadway
N.Y. 19

He said if I ever wanted to be sure of contacting him, I should write to him there and it would eventually be forwarded, wherever he was. That felt wonderful, as if he wanted us to stay in touch over long distances and for ever, as if he wanted to be sure of me.

I first met him last month when he came into the office where

I work. It's my first job since leaving Conti's. Mr Woodward is a theatrical agent, and he has arranged to have several plays put on at the Pembroke - including Norman's. Loads of writers and actors come in and say they want Mr Woodward to read their play or be their agent or something and this is good because they are always nice to me and I fall in love all the time.

It is a very small agency on the third floor of an Edwardian building at the Trafalgar Square end of the Charing Cross Road. To reach the office you have to go up in this tiny, cage-like lift in which four slim people can squeeze, as long as Mr Woodward is not one of them. I work in the tiny front office, which is also reception, and there is just room for my desk, an old, khaki filing cabinet and a small chair where people can wait for Mr Woodward. His office is behind me, and even smaller. His desk is covered with scripts, some well-thumbed, some still in their unopened envelopes, signed photographs, bundles of photographs of scenes of plays, bound with elastic bands and curling sharply at the corners, several spectacle cases, a rolled up spare tie and an inkwell with matching pen holder. I know that underneath all this is a blotter, which matches the last two, because Mr Woodward and I had a tidy up on my first day. It is my job to open the post in the morning, and Mr Woodward says I'm welcome to read any of the plays and tell him what I think. But when I do he doesn't say anything, just throws the script back on the pile.

My best outfit for work is my pink courtelle cardigan with my black pencil skirt and luckily this is what I was wearing on March 1st when Norman first came in. He is long, lean and gorgeous and I wanted to go to bed with him as soon as I saw him. I don't mind about him being bald. He is American, and like Ray you can tell this from his clothes, but his are much more elegant. He wore a black polo necked sweater, under a soft camelhair coat, unbuttoned, and his black, square rimmed glasses are almost identical to my own. He looks artistic, he reminds me of jazz, and of French films in black and white.

He told me the only thing left in his flat is his bed - all the rest of his furniture is being used for the set at the Pembroke. The Sunday Times had just been round to interview him about the play, and they took this very *Avant Garde* photo of him sitting cross legged on the floor of his empty flat wearing a black polo necked jumper and holding a vase. I can't wait to see it, and must make sure Mummy buys the Sunday Times as well as The Observer this week.

His flat is in Tite Street, Chelsea, which is where Oscar Wilde lived. He didn't even know that and he's supposed to be a playwright! Anyway, he spent ages talking to me, even after Mr Woodward was free to see him. He said I ought to come to Chelsea, he said I was the type, whatever that means.

Two days later, on March 3rd, he came to the office again - I had been hoping he would. I showed him in to Mr Woodward's office, and asked if it was OK to go out to lunch now. I hoped that Norman wouldn't be long with Mr Woodward, because I wanted to bump into him and by sheer coincidence (honest) I did. Or rather, he bumped into me, a few doors down from the office, and he asked me to have lunch with him. We were outside a restaurant called the Pop Inn and he said

'Shall we pop in?'

We ordered chicken soup, but I had trouble finishing mine and didn't even touch my roll and butter. He asked me to come to Chelsea and have dinner with him, and we arranged to meet in a restaurant called Berino's in South Kensington. Once again, I wasn't hungry, I was just so excited. Norman said he wasn't hungry either, and anyway we could eat later. On the way to his flat he told me that currently, he was a breast man! Most men get fixated on one part of the female body and stick with it, apparently. It could be bottoms, or legs or anything. But Norman changes every few months. Until recently he was a bottom man, but he was now more interested in breasts. I went all hot when he said this, because I thought he was going to say something about my figure, but he didn't.

We walk up to the first floor of 13 Tite Street, which is where his flat is. The first landing is - literally - covered in empty milk bottles, neatly crammed together - and unwashed, I notice. Those at the back are very dusty, at the front far less so. We have only a small area in which to tread to reach the next flight.

'What are all those milk bottles doing there? Why don't you put them out on the step?'

He looks baffled, as if I'd addressed him in a foreign language, and says

'Welcome to my humble abode!'

It is a huge space - the whole of the first floor - and contains a desk, a chair and a double bed. There is no carpet - just bare, unpolished floorboards, and yet it looked elegant. Avant Garde.

'This looks very Avant Garde!' I say

'All my furniture is on the set.' he replies, putting his arm around me and lowering me on to the bed.

He asks if he should come inside me or on my tummy. I don't understand the question at first, but he explains and I say my tummy. It wasn't that different from Ray really, the same sense of beginning something and then everything being over very quickly. But unlike Ray, Norman seems to expect more of me. It's almost as if he wants me in some way to join in. He looks a bit disappointed, cross even.

I asked him 'Was I alright?'

'Fine darling, fine. Put your clothes on - we're going out.'

As I dress, I wonder if I ought to have moved around a little. After we had taken our clothes off, I had simply lain down on the bed and waited for him to perform sexual intercourse on me. I ought to have been sexier. But how? How do you act sexy? How can I make him love me?

We eat at the Devil's Kitchen in Chelsea, where our round, white table has '...he who sups with the Devil must have a long spoon...' written in black italic script around the perimeter. I read this aloud, and Norman gives me a look. This is a business dinner, with a few other men in their thirties, and on the way to the restaurant. Norman has told me not to talk too much.

'We want to talk business, so just eat your food and don't say anything weird or stupid.'

I have soup and french bread, speak only when spoken to and smile. And listen. They are talking about the kind of screenplays Paramount is looking for right now. I suck my thumb. This is not something I would normally do in public, but recently, all over London there have been posters for the film *Baby Doll*. In the posters Carole Baker is wearing shortie pyjamas, which have sparked off a whole new nightwear fashion craze - some people even call them Baby Doll pyjamas. And she has her thumb in her mouth. I enjoy my thumb, still can't get to sleep without it and perhaps it is now OK to do it in public. Also, it could be a way of getting noticed without saying anything. It is. After a few minutes Norman says

'Don't suck your thumb baby - everyone will think I don't give you anything else to suck.'

This is really funny and we all laugh. I have no idea why. One of the men asks

'*Does* he give you anything else to suck?'

'No' I reply. Norman rolls his eyes. Wrong answer.

'Yes of course.' I simper, knowingly. More laughter. Right answer.

It's almost 7.30 and I'm furious now. Why did he make a date if he doesn't like me any more? Also, I'm starving - now I know he's not coming, my stomach is unclenched and I could eat a horse. We were going to go out to dinner. If he would just come now I might be able to eat before it clenches up again. Every time I am with him I'm too excited to eat, and he says why did I bother to order any food if I'm not going to eat it. But he isn't going to come, and I will have to go home because I'm ravenous now. Ravenous and foolish. I will not cry.

36

Crime On Goat Island

I was not a successful girlfriend. There were moments when Norman and I looked at each other - at a loss. We were in bed once, and he said

'Would you rather eat or be eaten?'

And I replied

'Oh I don't know! What a terrible question, I mean I wouldn't want to eat anyone - you mean eat them alive? While they are awake and watching you eat them? Where would you start - at the feet I suppose. Anyway, you couldn't eat a whole person - half an arm at the most. What would you do then? Say 'Thank you, wait there, I'll come back for the rest later. Oh, and would you mind sitting in the fridge to keep fresh!' But then I wouldn't want to be eaten either. It would hurt and I would die. Imagine someone ripping your flesh with their teeth, I couldn't bear it. Is this one of those moral questions, where you have to choose one or the other, and whichever you choose it reveals your true character? I really don't know, because I would hate both of them. But I don't want to die so it will have to be eat. I would rather eat. Which would you choose Norman?'

He didn't answer, he just looked at me, bewildered yet bored at the same time. I wondered what I'd said wrong - he had asked me a riddle and I had answered it. I could see he was trying to think of something to say. He actually started several different sentences unsuccessfully, but gave up, rolled his eyes and said 'Never mind.' in this ironical, grown up 'I'll do it myself.' voice. He jumped out of bed.

'Come on, get your clothes on, we've got work to do.'

There was a typewriter on the table by the window and Norman said I could type his screenplay for him. He wanted it done professionally before he could send it to Paramount. He knew I could type because I sat in Mr Woodward's office, with a typewriter at my desk. He may even have seen me bash a few keys, because like a dyslexic hunting for the spectacles they will never find, I have developed strategies to conceal my inability to type more than 15 words per minute. The main one was to do all my typing when Mr Woodward was out of the office, so he didn't hear how slow I really was. He probably did know really, he may have been old but he was not stupid. However, he liked me and he laughed at my jokes. Also, I spoke nicely, which was useful for answering the phone. But I think that the main reason he tolerated me was the Agency charged him an especially low rate - I was only 16 with a poor education, one O level and no experience.

Anyway, there wasn't that much typing to do, and what there was Mr Woodward would write out by hand for me, to be sure I got the spelling right. I think he often found it quicker and easier to pick up the phone.

Norman knew none of this. He was American, and could not imagine why anyone would employ a typist who could not actually type. He simply assumed I could do it and I was too terrified to tell him the truth. Also, typing his screenplay would involve several hours alone with him. So, I put the blank piece of paper in the machine, Norman pulled up the kitchen chair (his furniture was still on set at the Pembroke) and started to dictate. Fortunately, I had seen the cover pages of enough scripts by then to know how to set it out, so in capitals, one third of the way down the page, roughly centred, I typed:

CRIME ON GOAT ISLAND

'An Original Screenplay' said Norman.

'An Origanal Screenplay' I typed.

'Then under that put 'by Norman Thaddeus Vane' - you know how to spell my name, don't you?'

He got up to look over my shoulder.

'That's not how you spell original - Jesus - take a fresh sheet'

As I did so, I wished I had the nerve to ask him how you *do* spell it. He looked so angry, like Walter in one of his moods. It had started with the 'eat or be eaten' thing. I wanted to say

'Look I can't type, I can't spell, my education was rubbish and finished when I was 14 - after that it was all Voice Production and Musical Comedy. Typing makes me cry, please don't make me do it!'

But I longed for his approval, did not dare risk his further scorn. I could not speak. On the second sheet I typed:

'An Origonal Screenplay.'

'Original! ori-GIN-al! An *original* screenplay. I'm not going to have enough paper if you go on like this.'

He handed me a typewriter rubber - a disc with a smaller metal disc in the centre with which to hold it. The rubber was soft red on the outside, harder grey on the inside and I was not sure which to use. My hand was shaking. I used the soft red and it made a mark, so I rubbed harder with the grey and made a hole in the paper. A grey hole. He ripped the paper out of the typewriter and silently handed me a fresh piece.

It was humiliating. Nerves reduced my usual 15 wpm to about 10 and my spelling was unreliable. He began spelling out every word, letter by letter. I start crying.

'What's the matter with you? I thought you could type! This is going to cost me more in materials than paying someone.'

'I'm sorry.' I wailed. Norman was exasperated. I was obviously some kind of British flake, some kind of nut, something wrong with me. He didn't understand and he didn't ask. He said never mind - let's have some coffee - oh wait - I need sugar. He gave me half a crown and sent me out for two pounds of granulated.

'There's a deli round the corner, right and right again' he said.

It wasn't simply that I had no sense of direction - more that I had not yet learned the compensation skills. I had not yet grasped that I *had* no sense of direction. Since I was five, Reedham had been my whole environment, apart from holidays, when I learned each journey separately, like the words of a song, by repetition. Either by walking along with Billie several times till I knew it by heart, or walking slowly with an A-Z, gradually speeding up after a few days and eventually able to do it without the book. I could find my way around London, but not with the aid of any spatial skills, or any grasp of the compass points.

I don't know where I went, how I went there, how I got the sugar. I remember confusion, despair, a few tears, asking dozens of people and retaining nothing of what they told me. Walking round the quiet, red brick mansions on a hot and sticky day, eventually with a two pound bag of sugar under my arm. Endless. When I finally stumbled upon 13 Tite St somehow, Norman was coldly furious.

'Where the hell have you been? I nearly called the Police. What's the matter with you? Don't just disappear like that - Jesus - where have you been?'

'I don't know. I got lost.'

'How could you get lost, it's only round the corner, I told you where it was. There's no time for coffee now - I've got to go. Come on, I'll walk you to Sloane Square.'

I knew I had serious deficiencies as a girlfriend, but I still hoped he would take me on and sort of train me up. Take an interest in me, become my mentor, my teacher, my father. Even if I'd thought of saying that, I wouldn't have known how. Instead, as we walked to the tube, I tried to get him to tell me when he could see me again. He couldn't say. He explained that he had to get this screenplay typed somehow and off to Paramount before the guy he wanted to read it went off to New York. He couldn't think about anything else till that was done. I had to change at Earls Court, so he kissed me goodbye, said he would call me.

'When?'

'Sometime this week.'

'You've got my new work number?'

'Sure baby. Bye now.'

The agency had sent me to a new job, because Mr Woodward was unable to afford me any more. Norman's play had not been a success, the run ended early to cut their losses and the Pembroke would be dark for a few weeks. Mr Woodward explained what 'dark' meant, and also that with no box office, he wouldn't even be able to pay himself for a few weeks. When things picked up, he promised he would ask the agency for me again. He gave me a kiss, which was nice of him, and I didn't mind, even though he was fat and old and smelt of earwax.

The new job was in a proper office, half a dozen girls at typewriters in a blank kind of room. It was addressing envelopes. The others all had smaller, newer machines, but as the temp, I had the big, heavy old Remington, it was like walking in treacle. After an hour, the Supervisor came in to count my pile.

'Eight? Eight in an hour, is that all? That's seven and a half minutes for each envelope. You're very slow, aren't you dear?'

She looked in the waste paper basket. It was almost full of crumpled, brown envelopes.

'There's about *forty* eight in there, aren't there?'

'Sorry, I'm not used to this typewriter.'

'I'm fed up with the agency sending us girls who can't type.' she said to the room in general.

'Sorry.' I said again. This was the first job I'd had which was all typing - previously I'd been sent out as a clerk/typist and had managed, in various ways, to avoid much actual typing. This job was nothing but copy typing - typing addresses from a roneo'd list onto small brown envelopes and there was no way out.

'What's your handwriting like?' she asked.

'All right I suppose.'

'Let me see - write the next envelope by hand.'

She timed me, using the minute hand on the office clock.

'That took you 90 seconds and its legible enough. Since we're stuck with you for today, write them by hand. But I'm only paying the clerical rate - not the typist rate.'

Norman forgot to call me, so I had to call him. He had said he'd call some time that week and when it got to Thursday I couldn't wait any longer. Couldn't think about anything else. I called him from work. We were allowed to make personal calls in our lunch hour, from the switchboard phone in reception. With the receptionist listening. Someone else answered - another man - he asked who was calling and I gave my name.

Norman came on the line instantly.

'Penny - where on earth have you been?'

My heart leapt. He sounded angry, but really concerned. He had been really worried about me, wondering where I was, waiting for me to call. I must have misunderstood him when he said he would call me - I was meant to call him. At that moment, I knew for certain that he loved me, and I was almost delirious.

'Oh I started a new job - I gave you the number. How's the screenplay coming along?'

'Oh, it's you.'

'Yes, it's me, Penny.'

'I'm sorry baby - my wife is called Penny too, and I don't

know where the hell she is. How are you, anyway?'

His tone had completely changed, back into the way he normally spoke to me, cool and laconic. Half hearted. He had told me he'd been married twice and divorced twice and I'd concluded he didn't love either of them any more. He never told me that one of them had the same name as me.

'I'm fine. Which wife, the first or the second?'

'The second, we're getting divorced.'

'I'd really like to see you.'

'No can do, baby - not this week. Tell you what, I'll write you - OK?

'OK, don't forget.'

'Bye.'

So far, I'd had two letters from Norman, big, black inky writing, my surname spelt exotically - Wardmann - as if it were German or Jewish. No further letter arrived and I knew it wouldn't. I knew he wasn't going to call me again either. I knew we were through. But I couldn't help it. I stood in Reception a week later and called him again.

'I just rang to say goodbye - I'm getting married.'

'Oh really - anyone you know?'

'No, I'm not getting married, but I'm finishing with you, I never want to see you again.'

'My heart is broken.' He was actually sniggering.

'Goodbye, Norman.'

I saw him once more after that, but I thought about him for ages, and about his wife called Penny who he still loved but was divorcing. And who had disappeared. For that brief moment on the telephone, I had experienced what it was like to have a man in love with me, waiting anxiously for my call. Would anyone ever love *me* like that?

Incredibly, I was still in the same temporary job, still handwriting envelopes. There was a tremendous shortage of office staff in those days and we could get away with behaviour that would never be tolerated now. To save money and to stop myself thinking about Norman, I spent my lunch hours on the Remington, getting my speed up. Certain words which recurred in addresses - street, road, and all the counties, I could now type much more quickly, and I had developed a satisfying and noisy rhythm for postal districts, shifting up and banging the full stop in between S.W and 1. The supervisor softened and said no point in replacing me, since the next girl would be just as bad. If I stopped talking so much, she'd keep me another week.

37

Fitzjohns Avenue

Spring 1961

ALTHOUGH West End Lane was a better address than Minster Road, Walter felt Billie could still do better. Once again, we sacrificed space, but 37 Fitzjohn's Avenue, Hampstead was in a very grand building and, it was NW3! The three of us lived in one large room: two beds, one sink, one gas ring. I shared the larger bed with Billie and Tanya had the small one. Walter Gilmore was renting a room in Mrs Sherman's flat in Montague Mansions, Baker Street, W1. Postcodes were crucial to Walter. He spoke reverently of Mrs Sherman, who was a wonderful woman, he said, but so ill she could rarely get out of bed. We saw her briefly one day when we called for him, and realised that she couldn't get out of bed because she was huge, she must have weighed about 25 stone. In those days people that size were rare and remarkable and she was the fattest person we had ever seen. Walter explained afterwards that it was glandular. She summoned us into her bedroom and asked us the questions people ask children: What's your name, how old are you, where do you go to school...

At just seventeen I was weary of these questions. I replied to the recumbent mountain in what I hoped was a superior tone that I had left school and was working as a temp. in an office before going to University, which startled Billie and Walter, as it was meant to.

I had no intention of going for auditions as most of my classmates were doing, because by this time I was certain I didn't want a career on the stage. Conti's had been interesting, but its main attraction had been that it wasn't Reedham. I'd had a good time, gained confidence and learned a lot, but I never really wanted to go on the stage. Billie did. Billie longed to be an actress. If WW2 had not broken out when it did, she knew she would have been plucked from the chorus line and elevated to stardom.

After Conti's I was even more certain about what I wanted. I had not forgotten the humiliation of the Pat Glover Agency. I knew I looked wrong, but more importantly, I didn't want to do it, it seemed frivolous and old fashioned. Several of my classmates had got jobs as chorus girls in seaside shows - three of them were booked for Kidderminster for the summer season, and were tremendously excited about it - after that they planned to try for jobs in panto. I was fascinated to hear about it, and I wanted to get away from home too, but not as a dancer.

What I really wanted, what I wanted so much I could rarely say it out loud, was to go to University. Dancing - acting even - did not seem as glamorous to me as the academic life in a duffel coat and black polo necked jumper. Going on Aldermaston marches, anti-apartheid marches, reading difficult books on existentialism, discussing them in depth with serious, angry young men in coffee bars. Better still, in bohemian cafés on the Left Bank in Paris.

After we left Mrs Sherman's, Billie and Walter explained to me that they could not afford to send me to University. At present they were looking for a flat where we could all live as a family, and that would take all their money for a while. I saw no point in talking about it any more, obviously I had missed the higher educational boat by not getting to Grammar School and the one English Literature 'O' level I'd got at Conti's was to be my sole academic achievement.

Later, I discovered that you did not have to be at school to take exams, and there were other ways to get enough GCEs to qualify for University entrance. There were evening classes at local colleges, or even correspondence courses. Later still, I discovered that you could get a grant to go to University, which would pay for your tuition and your keep while you studied. But if Billie or Walter knew about these opportunities, they took care never to mention them. Billie often told us that in 1934, my father had won a scholarship to read History at Oxford, but had been unable to take it up, because it only paid for tuition, not for his books or his keep. It was not enough to be clever, you had to be rich to go to University. Even more important, all that studying would 'ruin your eyes', and mean having to wear even stronger glasses.

On 4th April 1961 I spent the night with Norman, the last time I saw him. He explained that he probably wouldn't sleep much because a man at the studio called John Klein had given him some tablets called Benzedrine so he could get his screenplay finished. He said he was going to stay awake till Sunday and get it finished. We had sex and I slept. We didn't have anything to eat - he wasn't hungry because of the tablets. I woke up to find him banging on the typewriter. He wanted to use up some energy, so he walked me to the tube. I knew it was over, and although I was sad and hurt, Norman did not look as attractive as he had at first. His breath smelt, he was bald and old and he didn't like me much. I had thought that because he was a playwright, he was an intellectual, but when I tried to discuss politics with him, he looked incredulous, then - very quickly - bored. He was not a man for Aldermaston. But it was months before I stopped thinking about him. I rang him a couple of weeks later, the person who answered said he had gone to the country to finish his screenplay.

I made the call from the cream painted telephone booth downstairs in the hall at Fitzjohns Avenue, and after I put the phone down, I sat there for a bit. It was a good place to be alone sometimes. The phone rang again and it was Ray Johnson. I'd not heard from him for about six months, he'd just evaporated. I'd never had a phone number for him. He said he had been to a lot of trouble to get my new phone number, and he was sorry not to have been in touch but he had been in prison in Amsterdam. I didn't ask what for, I didn't care. It could have been any one of a dozen sordid crimes. He asked when he could see me again and I said I had another boyfriend now and I didn't want to see him any more.

'But Baby, listen to me, I've got a present for you. I got you this adorable toy poodle, you'll love it.'

'I'm a bit old for toys, thank you.'

'It's not a toy, darling, it's real, it's called toy because it's so dinky. You're just gonna go crazy when you see it.'

'No I'm not. How irresponsible to buy a live animal for someone when you don't even know if they've got somewhere to keep it. I don't like pets, I never said I did.'

'But Baby, I really want to see you, I've missed you...'

I hung up on him. He was so - so *1960*.

I wonder now what Billie was thinking of, letting me spend the night away from home when I was sleeping with Norman. She had always left Tanya and me on our own during the holidays, and continued to do so after we left. Somehow this seemed to extend to staying away for the night, and I would simply announce that I would be staying the night with a friend. There was rarely any argument. Of course, she should not have allowed it without knowing exactly where I was. But to be fair, I probably lied most plausibly about spending the night with Ginny, and it must have been a relief to get rid of me for a few hours. Any three women living, cooking, washing and sleeping in the same room will get on each other's nerves. She and Walter were looking at flats in Baker Street. However, in that area they all required more 'key money' than Billie and Walter could find. Thinking they had found somewhere, she had given notice at West End Lane, but it fell through, and we'd had to find somewhere quickly. Walter saw this as an opportunity for us to move to a smarter address. West End Lane had been cramped enough, but at least we'd had our own separate kitchen in which we could eat.

We had been living a bed-sit life since we left 22 Minster Road. Walter took up a lot of Billie's attention, she was working full time, looking for a flat where we could all live together and planning her wedding. And I was being a teenage monster. We were all rowing with each other: Tanya and me, Billie and me, less often Billie and Tanya or Billie and Walter. But the main battleground was Walter and me. All sexual contact between us had ended at Minster Road, but we remained acutely aware of each other's presence.

I was trying to get Billie to stop buying South African fruit, and she was happy to boycott it when she remembered. But she didn't want me to tell Walter because it would only start an argument. He came in with a bag of South African oranges, and I made a remark. The kind of remark he was waiting to hear, so that he had an excuse to lose his temper. I didn't care, he was prejudiced and wrong. I remembered what he'd said about coloured women and getting them pregnant. I hated all his smug, racist remarks.

'Why not?' he would say, when he wished to justify doing as he pleased 'I'm free, white and forty.' He thought that was a funny remark. I no longer knew any black people, but wished I did so I could bring them home.

So he said something like 'What's that supposed to mean, young lady ? You think you're so clever, well let me tell you, you know nothing, *nothing*, so shut up!'

I was sitting on my bed at the time, and he stood over me, red faced and angry. I was afraid of him but couldn't resist. He was so stupid, and I had no idea about how to let it go graciously. I said apartheid was a disgrace, that boycotting South African products was the only way to influence them, that they shouldn't be in the Commonwealth. And he punched me in the jaw.

Billie told him off and he apologised to her. She said he should apologise to me, but he said no, not after the way I'd spoken and she said fair enough and she couldn't stand all this any more. So it was no wonder she didn't question me too closely when I said I would be spending the night with a friend.

Then she saw a job advertised in the Daily Telegraph, and said she thought it sounded perfect for me.

38

The Scilly Isles

Summer 1961

BILLIE bought the Daily Telegraph for the crossword, but unlike most people who say that, she really never read much of the paper, always did the crossword, and often finished it. In April 1961 she saw an advertisement for a summer job:

> **ST MARYS SCILLY ISLES** *Live in staff required for Hugh Town Milk Bar. Apply Pender, Kavorna Milk Bar, Hugh Town, St Mary's Isles of Scilly, Cornwall.*

Billie suggested that I apply for it, and I went to the library to do some research. Everything about the Scillies sounded great - it was in the Gulf Stream, so the weather was warmer than the rest of Britain, it was pretty, with lots of flowers - if I went there it would be a long summer holiday. Kidderminster would have been as good, or Colorado. Or Mars. Billie and I were fed up with sharing a bed, we were desperate to be apart.

The Milk Bar was actually a Coffee Bar. We served two kinds of coffee: Cona and Instant. Cona was 9d a cup made with ground coffee, filtered then left on the hot plate till it was used up. Instant was 5d a cup and made with a teaspoon of brown powder from a catering sized tin kept under the counter. The locals always had instant, visitors always had Cona, unless they specified otherwise. Part of the job was to know all the locals on sight, and very soon, I did.

Walking in off the High Street you came straight into the Milk Bar itself - a long counter with about eight stools, and on the left was the café itself, with dark wooden chairs and tables and a nautical theme. It's a cliché now, but at the time I thought it witty and bohemian. Suspended from the ceiling in drapes and festoons were fishing nets - stiff and dark brown. Caught up in them were large shells and a few round glass floats - the first I'd ever seen. Once in a while, Gilbert would get us to dust and rearrange them. On the walls were various nautical prints, which made me think that the Kavorna Milk Bar was a fairly recent incarnation. Before that it had probably been The Captain's Tea Rooms or something. Milk Bars had been a brief fashion imported from the United States and had never really taken off. In 1961 they were just giving way to Coffee Bars and the only other Milk Bar I'd ever seen was in the Kilburn High Road. It never looked as if it was doing much business. But the sign over the door now said The Kavorna Milk Bar, so Gilbert was stuck with it.

I was one of four girls recruited for the summer season. Annette was just starting her third summer season at the Kavorna, and she showed us what to do. We all slept upstairs, Annette had her own room, the rest of us were in two twin rooms.

Annette was engaged to Guthrie, Gilbert's younger brother. They were part of the numerous Pender family, which had been on the Scillies for centuries, the churchyard was packed with them. They were both short, dark, stocky and full of themselves, but while Gilbert was chatty, Guthrie was quieter. Gilbert always had some girl or other in his room with him - but never one of us - he was always careful not to mix business with pleasure. They were usually visitors, only on the island for a week or two, and we'd hear thumps and giggling from his room, then we'd bump into them in the bathroom, sleepy, embarrassed, still giggling. Annette said he had a wife on the mainland somewhere.

Guthrie was a fisherman and Annette would sometimes go out with him in his boat. She was beginning to despair of him ever marrying her, and was certain that, during the winters, while she was on the mainland, he was regularly unfaithful. She was a decent, friendly woman in her early 20s, with glasses and a matter-of-fact, slightly sardonic manner. She was very kind to me, which is remarkable because I must have pissed her off mightily sometimes.

Annette taught us how to make all the house specialities. When I rushed to tell her in panic that someone had ordered a chocolate spider, she showed me how to pour lemonade into a knickerbocker glory glass, then add a scoop of chocolate ice cream. Surprisingly, and very satisfyingly, the ice cream fizzed around in the lemonade, then you put two straws and a paper parasol on top and presented it. For a strawberry spider you added strawberry ice cream, and so on. I made one for myself, it was delicious, but the real work of art was the knickerbocker glory itself. I loved using the ice cream scoop, dropping each flavour cleanly into the glass so it didn't smear the sides and ruin the effect. At certain points you squirted strawberry syrup, then a bright green lime syrup and finally chocolate sauce on the top, crowned by hundreds and thousands and a maraschino cherry. I thought it should be a glace cherry, but we didn't have any of them. Then you perched a fan shaped Milady wafer on top and carried it - very carefully - to the customer. We served all day breakfasts and snack items, welsh rarebit, scrambled eggs, beans on toast and I learned to carry six full cups and saucers without a tray.

In the Scilly Isles I became seriously promiscuous. I was miles away from London and from anyone I knew. I had a steady wage, no bills to pay and in many ways it was a wonderful summer. The social life centred around the pub, and I went most evenings. I usually drank halves of mild, which cost 7d each. The other drinkers were locals, many of them fishermen, farmers and flower growers, but I hung out with those who like me, were down for the season, working in hotels and restaurants. We were a young, transient, bohemian bunch and we considered ourselves intellectuals, arguing passionately about the work of writers we might or might not actually have read.

Tony Armstrong was a poet and at the centre of this group. When sufficiently drunk he would stand on a table and recite his poems for us. I fell in love with him immediately and indicated in some not very subtle way that I was interested. He indicated in some not very subtle way that I should join the queue, which hurt and, of course, made me even more keen.

He was the kitchen porter at the Atlantic Hotel, opposite the Kavorna, and when I saw him stride down the High Street in his kitchen whites, I was overcome with lust and longing. If he crossed the road and entered the Milk Bar, I would rush breathlessly to take his order.

I had no idea that I should conceal my feelings or wait for a man to approach me. Even when I began to realise that I should, I didn't know how to do it. I still don't actually. So I threw myself at him in a way that makes me cringe with embarrassment when I think of it now. He was a young, heterosexual man without a regular girlfriend. I was a tall, slim girl with unruly hair and glasses, weird but not repulsive. And I was just seventeen. Against his better nature, he succumbed on the beach one night and on several subsequent nights, but he never really liked me.

For a start, I talked too much, and when a man is a poet, an intellectual, who knows about writing, he needs an audience, not a rival. One reason I did not listen attentively enough to his poetry, or have much to say about it is that I did not really understand it. Of course, I was immensely impressed that he wrote it, that he professed himself before the world to be a Poet and an Intellectual. After all, I wanted to be a writer myself. However, to my ignorant ear it sounded like some drunken bloke's ramblings. When he read aloud, he would have the poem written out on a piece of paper, and refer to it now and then, but what he recited often seemed to contain many more words than were actually written down. Also, the same poem seemed to change on different occasions. It would start off with the same few lines - something about anger and Yorkshire blood and true feelings misunderstood by the soft southerner. Tony was from Yorkshire. And then it would become something else - sometimes about going down the mines and manhood, other times about artistic sensibility misunderstood by money fixated capitalists. Tony had demons and he needed to talk them through. They were his artistic badge of honour, they were what made him interesting, what made him a poet. I could probably have been his girlfriend if I had just shut up, listened and admired. But I too had demons, and I too needed to talk them through, to drink too much, to stand on tables and rail against the injustice of the world.

People told me to act cool. Don't be so sensitive, stop trying to change the world, don't show your feelings all the time. I understood what they meant, but I never got the hang of it. I could see the advantage of saying little, keeping people guessing. If you are silent and look quietly amused, everyone thinks you're brainy, everyone wonders what you are thinking and men will think you are a good listener. Eventually they will ask you what you are thinking. Eventually, they will lean forward attentively to hear your answer. I was rarely able to wait that long.

Men expected women (or girls as we were called) to be good listeners; in those days, all the advice in the back pages of the womens magazines recommended this. Take an interest in his hobbies, go to football matches with him, read the paper every day so that he can have an intelligent conversation with you. Above all, be a good listener. Which actually meant, be quiet. You did not actually have to listen, but I did not yet know this. There was some trick to being cool and hiding your feelings, and somehow I couldn't learn it.

I had lots of sex that summer, lots of long, romantic night walks - after midnight there was virtually no artificial light on the island in those days - and we would wander all over the island, down on the beach, up to Penninis Head to gaze out over the ocean, through acres of mysembrianthemum, walking, talking and making love. Sailors, musicians, bohemians artists, three posh young hikers one after the other in their tent, a journalist friend of Tony's called Frank, a failed pop singer called John. I fell in love with a few of them, including a sailor called Brian from Caerphilly, who wrote to me several times and said he would come to London one day and find me again.

When I did fall in love, it only lasted till the next one. At that time, I wasn't ready for it. Too much anger and self-destruction. I remember those three Home Counties chaps in their tent. I'd picked one of them up in the pub and we'd done it on the way back to his tent, where I'd agreed to spend the night. When we crawled into the dank, sea-salt reeking tent, the other two woke up. I insisted on having sex with each of them as well. It is entirely possible that neither of them really wanted this. There was no light, none of us could see the others and we were all in various stages of drunkenness. The tent was a male place, and I wanted to be part of it in some way. I wanted to belong among the sleeping bags, the rough ropes and rubber smelling groundsheets, to be useful in this kind of life.

I remember feeling I wanted to give myself be used, like a clay vessel, to be of service in the world. I may even have embarrassed them all by expressing this drunken thought. At that time, in that tent, having sex with as many men as possible seemed a really useful contribution I could make. It was the one thing I was good at, the one way I could get a man's undivided attention, and - fleetingly - approval. The three posh lads were most embarrassed afterwards, and kicked me out of their tent very early in the morning. I wandered back to the Kavorna, hot from the early morning sun, sticky with semen and sand, damp blades of grass in my knickers and with a roaring thirst - but still too young for real hangovers.

One evening, early, alone and recently paid, I went in the

pub and asked for a whisky. Then a gin, then a brandy. I worked my way through all the spirits, in precisely the way I knew you should never do. Never mix grape and grain Walter Gilmore used to say. I wanted to see what would happen. With grave amusement the barman served me everything I ordered. At some point I passed out and was apparently carried out over someone's shoulders, dumped on the back of his lorry and driven back to the Kavorna, where I was carried up the stairs and dumped on my bed. I remembered nothing about it, and woke the next day bright and breezy, but extremely thirsty. Annette told me what had happened and found it remarkable that I had no hangover.

'I don't have hangovers.' I told her, ignorant and smug.

One night I walked up high on Penninis Head with John, the bitter and disillusioned pop singer, he told me the sad story of how he had written a song, which had simply been stolen. He had known nothing of copyright law, had no agent or manager and had simply recorded his song and sent it to the company. They did not reply or return the tape, but a few months later, his song was high in the charts, performed and ostensibly written by an established singer. John had no way of proving that he had written it, and the record company claimed never to have heard of him.

He would not tell me the name of the singer or the song, but he did ask tentatively what I would say if he started to make love to me, and I said why didn't he try and find out. Afterwards, we sat among the dunes, smoking cigarettes and talking some more about how cynical we were, how evil and corrupt the world was. I wanted to hurt myself. I asked John what would happen if I stubbed my cigarette out on the inside of my ankle. He replied that I'd burn myself, which was not the answer I wanted. The answer I wanted was 'No, don't hurt yourself, don't burn yourself' but he didn't say that. So I said

'Shall I do it, then?'

'If you want' he said, puzzled, but not very interested.

So I did, I stubbed my cigarette out on the tender white triangle inside my right ankle, making a round burn, the pain giving a satisfying release of self-loathing. Punishing myself, spoiling myself. Nobody cared.

I had a scab and a scar for a while, then it disappeared completely. But the body remembers, and forty years later, it reappeared, a precise disc of red thread veins.

39

Fulham

November and December 1961

I returned from the Scillies in September 1961, full of attitude, wearing a long, navy fisherman's jumper and a new sense of independence. At first I was glad to be home, glad to be back in London, but dismayed that we were all still living at Fitzjohn's Avenue and I still had to share a bed with my Mother. After my long summer of freedom and adventure, this was hard. Walter and Billie were married now, but still living separately and flat hunting every weekend. He was very keen on what he called a 'mansion flat' for which 'key money' would be required. He was also very keen that I should get a job and stop 'sponging off' my Mother.

I was keen on this too, and Billie suggested I start temping again. London in those days had an insatiable demand for office workers. The Evening Standard always had columns and columns of advertisements for Secretaries, Shorthand Typists, Copy Typists, Clerk Typists and even Typists. All these jobs had a common requirement, not difficult to spot. You had to be able to type.

A very nice lady called Marion Barton ran a small Secretarial Agency in Kensington Church Street called Personal Services. It was she who had sent me to Mr Woodward and later to the place where I ended up addressing envelopes by hand. I went back to her and asked if there were any jobs.

'Loads of jobs if you can type, darling. What's your speed like these days?'

'Oh, about 50 word per minute' I lied 'But I've probably grown rusty over the summer, so let's say 40.'

'That's good enough. Look, I know it's a bore darling, but I've started giving everyone a typing test before sending them out. Employers get a bit shirty when I send them typists who are too slow – would you mind?'

'Oh not at all!' I replied airily, confident that somehow between now and the moment my fingers touched the keys, a miracle would occur.

She sat me in a corner with a small manual typewriter – electric typewriters were still very expensive and rare – and left me to it. The sound was painful, a few hesitant bashes on the keys, followed by a deep sigh, the crick-crick of rolling up the carriage to rub something out, then crick-crick back down again and another bash. Slowly, irregularly, I copied the first few lines of the letter, word by excruciating word.

To Marion's credit, she gave me a full 10 minutes, before walking over and asking brightly how I was getting on. She was a nice looking woman in her early thirties, with impeccable manners and I had a bit of a crush on her. I would have loved to be one of her best typists, one of her star girls, who could take shorthand like lightening and type like the wind.

'Oh dear' she said 'you *have* lost your speed over the summer, haven't you?'

Of course, we both knew that I had never had much speed to begin with. I'd never even learned to type. But Marion was a kind woman, and for some reason, she seemed to like me. She was also in need of typists. She asked if I would like to sit there for a few hours and practice on that typewriter, and get my speed up. She suggested that I type the alphabet over and over again, as she believed this was the best way to get to know where all the keys were.

I stayed for the rest of the day doing that, and it did help, but I had also seen an outfit called 'SIGHT AND SOUND – LEARN TO TYPE IN 24 HOURS' advertised on a big yellow, black and red hoarding, somewhere near Oxford Circus. It turned out that these were 24 separate hours, so you did not become a typist overnight. For 24 separate hours, you sat with other aspiring typists, a surprisingly high proportion of whom were male, in a large room full of desks with typewriters on them. All the typewriter keys were blank, so there was no point in looking at them. On the wall in front was a huge chart of the keyboard, and you were meant to look at this, and thus become a 'touch typist.' A tape-recorded voice yelled the name of the key and you bashed that key. Rhythm was the thing. Bash, bash, bash. All together.

It worked though. I told Marion what I was doing, and she started sending me out as a Clerk Typist and Switchboard Operator. With my first weeks wages I bought a pair of mauve, pearlised winkle pickers from Dolcis. Even though I had to walk up stairs with my feet splayed out in the ballet First Position, I loved those shoes passionately.

But that one room in Fitzjohn's Avenue was getting on everybody's nerves, especially when Walter was there. He and Billie took the armchairs, Tanya and I had to sit on the beds, and be very careful what we did and said. I was 17 and I'd had enough. Now that I was earning my own money, I looked for a room, as far away from Hampstead as possible.

Marion had found me a job working at Hotpoint in Perivale, West London, and during my lunch hour I saw a card in a tobacconists window, advertising a Single Room. The rent was 35/- a week, just a bit more than I was already giving Billie from my wages. The address was 1, North End Road, Fulham and I went there one evening after work and knocked at the door. A lady in her fifties opened the door. She must have been wearing the same clothes for the last twenty years, since the thirties: flowered overalls, wrinkled lisle stockings and tartan slippers. She wore her greying hair in a hairnet. I asked if the room was still available, and she said, yes, would I like to see it?

Everything about the house was pre-war. The hall smelled of cabbage, earwax, unwashed hair and old gas fires. The room was on the first floor, it had a single bed under a window, with a stained green satin bedspread, a table with a dark red chenille cloth, an upright chair, a fireside chair, a cupboard and a chest of drawers. There was a gas fire, a gas ring and a gas meter, which took shillings. There was green lino on the floor and a grey bedside rug. Along the hall was the bathroom, with an old roll top bath and a huge, white enamel, gas water heater. The heater had the word Ascot in black on it, with huge capital A and a flourish beneath.

The room wasn't very nice, but I didn't care – I could have it all to myself and do whatever I wanted. I said I would take it. The lady's name was Mrs Coombs, she was not of the generation which used first names with everyone, and always called me Miss Wardman. When we stood talking to each other, she always folded her arms. She asked how old I was, and I lied and said 18. She was a bit nervous about that, she said a girl of my age should be living at home, and that she didn't want the responsibility. I had no idea what she was talking about. However, I was nicely spoken, which impressed her, I was clean and I was working. She can't have had anyone else interested in the room. We agreed I should move in that weekend, and I handed over 35/-

Billie and Walter were out flat hunting when I packed and left, and I must have landed Tanya with the task of announcing my departure.

I had never slept in a room on my own before, let alone lived by myself. I loved it. I sat at the chenille table to write letters and my diary. I cooked baked beans on the gas ring and made toast in front of the fire. On Saturdays I walked down North End Road to Lillie Road, where there was a huge market, and returned with nothing but fruit, which you didn't have to cook. I discovered you got a huge amount of food for very little money if you didn't bother with things like meat or potatoes.

I started buying every copy of Vogue as soon as it came out, and sat in front of the gas fire devouring bananas, and every word of the magazine. I spent ages in the bathroom. I shared it with Mrs Coombs, but she wasn't a great one for ablutions. Once she confided that she never washed her hair, but went to the hairdressers every fortnight where they did it for her. She wore it in that war time style, sausage curls round the back and sides, straight on top, wave at the front, all held in place with a hairnet. I never saw her without her floral overalls.

She gave me a rent book, and signed her name 'E. Coombs' in curly, old fashioned writing, beside each week's payment.

I became friends with a girl at Hotpoint called Jennie. She was unmarried, pregnant and desperate to 'get rid of it'. She was engaged to the baby's father, Tony, but they each lived with their parents and said her father would kill Tony if he found out. She'd heard that if you drank lots of gin and sat in a hot bath, you could get rid of it that way. She and Tony came round to my room one evening with a bottle of gin, and after a few pleasantries, went into the bathroom. They were ages. Eventually they emerged, just in time to get the last bus home. Jennie was a tall, slim girl with an impressive, dark brown beehive, which had collapsed in the steam. She was drunk in a puzzled, immobile kind of way, she just stood and leaned on Tony. Tony was an early Mod., with short blond hair, trendy short overcoat and a permanently worried look. He thanked me, and steered the silent and comatose Jennie thud, thud, thud, down the stairs. She never turned up at Hotpoint again, and I have no idea if it worked.

I had no radio and my evenings were spent reading and writing. For five weeks I had no contact with home, and for most of that time I didn't miss them. But Christmas was coming, and when I saw the fairy lights and heard the

Christmas Carols at North End Road Market, I suddenly wanted to see my family. So one evening I went home to Fitzjohns Avenue for a visit. Billie and Tanya were delighted to see me. Walter wasn't there, and we spent a happy evening, saying sorry and catching up. It got late, so I stayed the night and went to work from there in the morning.

When I returned to North End Road the following evening, I found a note in my room:

'Please take one weeks notice from today's date, signed E. Coombs'

When I moved in, Mrs Coombs had told me that she always locked the front door at 10pm sharp, but since I had always stayed in, this had never been a problem. Now, it seemed, this remark had been code for 'no staying out after 10pm'.

I went downstairs, knocked on her door and explained that I had spent the night with my Mother. She said she did not believe me, and please would I be out of the room by Friday. I was really hurt. Obviously I had offended her deeply in some way, but I never really found out what it was. Perhaps it was my age, and the responsibility thing, but if so, why throw me out with – as far as she knew – nowhere else to go?

I rang Billie and asked if I could move back home.

'Of course you can darling, and guess what? – Walter and I have finally found a flat! It's in Maida Vale, we're moving in two weeks time, we can be there for Christmas, and you and Tan can each have your own room!'

40

Tanya Discovers Walter's Cycle

Winter 1961-62: *Maida Vale*

'BILLIE, you know, I can understand it when men interfere with girls, touching their breasts - that's natural - I can understand that. What I can't understand is why they want to fiddle around with their vaginas.'

Walter is in bed, reading The Sunday Times, and something in it has given rise to this most unexpected remark. Billie has just come into the bedroom with a cup of tea. She is as baffled as I am. Hands him the tea.

'Careful, it's a bit full' she is playing for time. I pretend to be still reading the paper, pretend I haven't heard.

'I mean, what sort of man wants to go poking around down there?'

'*Not* in front of my daughters if you don't mind.'

'Oh, sorry. It's a bit full dear.'

'Yes, drink a bit down, it shouldn't be too hot now.'

Suddenly I know exactly what he is talking about. He is explaining why, when I used to read aloud to him at Minster Road, he only ever touched my breasts and never ventured below the waist. It's wasn't because he knew it was wrong, it was because below the waist is something no man wanted to touch or look at. I had had sexual intercourse with lots of men since we lived at Minster Road. Ray never even took my knickers off, just went between the elastic. And Norman hardly looked at me, just took my clothes off, told me to lie down and just did it. The boys on the Scillies had been much the same, sex was a swift and grunting function.

I am hot with shame. I realise that for some reason, Walter wants to convey to me that he finds vaginas disgusting, but he apparently finds it easier to do this by saying it to my Mother in my hearing. If he does, then all men do, and this is what Walter wants me to know. No wonder Norman looked disappointed after we'd had sex. I am embarrassed, I feel ugly, but I notice with gratitude that Billie neither agrees with him, nor with him raising the subject in front of me.

Sometimes on Sunday mornings, Tanya and I get into bed with them for tea and toast and the Sunday Times. Despite our easy physical proximity, there is the usual tension between us, the risk on Sunday morning is usually from the newspaper. Either I will say something to upset Walter, or he will say something to upset me and unable to button my lip, I will say something to upset him. Either way, he and Mummy will agree that it is my fault. Even Tanya sometimes sides with them.

'Why don't you just ignore him - I do.'

The something that one of us says is always political, usually about the Colour Bar or CND. I feel so passionately about these things, I just come out with it, knowing he will blow up and shout at me, his face red and roaring, his finger pointing right in my face, shouting.

'You shut up, *shut up*, you are an ignorant child who knows nothing. That's all.' I am always afraid he will hit me, and very occasionally, he does. It's quite hard and it does hurt, but not that bad in itself. It's his anger that brings about the fear, the trembling and the crying. The anger always belongs to him, the tantrum is his show and he decides what it's about, when it starts and when it ends. He shouts, and flails and points and hates me, tells me to get out of the house, that I am nothing, *nothing*, and it always ends in the same way. He says 'That's all!' and leaves the room. 'That's all!' means he has decided that the confrontation is now over.

I have to withstand his anger and control my own. It is agreed among the four of us that Walter inevitably will lose his temper; that it will be because of something I do or say, and that the rest of us must keep calm and not react. He loses his temper because he cannot help it. I lose my temper because I have not learnt to control myself.

After he has said 'That's all!' and slammed out, he follows Billie around the flat.

'Why does she do it Billie? Where does she get these communistic ideas from? What's the matter with her?' He is never able to grasp that these ideas originate from Billie, and ultimately from my father. She is the one who, in 1956 refused to buy us Union Jack flags for Empire Day.

'The Empire is nothing to be proud of, you know. The British have abused, enslaved and exploited coloured people, invading and colonising their countries. I don't want you parading up and down singing nationalistic songs. That's how wars start.'

In the end she had relented and bought us the tiniest flags she could find - postcard size - their sticks flimsy like lollipop sticks. On Empire Day I converted the shame of my tiny flag into a manifesto.

'I didn't really want a flag, I've only got one because they made us. The Empire is nothing to be proud of, the way the British have treated coloured people is very unjust. We just walked into their countries and took over, stealing everything, when it wasn't even our country. And they weren't even emancipated or anything.'

The other girls at Reedham had listened, their mouths hanging open, as I ranted on, a passionate 12 year old misusing long words, indignation personified. When I'd finished, someone said.

'You're mad.'

'And you're ignorant.' I'd retorted.

On Sunday mornings in Maida Vale, I am usually safe commenting on Arts subjects or Fashion. I am deeply interested in fashion, but I can't afford the clothes in the Sunday Times, and anyway fashion is rather a frivolous subject for an intellectual. I would really like to be taken seriously as an intellectual, to be respected for my mind, to show them I'm really far more *au fait* than they are. So I suggest visits to the Royal Court Theatre, or ask Walter if he has heard of Jean Paul Sartre. He might make derisory remarks about Angry Young Men, long hairs, egg heads and highbrows, but he's so ignorant, so ridiculous and irrelevant, he doesn't care if he makes a fool of himself, and if he's in a good mood I can even tease him a little. I asked him once if someone could be a longhair, and an egg head *and* a highbrow, and he said yes, and we had a lot of fun establishing exactly where the hairline of such a hybrid should be, how long the hair and what the female of the species would look like.

But on other days everything is so tense that anything I say will send him into a rage, and I am just beginning to realise that his rages are not necessarily in response to my remarks, even though everyone thinks that they are. Mummy is always begging me 'don't answer him back, don't rise to it, just let it go.' I really try. I *really* try. Yet, when he has a bad mood he will blow up eventually, inevitably. He looks for things to be angry about.

Once Tanya and I wanted to listen to *Saturday Night Theatre* on the Home Service, so we asked Mummy if we could borrow the kitchen portable radio.

'Can we listen to it in the lounge, we want to do a jigsaw puzzle on the table?'

Mummy went into their bedroom to ask Walter.

'Yes, but Walter says you've got to bring it in to the bedroom by 10 o'clock so he can listen to the news.'

We finished the jigsaw and sat, side by side on the sofa, listening to the last two minutes of a gripping, 90 minute whodunnit. Just as the murderer was about to be unmasked, Walter crashed in, eyes bulging, dressing gown flapping, shouting.

'I *told* you to bring it in at 10 o'clock. In future - do as you're told. That's all!' picked up the radio and slammed out of the door.

We stared at each other, overcome by the injustice.

'It isn't even 10 o'clock.'

'It isn't even his radio - it's Mummy's.'

I wanted to go in and tell him his clock was fast but Tan restrained me, and for once, I listened.

'But he won't stop being in a mood till he's had his real tantrum, so he might as well have it tonight and get it over with.'

'What do you mean?'

'Haven't you noticed, he gradually works up to them, getting more and more short tempered and cross? We try to placate him, Mummy tries to distract him, but she never succeeds. We say nothing, stay in our rooms, best behaviour - don't we?'

'Well, some of us do! No, I know what you mean. But it's no use, he'll always find something.'

'Exactly. He always finds something. Then he blows his top, shouts at us, tells us to find somewhere else to live, slams doors, goes on and on at Mummy and we're all scared and crying. Then everything goes quiet.'

'And he wakes up next morning all smiling and friendly…'

'…And we're supposed to act as if nothing's happened. Then he's all right - till the next time.'

'How long is he all right for then?'

'Oh, let's see - about 3 weeks? What do you think?'

'Yes, I suppose. Then he starts getting moody again. He

gets moody for about a week - doesn't he? Or until somebody upsets him.'

'You know what?'

'What?'

'Three weeks and one week makes four weeks - 28 days - he's got a monthly cycle!'

Our shrieks of laughter brought him storming in again and this time he had his real tantrum, let it all out. I cried myself to sleep.

Next morning, he was all smiles.

41

Ladbrokes

Spring 1962

It seemed that my education was finished, and that, like Billie, my career was to be a Secretary. I was a mediocre typist and never learned shorthand, but I looked good, spoke nicely and could spell, which was always enough to get a temporary job. For a permanent job, qualifications and interviews would be required, but West End Employment Agencies were always desperate for a girl – any girl – they could send out right now. Especially on a Monday morning.

The West End in the early sixties had as many Employment Agencies as it now has Mobile Phone shops. Each man with any status required a Secretary, those lower down the ladder would share one, and those on the bottom rung used the Typing Pool. Then there were Receptionists and Telephonists. In a smaller company, these would be the same person, but if the roles were discrete, the Receptionist was always the more attractive girl, and the Telephonist was kept out of sight, often in a kind of cupboard, behind the Reception area. The other women's jobs were Clerks and Filing Clerks. Very occasionally, I came across a 'woman boss' but mostly, men were the bosses and women were girls.

The hierarchy for both genders ran parallel, so at the pinnacle were Executives and their Secretaries. He would have a massive office and huge desk, elegantly clear of any evidence of work, and she would have her own, smaller office, adjoining his. If there was an electric typewriter in the company, this is where it would be. Being Secretary to the Big Cheese made you Head Girl, and all the other girls had to do what you told them. The lowest rung for typists was the Typing Pool.

In the Spring of 1962, Marion Barton found me job as a temporary Clerk for several weeks at Ladbrokes, the Turf Accountants in Savile Row. She told me to report to Miss Bennett, Secretary to Mr Duncan. Marion did say Miss Bennett was very nice, but then, Marion said everyone was very nice. I expected her to be one of those shrivelled and hair-lacquered Senior Secretaries, for whom temps were no more than pond life. Based on past experience, I would probably exchange two words with the exalted one, be passed on to another 'girl' who would show me to a small dusty desk behind some filing cabinets and give me some work, explain it if I was lucky, and henceforth Miss Bennett would have nothing to do with me.

But she came to Reception to greet me, and as we walked along the hushed yet sporting green carpet, she asked if I would mind working in her office with her!

She wanted me to do cheque clearing: I had to go through the giant Coutts cheque books, empty but for their stubs, and check them against the bank statements, to see if and when customers had paid their winnings in. Miss Bennett explained to me why I was doing this. A cheque is only valid for six months after it has been issued, so if a punter failed to cash in his winnings within six months, I had to put a cross in red ink on the cheque stub. When a cheque had cleared, I put a black tick on the stub. This was meant to be Miss Bennett's job I think, but she didn't like doing it and a backlog had built up, so they hired a temporary clerk, and that was me.

Miss Bennett must have been in her fifties, and I so admired her style. She was always well turned out: her dark hair was never too long away from the hairdresser. Her crisp coral lipstick matched her nail varnish; her crocodile court shoes – high heels always - matched her handbag. She was easy and confident enough to be charming and good-natured towards everyone.

Ladbrokes was just as you'd imagine a gentlemen's club: thick green fitted carpets, dark wood panelling, leather armchairs with buttons in the dimples and the rich smell of Mansion polish and cigar smoke. I loved it there, and for some reason, they loved me. Miss Bennett cleared a small antique desk in the corner of her office, by the door, for me. Her office was next door to the Boardroom, and Mr Duncan was just across the corridor. He didn't seem to have much to do, and was always popping in for a chat. They had obviously known each other for many years, probably from before the War, and their relationship was easy and intimate, yet tremendously courteous. And they often included me in their conversations, asking for my opinion, answering my questions and making me feel like a loved and indulged daughter. They listened to my political outbursts with a kind of grave amusement and never told me I didn't know what I was talking about. At the same time, they would not be drawn on my pet topics: nuclear weapons and apartheid in South Africa, so we never got into an argument. I have no doubt that they were both right-wing Tories, but of the old fashioned, tolerant and well-mannered school.

This was a paradox. I really liked these people, and yet I held their political opinions to be abhorrent. It was something I'd never thought possible. I could not use Billie's friendships as a yardstick – she had none. Tanya and I had recently become aware that our mother had no friends. There were 'girls' she worked with and sometimes had lunch with, but she rarely saw them outside the office, and very few people who were not family ever telephoned or visited.

From people like Miss Bennett and Mr Duncan, I learned how good manners grant dignity to everyone. At Reedham the adults lectured and shouted, at family gatherings my Uncles ranted on about politics, rarely listening to each other, all shouting at once. At home, there was Billie's stream of consciousness. We just absorbed it all, waited for her to draw breath and then started on our own version. We did have conversations, of course, but Billie didn't really listen to us much. Like all van Tinterens, she was merely waiting for us to stop speaking so that she could deliver her next remark. It was the way she had been brought up and it was all she knew. And thus, it was all we knew.

Sometimes at Ladbrokes there would be delicious and dainty food left over from Boardroom meetings – scotch eggs with bright orange crumbed coating, chicken and mushroom vol-au-vents, sausage rolls with golden pastry and salty grey filling, cucumber or fishpaste sandwiches with the crusts cut off, all set out on paper doilies and garnished lavishly with small bunches of parsley. Often there was cake as well: small chocolate éclairs with real cream inside, slices of pink and yellow Battenberg and *petits fours*, and once - after a big win - Mr Duncan came in with two glasses of champagne - one for Miss Bennett and one for me.

Towards the front of the building, was a huge room where all the clerks sat taking bets on the telephone. People who had accounts at Ladbrokes could bet on the phone, they all used a '*Nom de Plume*' but their identities were no secret, there were files with their real names on, cross referenced with a card index system. All the Royals had accounts, and if you wanted, you could look up how much - for instance - the Queen Mother had lost or won, which horses she had bet on and whether or not she had paid. Usually not, she was a famously slow payer. But that was later, when I had cleared all the cheques, and I had to leave dear Miss Bennett's office. Ladbrokes was in transition at the time, there was a young man called Gerald Green, a relative of the owner Cyril Stein, who seemed to have recently taken charge, and that may have been why they wanted the cheques checked, to calculate how much money was in the bank. Until 1961, off-track betting had been against the law, but when Betting Shops became legal, Ladbrokes was one of the first to open.

Tony Connor was a senior Betting Clerk in the Telephone Room, and he would stand, leaning in the doorway of Miss Bennett's office, flirting with me. He was 24 and I really liked him. We would have lunch, walk around Soho, talking about everything. He told me all about betting and odds - it was a world he knew everything about. When Tony was nine, his father had won a huge amount of money on the football pools, had given up his job and moved the family to the South of France. For a year or two - it must have been just after the war - Tony had not gone to school, but had played on the beach, and hung around in casinos. He learned to gamble and to speak excellent French. When all the money ran out, the family returned to London, his father got his old job back and they carried on with their lives as before, as if all that money and the South of France had never happened.

Of all the boys I went out with, he was the most relaxed, the easiest, the most fun. We had sex of course (quick, warm and friendly on a single bed in his grotty little room off the Tottenham Court Road), but we also really enjoyed each other's company. We sang French nursery rhymes as we walked along the street. He was the only bloke I had met who would play silly games, like 'I'll hum the tune and you guess the words.' I knew every song he hummed except 'I don't want a Ricochet Romance' a song I had never heard of. I had never heard the word ricochet either, and he explained it to me. He was a bit of a sharp dresser, wore a short navy raincoat, which I thought quite continental looking. When we got back late from lunch, we never got told off, just a few rolled eyes. He said this was because he was the best betting clerk they had - could calculate odds in the blink of an eye. He could work out accumulators in his head. In pre-calculator days, he was an immense asset to the company and could get away with a lot. So could I while I was in Miss Bennett's office. When the cheques were finished, she said it was a shame to let me go, and she asked Gerald Green if there was anything else I could do. I was hoping to be sent to the Telephone Room and be taught how to take bets, but instead, he sent me upstairs to the grey filing room, where we filed betting slips and made up the monthly accounts. I still went out with Tony, but there were no more long lunches. On reflection, I think he probably had quite a serious gambling habit, although he never mentioned being in any kind of trouble. I imagine his father - and later Tony - always trying for another big, life-changing win.

Among the friends I made while hanging around in the Telephone Room, was Muriel Murphy, a small, sharp nosed young woman with dark brown eyes, white skin and straight, dark hair, almost black. Like many short women, she added height with very high stilettos and a high beehive hairdo, aggressively backcombed, with long straight dangly bits hanging in front of her ears. She was from Dublin, a little older than me, and I was in awe of her speed and confidence on the phones. With a cigarette hanging from the corner of her mouth and a pile of forms in front of her, she would take call after call, black receiver in her left hand, scribbling away in pencil with her right:

'Yep, yep, right – two-to-one-on – right!'

Like all the other Telephone Clerks, she kept an eye on the big blackboard, where the odds were chalked and constantly updated by a man who wore white overalls over his dark suit, to save it from the chalk dust. There were about twenty young men and women on the phones, and this was the hub of Ladbrokes, where the money was made. I wanted to work on the phones not just to be near Tony, but to be where men and women worked alongside each other on equal terms. It seemed quick, tough, worldly and glamorous. It was also quite well paid. After work, I'd often go to the pub with the Telephone Room crowd. Muriel, and I were never close friends, she was friendly enough, but quiet, and without the warm and garrulous character so often associated with Irish people. Then she invited me to her party.

42

Nevern Square and Neuilly-sur-Seine

August-October 1962

MURIEL shared a flat in Nevern Square, Earls Court. Like everyone I knew who could afford a good address, she lived at the very top of a very tall building. After climbing all those stairs, the first thing I needed was a cigarette! Muriel had a dark and tiny room with a single bed and as far as I know, she never drew the curtain. A single, central, naked bulb, a small table, crammed and piled with cosmetics – including several open pots of Muriel's signature bright green eye shadow – are what I remember. In this room she and I got ready for the party, while she told me about her brother Derry, (short for Dermot) home on leave from the Air Force and arriving any minute. She wanted us to meet.

'He's stationed out in the country, and he never gets to meet any girls on the base. So he told me to invite some girls tonight, you know.'

'How many have you invited, then?'

'Oh, I don't know. I expect the others will be along later.'

'How old is he, then?'

'Twenty four. But he's young in his ways, like.'

I never found out what she meant by that. A few hours later, Derry and I were on a pile of coats in Muriel's small bedroom, while the party went on in the rest of the flat. I think we locked the door. Not my first time, but my first truly erotic experience. He put his hand between my legs and found my clitoris. I had never found it myself, and was delighted and excited. I had been having sex for ages, but this was the first time I'd joined in. He smiled at me, he talked to me, he took his time. This felt like real sex, with feelings going on in it, real grown up, sexy sex.

He had white skin like his sister, but his curly hair was dark blonde and cut short. We wrote to each other and met whenever he got leave. We went to a dark jazz club in Soho, where the floorboards were bare wood. We danced a bit, we drank a bit and I talked a lot, shouting into his ear so he could hear me above the music. I could not understand why he was in the RAF – the armed forces, for goodness sake! Didn't he care about Britain's Nuclear Weapons? He didn't seem to know much about them, which shocked me deeply, and I felt it my duty to inform him as fully as possible. I had heard that you could get high if you dissolved aspirin in coco-cola, so stirring the two stubborn white tablets into the sticky brown fizz with my finger, I expounded on the evils of nuclear warfare, the escalation of the Arms Race and the vital importance of Nuclear Disarmament. The floor shook with earnest young jivers, but Dermot and I sat crouched together on the narrow wooden bench, which went all around the room, while I preached World Peace into his ear for hours on end.

Dermot wrote several letters and cards to me from Cyprus, where he was briefly stationed. He sent presents: a plate to hang on the wall, with different Cypriot scenes all round it. I considered this in rather poor taste, but I loved the pink silk pyjamas.

'They are too short for you!' cried Tanya.

'Well, nobody is going to see me in them, so it doesn't matter.'

'You look like a stupid refugee with those trousers flapping round your skinny legs.'

Which is why I never wore them, and Tanya got them.

Billie was once again trying to think of ways to get me out of the house. It was August, and she and Walter had a holiday in Ireland planned, but before she left, she showed me an advertisement in The Daily Telegraph for an *au pair* in Paris. Somehow, we had agreed that this was the best step for me. I would learn French, which was as good as going to University, says Billie. Better, in fact, as I would not have to 'ruin my eyes' with studying.

I got my passport photo taken on the fourth floor of Selfridges, Oxford Street. After careful thought, I wore a black polo neck and my new, beatnik glasses, with heavy, black, square frames. Billie helped me make an A-line pinafore dress in light brown, herringbone tweed, and there was something about the way she said 'pure wool', which made Tanya and me wince. I really liked this dress. Teamed with a toning, mustard coloured polo neck, it was my best outfit and the one I planned to wear to travel to Paris.

I know Dermot asked me to marry him, and that I turned him down, saying I didn't love him. I know this because he refers to it in one of his letters. However, I don't remember it. I do remember that in the early summer of 1962 he came to a family party at Maida Vale, and sat in the corner, chatting politely to aunts and uncles over tea and sandwiches.

In late August, while Billie and Walter were in Ireland, Dermot and I were again in that same room, on the same sofa where the aunties had sat just a few weeks before. With time and privacy, we took off all our clothes and took our time. I remember us standing naked, our arms around each other, and running my hands down his back. The feeling of it drove him wild. From such a simple thing came so much pleasure. That weekend I learned that I could take the initiative, and it did not have to be an explicitly sexual gesture – affection, touching and laughter were part of it too.

I had read about a woman's fertile period, and knew that I was 'safe' from pregnancy for about 10 days after my period, and for about a week before the next one. I had been getting away with this since I was 15. The weekend we spent together was not exactly 'safe'. It was a bit borderline actually. I asked him to pull out before he came. What could possibly go wrong?

Dermot did pull out the first and second time we did it, but we had the whole weekend. We couldn't stop. On the sofa, in the kitchen, tangled up in the sheets on my single bed, in the hall. The only place we did not do it was Billie and Walter's bedroom. Revolting thought.

As soon as they returned from Ireland, we got a phone call. It seemed the Roger-Vasselin family were urgently looking for an English au pair, and within a few days of Billie and Walter's return from Ireland, I was on the plane.

Paris in early October 1962 was sweltering. Madame Roger-Vasselin was English and she, Monsieur and their 3 children lived in a noble and crumbling pile in Neuilly-sur-Seine, where the maid Claude and I looked after them. Claude took them their breakfast in bed, I got the children up, prepared their *chocolat* and breakfast and looked after them. Caroline was seven, the twins Nicolas and Christopher were five. One of my duties was to wipe their arses, something they were not allowed to do for themselves. After they had finished on the toilet, they called out what they had done, and I had to come and wipe as appropriate.

If they had simply done a pee, they would shout

'I've done tinkles'

If they had done a poo as well, it was

'I've done tatterball tinkles' and I'd have to go running in to clean them up. This wasn't too bad for the five year old boys, but Madame would not hear of Caroline learning to see to herself. She's nearly 60 now - I wonder how she manages.

The Roger-Vasselin family were proud of their monumental helplessness. Madame boasted that when she was in hospital having the twins, Monsieur came down to the kitchen to make coffee for himself. They were between maids, and Caroline was with her grandmother, so he was alone in the house. He had spent some time in front of the stove, but eventually, unable to turn it on, he went out to the café.

The idea of coming to Paris was that I should speak French with Madame and the children. However, during the swift interview process, I had missed an obvious reason why this would never happen. Madame was English, and all the children bi-lingual. They spoke nothing but English to me. As an au pair, I had hoped to glean a little French conversation at meal times, but there was none of that *en-famille* nonsense with the aristocratic Roger-Vasselins. Claude served them lunch and dinner in the dilapidated, swagged dining room, then she and I sat down to eat lunch in the kitchen, jumping up every now and then when Madame or Monsieur rang the bell. Madame and Monsieur always had a cooked lunch, but Claude and I had the same every day: *baguette, beurre* and *camembert,* and a glass of *Nicolas vin rouge de table.* The baguette was always warm and crusty: Claude rose early each morning to buy bread and croissants for breakfast, but it was my job to buy the lunchtime bread. Claude would go out again at about 5pm to buy more fresh bread for dinner, and – shockingly - would throw away any unused bread after each meal.

Claude was one of the two people in the house who did not speak English, but she was not chatty, and I think she found conversation with me hard work - and anyway, it wasn't her job to teach me French. The other person was Monsieur, and he never addressed a single remark to me in any language.

I was allowed out after the children were in bed asleep, but when Monsieur came home from work, he wanted to play with Caroline, so I had to get her out of bed and bring her, grumpy and half asleep, to the dining room, then wait till they called me to put her to bed again. So I didn't get out much, or manage to enroll in any French classes. I spent most of my free time lying on my bed, reading a copy of *The Houses in Between* by Howard Spring, which I found in my room. I had brought some special soap from London: Yardley's English Lavender.

When I took it out of the box, the soap was a surprising colour, not the white or lavender you'd expect, but beige. I washed at a sink in my room, and the scent of Yardleys English Lavender soap, even to this day, brings back the chalky, steamy feeling of that October in Nueilly-sur-Seine. It takes me back to the heat, the arse wiping and the way the smell of Gauloises made me feel sick, especially in the mornings.

I abandoned the Roger-Vasselins, and booked into the YWCA, where I shared a room with an American girl. After weeks with nobody to talk to, I jabbered at her nervously nonstop. Did I confide in her about what was really worrying me - my period being late? Not at all, I didn't even mention it. Instead I lectured her at great length about the evil of Nuclear Weapons and American foreign policy, as if she, poor girl were entirely responsible for it. She eventually conveyed that my conversation did not interest her, in terms far more polite than I deserved. I decided that she was a typical American, arrogant and ignorant.

At the YWCA I read a notice about the Cardew Club, a place where young English women in Paris could meet socially. I joined immediately, and spent an evening in a comfortable sitting room, with a real fire and several friendly English girls. Some were au pairs, but not all, and they all seemed so confident about living in Paris. A cheerful, Home Counties sort of girl called Gillian Rumsey befriended me, and I soon confided in her my fear that I might be pregnant. She said I should see a doctor straight away, just to make sure.

'Look, it might just be a reaction to the change of food, the change of climate. Periods can be irregular for all sorts of reasons! No point in worrying yourself sick until you are absolutely sure, you know.'

Next day Gillian took me to a Doctor she knew of. Her mother had given her his name and address, in case she required medical advice, and we went there together on the Metro. It was a very grand building, in a very grand part of Paris. The Doctor wore a morning suit, his office was large and ornate, and he sat behind a marble desk with curly gold legs. I think even Gillian was overawed. It didn't take long. A few questions, a very brief examination on the couch behind a screen, then he picked up his important Mont Blanc fountain pen and wrote a few neat words on his headed notepaper. He folded the paper over and handed it to me:

'Congratulations, Madamoiselle Wardman, I confirm you are pregnant, and your baby is due at the end of May next year.'

On the way out, his Secretary relieved me of 10 francs - all the money I had.

Back on the Metro, Gillian gave me her address in England and asked me to write to her if I needed any more help. I thanked her and said I would have to go to the British Consul and ask them to ship me home, because I couldn't get another job now. I think she felt a bit guilty about the Doctor taking all my money, because she gave me a couple of francs and two metro tickets from her carnet. Somehow, I found the office of the British Consul. A young man in a suit gave a world-weary sigh, and handed me a form to fill in.

'We require you to hand over your passport, which may be returned to you after you have refunded the cost of your passage home.'

'What do you mean *may* be?' I asked, pushing my luck.

'The passport is the property of Her Majesty's Government. When you have repaid the cost of your passage, it will be decided whether or not it should be returned to you.'

We glared at each other. Then, showing uncharacteristic wisdom and restraint, I decided not to pursue the point, and handed over my passport. In return, I received a rail voucher to Calais, a ferry ticket to Dover, and a train ticket to London.

I don't recall the train journey, but it was the end of October, and the channel crossing was very rough. The few people on deck, perhaps hoping that fresh air would relieve the nausea, were clinging to the rails. Many were below deck in the bar, wedged tightly together, smoking and attempting to drink spirits. I spent most of the crossing in the Ladies Toilets, rinsing out the only two enamel bowls there were, and passing them to the next person to throw up in. When a dear old lady heaved up her dentures, I fished them out, ran them under the tap and returned them to her. The floor was sticky with vomit, and like everyone else, I was sliding dangerously about in it, but even if I'd been able to find a mop and bucket, there was no time to wash it. All sorts and conditions of women sat groaning on the toilets, the doors all open so I could dash in and out with a basin, or leaning over the washbasins, ready for the next evacuation. It didn't occur to me at the time, but being pregnant, I should have been more nauseous than anyone. Instead, I felt fine, and there was relief at having something useful to do among people who were grateful to me, knowing nothing of my shame. And happy for once not to think beyond the next few minutes.

I had not expected the Police Escort at Dover. As we stood in a wretched, vomit-reeking huddle, whipped by the wind and waiting to disembark, two Policemen boarded and asked for me by name. Some of the female passengers, to whom I was a minor heroine, looked incredulous to see me leave, ahead of everyone else, under a Police Escort. I've never since been through Customs and Passport Control so swiftly.

The Dover train got in to London at Liverpool Street. Fortunately, I had enough English money for the tube. To Billie's astonishment, I arrived back at Maida Vale at the end of October, exhausted, defiant and sulky, my figure concealed by my trusty, long, navy fishermans sweater. Claiming to be a beatnik, I wore it all the time.

43

The Scarlet letter

Maida Vale November 1962 – January 1963

AT home, the only person I told was Tanya. Years later I discovered that every night in late 1962, Billie heard my little sister crying on the other side of her bedroom wall. While I slept, my mother would go in to her and ask

'Tanya, what's the matter, you must tell me.'

and every night Tanya replied

'I can't, I can't tell you.'

And every morning after our mother had left for work Tanya would implore me.

'Tell her Penny, please tell her.'

and I would say

'I promise to tell her tomorrow.'

Soon after I returned to London, I started temp work again, this time as a clerk in a large government office. I sat by a big window in a room of perhaps 10 or 12 clerks, all women, and sorted endless piles of white index cards into numerical order. It was a job where you could easily work and talk, and the room was rarely silent. I still had no idea that as a temp., and a new, young person, the wisest and most courteous course was to start off by smiling a lot and speaking only when spoken to. It did not occur to me that my life and my views were perhaps not all that fascinating to the entire room. I was the daughter of a garrulous, friendless and solipsistic woman, and so I believed that these people were entitled – nay, longing - to hear from me.

At the end of the room, facing the rest of us, sat Mrs Gee, our Supervisor. I never really knew if her surname was Gee, or if, as was quite common in those days, something else beginning with G, affectionately shortened. In the early sixties, the use of first names was encroaching rapidly, but many older people did not feel comfortable with the familiarity of it. One way of achieving informality without resorting to Christian names, was to use the initial letter of the surname, and there seemed to be many women of a certain age called Mrs B, Mrs T or Mrs Mac.

Tanya was the only member of my family I told, but I dealt with my worry and fear by talking about my pregnancy to this room full of women. It was all very shocking to them: my unmarried state, my middle class accent, my left wing views, the way I had simply gone to the British Consul in Paris when my money ran out and demanded to be shipped home, the confiscation of my passport and the way I'd been marched through passport control ahead of everyone else, by two uniformed officers. As I airily described all this, I saw myself as Becky Sharpe, living on my wits, outside respectable society. They were good women, respectably single, engaged or married, and I enjoyed shocking them, and being the centre of attention.

Other women had stories too, of course. Mrs Gee longed for grandchildren, and her daughter, after two miscarriages, was pregnant again, and coming up to the crucial three month stage. Entirely self centred, I made no connection between her story and mine. Others in the room, wiser and more empathetic than me, probably had, and braced themselves. One day someone asked me what I would call my baby. I had just finished reading 'Brideshead Revisited' and decided on Sebastian for a boy. I wasn't going to have a girl. Before that it had been Dmitri, and I'd not entirely relinquished this. So I replied:

'Well, either Dmitri or Sebastian – I'm not sure.'

Mrs Gee looked up, and - sharp as a knife - said

'Yes, and it will be a little Se*bast*ian, too, won't it!'

That silenced me, and the whole room.

Mrs Gee continued.

'It makes me so angry that girls like you get pregnant so easily, and you don't even want it. You've got no morals, you just do it like animals, no self-control, and yet a good girl like my daughter, who waited till she was married, can't seem to hold on to any of her babies. It's wicked, that's what it is, and you're wicked too!'

Walking back from Maida Vale tube one evening in late 1962, I was worrying deep inside about my pregnancy. By now I thought of nothing else. I was still hoping for a miscarriage, thinking about ways to get money for an abortion, who could I ask, who would know, which friends had ever mentioned tablets you could take or a doctor who would do it - I screamed.

'Oh My God!'

There stood a tall man dressed in a dog collar and a long, black gown. He had been standing just inside his gate, watching people go past, and in the fading light of the November evening had loomed suddenly into my vision. He apologised for making me jump and we started chatting. He was only a few years older than me, but had quite a pompous, superior manner and a very upper class accent. He seemed to think that by exclaiming 'Oh My God!' I was expressing religious tendencies, and he was eager to explore these with me. I could not convince him that it was a meaningless expression, because of course, for him it was not.

We flirted around with this for five minutes or so. I explained why I did not believe in God. He said well, you may not think you do, yet when afraid, your first natural response is to call upon Him. He was tall, dark and handsome, he was well educated and seemed intelligent, and best of all - he wanted to talk to me! Already I was half in love. I wasn't sure if he was Catholic or not - not many Protestant priests wore floor length robes. If he wasn't a Catholic, he might take pity on me and marry me to give my child a name.

After that, I always stopped to chat whenever I saw him. He would try to rekindle my Christianity, I would counter with Socialism, Atheism and CND. He told me he had only recently started at St Saviours, Warwick Avenue. I asked if it was a Catholic church, and he replied 'Anglican' which left me none the wiser. His name was the Reverend Addison, he was as passionate about his beliefs as I was about mine, and we each enjoyed rehearsing the power of our arguments to the other.

My clothes were getting tight. I'd been wearing a roll on since Christmas, and already I had difficulty getting it on. The sweat it generated trickled down my bum crease, giving me a sore.

At home I was uncharacteristically silent and withdrawn. I couldn't tell them, but I had to tell someone, other than the women at work, someone who would have to help me. One day after Christmas, as I saw the Reverend Addison standing by the gate and decided he was the perfect confidante. I didn't think about what I was going to say, I just decided as I approached him and said Good Evening that he was the person I would tell. He was almost my age, he liked me and his profession meant he had to listen. I said I was worried about something and could I confide in him. He looked interested and serious, but also pleased, because this is what he had come to London for, what he had become a priest for - to help people with their doubts and worries. Perhaps he hoped I was thinking of becoming a Christian, or at least a churchgoer.

As soon as I told him, his face changed. Everything changed. We were no longer equals. He said 'You'd better come inside.'

I went down the basement steps, into his huge living room and while he made some tea, he asked me all the necessary questions. He took a few notes and gave me his phone number, then he said I must do two things immediately: go to the doctor and tell my mother. From then on he became a social worker and there was no more amusing talk of religion or politics. He said I had disappointed him. It probably did not occur to him that he had disappointed me, too.

Dr Beeton was young and Scottish and as soon as I told him his manner towards me changed as well. All women remember how, as they metamorphose from child to young woman, men treat them differently. A few become more distant and more hostile, but most become friendlier, more interested. This was now suddenly reversed, I felt it sharply and I minded.

For a girl in trouble in 1962, a Moral Welfare conveyor belt existed and inevitably I got on to it. I was allocated a Moral Welfare Worker who found me a place in a Hostel for Unmarried Mothers in Warwick Way, Victoria. I need not have gone there, I could have stayed at home with my family in Maida Vale, but it would be awkward for all of us, and easier if I left. First, I arranged to move in there, then, just after Christmas 1962, I told Billie.

Billie was not normally a woman who embraces the cliché, but she came out with them all that day. She even actually uttered the words:

'How could you do this to me?'

Indeed, the whole circumstance was freighted with the stereotypical phrases of that time. I was 'in trouble' and Dermot was 'the man responsible' or 'the putative father'. Was he going to 'do the right thing?' Would he 'face up to his responsibilities?' Now that I had 'brought shame to this house' was he going to 'make an honest woman of me?'

She told me to write to Dermot saying that I would now like to marry him please. He wrote back saying how shocked and sorry he was, and arranging to meet me. He had not heard from me for four months, now here I was back from Paris, pregnant and blaming him. Understandably, he was cautious.

There were a few days before I could move in to the Hostel, and while I remained at home, Walter could hardly bring himself to speak to me. His feelings for me had always been complicated, and my pregnancy made them more so. Having sexually abused me when I was under age, he must constantly have feared me telling Billie. This could have meant not only the end of his marriage, and the loss of his home, but the possibility of prosecution and even imprisonment. At the time, I didn't realise it, but he must have been terrified of me for that reason. Fear like that translates very easily into hate.

Although he obviously would have liked to, he had not had sexual intercourse with me. No doubt, he therefore had imagined I was still a virgin. The news that I was pregnant with no plans to marry would have indicated to him that I was 'easy' and had allowed someone else to take what he wanted, but had denied himself.

There was something else, too. I was cleverer than him, and could run rings round him in most arguments. Actually, so could Billie and Tanya, but they were able to keep quiet, and somehow I wasn't and neither was he. When the four of us were in the room together, Billie and Tanya were walking on eggshells and it must have been a huge relief for them when I went to Paris.

Instead of addressing me directly, he would berate Billie in front of me.

'What's the matter with her Billie? How could she do a thing like that? How could she have got herself pregnant? Does she even know who the father is? Is he the only one? If not, the father could be anyone, no wonder he won't marry her! How many boys has she been with?'

Mostly I managed to keep my head down throughout all this, listening to my Mother justify my actions to him, without too much conviction. Sometimes I would retaliate, he'd make as if to hit me and then, remembering my delicate condition, slam out of the room instead.

Billie was in shock. She kept repeating:

'How could you do this to me?'

Sometimes I said 'I'm sorry Mummy'; sometimes I ignored her; sometimes I retaliated:

'I didn't do it to *you*, I didn't do anything to *you*, you stupid cow. This isn't about you, it's about *me*. And my baby, and what is going to happen to me. You don't care about me, you just care about what people will think, and what stupid Walter says. Leave me alone.'

Despite my pathetic attempts to insist it was my problem, I was not in a position to solve it. I had no home apart from here, no permanent job and no savings. However, much I might resent it, I was once again in the position of a child. After a brief interlude of freedom, the adults around me once again had all the power. And all the best lines. Billie moved centre stage. It became her tragedy. I spent a lot of time in my bedroom avoiding Walter. Tanya too, stayed in her room, out of his way. Tanya was the only person whose life had improved in any way by my announcement. Of course, there was a horrible atmosphere, but now, at least she didn't have to worry about what would happen when Mummy found out.

Billie worried away at her problem; sometimes to Walter in the Lounge or their bedroom, sometimes she came into my room with some scheme, which often involved me posing as a widow or going to work as a Cook Housekeeper in the country where they wouldn't ask too many questions - redolent of an Agatha Christie plot. She was very keen that I did not return home until I was either married or no longer pregnant. I told her not to worry, I would soon be at the Hostel, where I would stay all the time and be glad not to darken her door. I asked why on earth she cared about our neighbours, since she didn't speak to or even know any of them. That wasn't really what was bothering her. What she was really worrying about was what she would tell the van Tinterens.

One part of her was dying to, the part of her that was proud of becoming a grandmother, and of course, all the drama of the circumstances. The whole affair was guaranteed to get the attention of her siblings, and even some sympathy too. Her elder sister, my Auntie Marie had faced the prospect of a 'premature' first grandchild a couple of years previously and had written to Billie that my cousin Susan would be getting married quickly and quietly to her boyfriend David, and would become a mother shortly after that. We had received that very long and detailed letter at 22 Minster Road, and I didn't really understand a lot of it when Billie read it out to me. I was surprised that Auntie Marie was able to report - verbatim - conversations between Susan and David at which she could not possibly have been present. It seems it had all been a silly misunderstanding and they had been going to get married all along. I was just 14 at the time and a lot of it went over my head. Billie said it didn't matter very much since they were getting married anyway, but it was still a terrible thing and Auntie Marie would have to stop putting on airs now.

Now she was going to have to tell Marie that I too was pregnant and would not be getting married at all. Now Marie could resume her airs with knobs on. As it turned out, I told Marie myself. The Hostel for Unmarried Mothers was at 77 Warwick Way, Victoria, SW1, and on my way back there one evening, I bumped into my Auntie. I don't know why I had not thought of this possibility before, because I knew she worked in Victoria. Nor do I know why I told her everything, but I did.

Once Marie knew, everyone would soon know, so Billie seized the initiative and telephoned my Grandmother.

'Please sit down Mother, because I have some very bad news for you.'

'Oh my goodness, what is it, what has happened?'

'Are you sitting down?'

'Yes, yes, what is it?'

'Penny's expecting a baby. And there are no marriage plans.'

'Oh, thank goodness! I thought you were going to tell me someone had died.'

What Billie never realised, and I only discovered a few years ago, was that my grandparents had married just three months before the birth of Tina, their eldest child. They were both from Amsterdam, and thoroughly urban. They knew it didn't matter at all, and had only married when it looked as if it would make their lives as parents in a foreign country, easier. They concealed this late marriage from their respectable and rather narrow-minded suburban children, by claiming to have been married a year earlier than they actually had.

The Hostel was a grim place, made all the more so by the short winter days. Somehow, about a dozen girls were packed into the tall, Georgian house. I shared a room with two others. The lights went out at 10pm, no exceptions – it was Reedham redux. We said grace before meals, took turns laying the table in the gloomy, basement dining room with pale green, ridged and institutional china, then washing it up and putting the things away in their appointed, cream and green places. On the edge of the kitchen shelves, were slightly grubby strips of fraying, flesh coloured sticking plaster, with 'cups' 'saucers' and 'plates' written on them in biro. The Warden and her Deputy were Christian women, who agreed with my Moral Welfare Worker that living in this Hostel was a privilege. A few girls were forced to leave for 'bad behaviour' such as not taking their turn on the housework rota or staying out late. Conforming was easy for me, I just slipped back into Reedham mode.

Tanya came to see me a few times while I was there. Visitors were not allowed inside the Hostel, so we had to meet at Victoria Station. We went to the Cartoon Theatre on the station, then she would walk me back to the Hostel. She had just started her foundation year at Art College.

Dermot also came to see me once. We went out for a drink, then he walked me back, and we stood on the steps to kiss goodnight. The evening was very cold.

'Can I – would you mind if I felt it?'

'What – the baby?'

'Yes, I've always wondered what it felt like. Is it hard or soft, like.'

I undid the horn toggles of my duffel coat, he slipped his cold hands under it and felt our baby. We grinned at each other in delight. We had five minutes before ten o'clock, but the Warden was twitching the net curtain in the front window and Dermot had a train to catch, so we said goodnight.

I only saw him once more after that, when he came to see our new baby.

I lived at the Hostel and continued going out to work, until mid-April, six weeks before the expected date of confinement. Then I went to St Mary's Mother and Baby Home at 153 Stamford Hill, an Anglican Convent, which earned its living by caring for Unmarried Mothers and their babies.

44

The Agreement

IN early 1963, walking down the Strand, Billie bumped into her eldest brother Frank and his wife Siobhan. This was a big surprise, because they both famously hated London, and never visited. However, on a whim, and in the coldest month of the year, they had caught a train from Faringdon, Berkshire to spend a day in London. They were just in time, too, because on 27 March 1963, Dr Beeching published his report on the future of the railways. Entitled 'The Reshaping of British Railways', it presaged the closure of one-third of the country's 7,000 railway stations, including Faringdon.

Billie blurted it all out. Her Tragedy. My Mother was the fourth of eight children, Frank was the third and the eldest boy. He was her big brother and she still wanted to impress and please him. The more he refused to be impressed and pleased, the harder she tried - it's a classic technique and worked a treat, everyone deferred to him. Think of Maggie Tulliver, trying to propitiate her brother Tom in *The Mill on the Floss*.

Frank had two bossy big sisters: Tina and Marie. Perhaps he felt he never received from them the respect and deference due to him as the eldest boy. I think he tried to extract some of that deference from the next one down, by criticizing and withholding approval from Billie. Tina emigrated to the US early in WW2, and Marie, who had once visited Tanya and me at Reedham, when she lived in Wallington, was now divorced from Uncle Dick, and had moved to Streatham.

Frank and Siobhan's marriage was not good. I know this because soon after this meeting in London, Siobhan began to confide in me, telling me things about their sex life I really did not want to hear, but was powerless to prevent her revealing. He was 18 years older than her and had recently recovered from cancer. They already had three children, all girls. When Billie told her of my pregnancy and the plans to have the baby adopted, Siobhan cried out, in the middle of the Strand

'Oh please, can we have it?'

'Yes, of course!' replied Billie, magnanimously.

And so it was settled.

My Mother gave me the good news.

'Frank and Siobhan have very kindly offered to adopt your baby. It means it can stay in the family and we know it will be well brought up.'

This sounded like a way out to me. I was ridiculously flattered that the important van Tinterens were taking any kind of interest in me at all, and Frank and Siobhan started to pay me lots of attention. They invited me down for visits without my Mother. Siobhan was convinced that I was going to have a boy.

I went down by train to Faringdon to spend a few weekends with them in the later part of my pregnancy. They treated me just like a grown up, and accepted me as one. More than this, they actually seemed to approve of me. I was so unfamiliar with attention, let alone approval from adults, it went straight to my head. I would help Siobhan in the kitchen and with the children, and in the evenings, after the girls were in bed, we grown ups sat, listening to Alfred Deller and Clancy Brothers records, drinking Siobhan's home made parsnip wine and talking. Mainly we discussed politics, because as van Tinterens we were aware of few other topics.

However, we also talked about my baby's future. There was one phrase without which no discussion was complete.

'The baby must come first.'

They were both concerned about Frank's age, which could be an obstacle. They were also worried that I would change my mind.

'You must come and visit whenever you want.' I remember Siobhan saying.

'Our door will always be open to you, I want you to remember that.' said Frank.

'And I will come down and help you with the house and children any time you want.' I eagerly promised.

How the bonhomie flowed.

However, apart from the fact that they were relatives, whom I had known all my life, I actually knew very little about these people. Of course, I remembered how Uncle Frank had looked after Tanya and me when we were little, and now I thought he would resume that role as father to my baby and to me. I thought Siobhan would be a kind of elder sister, or something. She loved being a mother, and was bursting with confidences and advice. She no longer mentioned my accent, and Jenny was doing very well at school, no sign of brain damage. The atmosphere in their house became jolly and welcoming, and the children were always overjoyed to see me. Here at last was the family I'd been searching for. I thought they were all wonderful. And of course, I was tremendously grateful.

At home, my Mother - apart from making clear what a tragedy this had all been for her, and how brave she was being – explained in great detail how impossible life was for the unmarried mother and how I would never be able to cope. Not once did she offer to help me in any way, or suggest that I kept the baby with me at home, and I knew better than to mention the possibility. Billie was not a woman who enjoyed having children around for long. If she had broached the subject with Walter, who had never had children himself, he would almost certainly have refused to consider it, but somehow I don't think she did ask him.

Frank explained to me exactly why Dermot did not love me, and spent a lot of time making sure I understood this. Because he had 'got me into trouble' Dermot did not respect me. If he really did love me, he would walk miles to see me as he, Frank, had walked miles to see Siobhan when they were engaged. Frank had not been in the RAF of course, as Dermot was, and did not therefore have to wait until he got leave before he could go on a date, but I didn't think of that then. I admired my Uncle Frank very much, and basked in his new found approval. So I thought he was probably right, and Dermot did not love me. Frank handled the legal side, obtained the necessary forms, and told me what to do.

He wrote: 'Don't listen to Marie too much. She always tends to confuse me with rather too much talk and I feel she might do the same for you. Don't be influenced into changing any plans, because nothing that Siobhan and I are doing bolts any doors, nor ever will, against you. We are however joining with you in shouldering this load...'

I was to be permitted to become part of their family and be treated as an equal. I stopped calling them Auntie and Uncle and started using their first names. They presented themselves to me as a complete and happy family – something I had never had. They were blood relatives and I had every reason to trust them. Billie trusted her brother and I still trusted Billie. Auntie Marie was the only one who had any thought for how I might feel, and I can now see why Frank would not want me to listen to her.

Like all van Tinterens, Marie talked too much, but because their own monologues were about public, rather than private matters, and she read the Daily Express, her siblings held Marie to be a simple chatterbox, and they despised her right wing politics. It's true that – influenced by Billie and my Uncles - I perceived her then as a silly and superficial snob, but as I was soon to find out, she could also be warm, sympathetic and far more human than the rest of her siblings, something for which they never gave her credit.

Babies born to unmarried mothers were called 'illegitimate' and there was a record number in 1963. Lady Carrington, Head of the British Association for Fostering and Adoption said, in a Sunday Times interview in the early eighties, that there were so many illegitimate children up for adoption in the mid-sixties, that they sometimes placed babies with parents who were not entirely suitable – whatever that means.

I must have presented a paradox to those adults. Despite their atheism and left wing politics, Billie and her siblings believed sex outside marriage to be a sin, and I know they looked down on me and considered me of even less worth than I was before, when I'd simply been a Children's Home girl with a bad accent. In their view, I had 'ruined' my life. Ironic, really, considering how concerned they had all been about my life up until then.

At the same time, I was more powerful than I knew. I had something they wanted, so they could not risk alienating me by delivering lectures on my morals. All the adults apart from Marie, lacked the insight to grasp that behind my confident exterior was a disturbed and emotionally deprived child with little idea of family life, who longed for parents (one of each) to cherish and value her. At that time, Frank and Siobhan seemed to be possible parent substitutes, and, believing that this was what they were offering, I agreed to let them adopt my baby.

Recently, I found a letter from my Mother to Frank. She often kept carbon copies, and in this letter she breaks the news of my pregnancy. So, the accidental meeting in the Strand was a lie. I wonder why they bothered. But this is what I believed at the time, and I was profoundly grateful to this kind couple for taking me and my baby into their family – I was home at last.

45

St Mary's, Stamford Hill

May 1963

A large square room with half a dozen sofas and several armchairs around a central coffee table. Fourteen or fifteen young women sit around, doing their nails. The coffee table is covered in bottles of acetone, rolls of cotton wool, lots of little bottles, as well as smoking paraphernalia. Every day Sister Mary warns us about setting the place on fire, and every day we promise not to put the matches and the inflammables together on the same table.

About half of us are in the final stages of pregnancy, and there is very little for us to do all day. Nail culture thrives.

'What's that colour then - that Revlon?'

'Brazen Bronze'

'Oooh it's lovely. Give us a go'

'You've only just let that Wild Cherry dry'

Hysterical laughter 'I know, but I'm fed up with it now'

'How much is that Brazen Bronze then?'

'Seven and six, so go easy'

'Who's got the remover? Careful!'

'Oh bugger, I've smudged it now. Never mind, I fancy that pink anyway, after you with the remover'.

The girls with bitten nails try to read.

'Shut up with your bleeding nail vanish – stinks the place out'

They are ignored.

Those who are no longer pregnant don't laugh much either. Their babies are upstairs in the nursery. They don't do their nails a lot, so that they can pick up their babies as often as possible. We all know exactly how old each child is and how many days each girl has left. As her time gets nearer, we start to treat her as a bereaved person. They are supposed to let the babies sleep, but are allowed to hold them whenever they want and during the last few days before the babies are taken the mothers often stand in the nursery for ages, holding them, staring out into the garden.

'What time are they coming tomorrow, Chloe?'

'Ten o'clock' replies Chloe, so white her freckles become really prominent.

'When are you going?'

'My Dad's coming to pick me up at 11 and take me home'

'What has he told the neighbours?'

'Oh I'm supposed to have been working abroad. Can't remember now where I said. Switzerland I think.'

'Still it will be nice to be home with your Mum and Dad again won't it?'

Suddenly Chloe starts to howl and the Mums all gather round, being careful of their wet nails. 'Never mind, you've got his photographs, you'll never forget him, he'll go to a lovely home and he'll be well looked after. It's the best thing really.'

Those of us who have not yet had our babies are less sympathetic. We cruise along giggling, buoyed up on waves of hormones. We know that we will be in Chloe's position in two or three months time, but anything could happen before then. Our parents could relent and let us have the child at home. He could leave his wife and marry us instead, as he promised. Meanwhile we keep ourselves slightly apart from the mothers about to lose their babies, in awe of their grief. Our bellies are fat, our ankles are swollen, our hair is greasy because we are only allowed to wash it once a week. Our maternity smocks are borrowed and our shoes are sensible. Nails are the focus for all our grooming - they are perfect.

The songs from that time are potent. *Please Please Me* was at the top of the charts, but for us, the killer was Andy Williams *Can't Get used to Losing You*. We had the radio on all the time; and every time it came on, those first staccato chords would silence the chatter, and we would start to sing along quietly.

Guess there's no use in hanging round

Our babies are to be adopted by barren middle-aged women who can give them a good home. We are bad girls and these respectable married women will make better mothers than we ever could. The baby must come first. We keep telling each other we are doing the right thing. For the baby.

We join in with Andy Williams, but one by one, our voices crack and we start to cry. Chloe has the strongest voice, and perhaps the strongest spirit too. She finishes the song alone, while the rest of us wrap our arms around each other, .and sway, sniffing and sobbing to the music.

Can't get used to losing you.

Very soon, the crying is overtaken by hysterical laughter.

46

May 28th 1963

IT'S after supper on Monday 27th May and I cannot sit still. I've been like this all day. Straight after lunch I went shopping, saw a double cucumber at the greengrocers and simply had to have it. Two cucumbers had fused together along their length like co-joined twins. In this terribly hot weather, I sat with the others at tea-time, and crunched the entire cucumber as if it were a banana. They all had crisps, biscuits and ice-lollies, and regarded my peculiar appetite as a sure and certain sign.

'When are you due, then?'

'Tomorrow – May 28th.'

'You'll probably go into labour tonight, then.'

'Not necessarily, you can be up to two weeks overdue.'

And our conversation falls back into the favourite, the only subject.

'Castor oil – that brings it on.'

'That's an old wives tale, it's a laxative, not a – what do you call it?'

'Yeah, but it works, though, uses the same muscles. Makes the baby slip out easy.'

'I hope my baby's early, I just want to get it over with now.'

'Hey Sheila, how overdue are you now?

'Ten days, *and* I tried the castor oil, which is disgusting. It would be this hot weather, too, I feel like a beached whale.'

Sheila sits on the sofa, weighed down by her stubborn bump, fanning her red face with a knitting pattern, her bare legs wide apart.

'If I don't start soon, I'm going to go mad.'

'How will we know? Ha ha! Anyway, they never come on the EDC, it's usually early or late, my Mum says.'

'What's EDC?'

Everyone, in unison: 'Expected Date of Confinement.'

After finishing the cucumber, I went upstairs to my room and re-packed my hospital bag. I was glad to have a room of my own, because sometimes, younger girls had to share. It had a single, iron bed, a chest of drawers and a small wardrobe. There was lino on the floor and a rag rug by the bed. I loved its convent-like simplicity.

We had to have our bags ready at least a week before our EDC, and there was a list of what we had to pack: a nightie which opened down the front; two nursing bras; three pairs of knickers; a packet of maternity sanitary towels. I was replacing all this in my bag when I felt a strong belt of muscle flex around my back and onto my abdomen. It was like a kind of internal corset. I'd had a few of these in recent weeks, but somehow I knew this was it. I called Sister Mary.

The nuns at St. Mary's were Anglo Catholic, like the Rev. Addison, and I had begun to realise that this meant High Church and Posh. Sister Mary - a nurse as well as a nun - was young, jolly and kind. She was also frightfully upper class. Although the same age as some of the older girls, she somehow contrived to be universally loved. She relished the drama of birth and always got very excited when a labour started.

'Oh good, this is perfect timing Penny. I'm so glad you told me now, rather than getting me out of bed later. Just give me a minute and I'll be back.'

She returned with a cup of tea for us both, with two sugars in mine. She sat on my bed, took off her wristwatch and we started measuring the time between contractions. I will never forget the two hours she spent with me at the start of my labour. During the long minutes between contractions, I told her my plans, and she heard me with patient, uncritical attention. I told her I really wanted a boy, because there were so many girls in our family already. Not only were males more important in the world, they were rare and precious in our family. She thought Sebastian was an excellent name.

'One of my favourite saints.'

By 10pm the contractions were about fifteen minutes apart, and Sister Mary said I should get ready, and she would drive me to Hackney Hospital, where all St. Mary's' babies were born.

'That means they are all true Cockneys, you know – born within the sound of Bow Bells.'

Sister Mary took me into the Labour Ward and kissed me goodbye.

'You'll be back with us before you know it, with your beautiful Sebastian.'

In the Labour Ward, a nurse showed me to a bed in the corner and showed me the cord I should pull when I felt I wanted to push.

'Don't keep pulling it, please, Miss Wardman. You girls from St. Mary's are always ringing the bell too early. We do have other patients as well as you, you know. Wait till you really can't help pushing.'

She drew the curtains around my bed, and checked the other two women in the small ward, neither of whom I could see. Opposite me, a woman with a West Indian accent:

'I'm doing fine, thank you Nurse. This is my seventh now, you know.'

'Well done Mrs Joseph, just pull the cord when you're ready to deliver. Now then Mrs Ryan, how are you getting along?'

The Nurse had moved over to the other bed, where a woman with an Irish accent was having her first baby.

'Oh it's terrible suffering, Nurse, it's pure purgatory. I'm paying for all my sins now, aren't I?'

'Nonsense! You've not sinned Mrs Ryan, *you're* a married woman! Let's have a look at you – ah yes, you won't be long now.'

Mrs Joseph's technique for riding contractions was to hiss her way through them. She gave a deep intake of breath and then a long, loud hiss until the contraction subsided.

Mrs Ryan simply yelled.

'All the Saints preserve me, I'm going to split meself in half'

'Holy Mary, Mother of God, I'll never let him near me again!'

I found all this theatre distracting and distressing. Needing to focus on my own contractions, I decided immediately to separate myself from them by making as little noise as possible. I had read a book about how breathing could help you through labour, and retreated deep inside myself, concentrating on breathing deeply and regularly through each contraction. I had no way of timing them. I dozed between contractions at first, but soon my whole concentration was on what I was doing. I realised that night why it is called 'labour.' Everyone has a different experience – for me, it was not strictly speaking pain, but it was terribly hard work.

As the night drew on, I was dimly aware of the other two being wheeled off to the Delivery Room, first Mrs Joseph, hissing like a steam engine, then Mrs Ryan shouting, confessing and calling upon the Holy Virgin to save her.

I had wanted to push for a long time before I pulled the cord, to avoid being told off. Throughout that long night, nobody came to check on me, and I was grateful for that. I expected no sympathy from the Nurse, who was far too much like Matron White at Reedham, all pursed lips and judgement. It seemed that Unmarried Mothers were not popular, and were expected to behave badly. I didn't want to conform to the stereotype.

Only when I was already pushing, did I pull the cord.

'Miss Wardman, what do you think you're doing? I told you

not to pull that cord. Let me have a look – oh my God, she's fully dilated – we won't get her into the Delivery Room in time – quick, roll on to the trolley, dear.'

In the Delivery Room, on my back, my knees up. The book had said the baby's head would feel like a grapefruit in the birth canal – and it did! In honour of the occasion, and just for today, the vagina becomes 'the birth canal.'

'Don't push yet. I know you want to, but don't.'

I would have said 'Yes Miss!' but could not spare the breath.

'Wait for the next contraction, here we go, deep breath in and you can push now.'

Her permission was entirely superfluous. I had no option but to push, and my baby was born at 5.05 on May 28, just as the sun came up.

'It's a girl – let me weigh her, then you can hold her. OK – seven pounds 12 ounces.'

And there she was. Her eyes closed, her nose swollen, a small blood streak across her forehead, her fists doubled up, she looked like a boxer after fifteen rounds. Her skin was white, her hair was pale ginger and in a part of my heart, which was not available to me, I loved her immediately. My available heart healed over that place, making sure I didn't feel too much.

I knew what was coming. I knew I would not be allowed to keep her. I had already learned to perform acts of separation between mother and child without showing, and eventually without feeling, any emotion. I had spent my whole life preparing for this.

For reasons I now forget, I had always liked the name 'Milly' but nobody else liked it much, especially Billie – perhaps because it rhymed with her own name. So, just in case the boy I had planned to call Sebastian turned out to be a girl, I'd decided to call her Emily, which I would shorten to 'Milly'.

Opposite me in the Maternity Ward was Mrs Ryan with her firstborn son. Our babies were in cots by our beds, so we could pick them up whenever we wanted. A midwife came round to show us how to breastfeed. Since Billie had fed us both herself, and I had seen my Aunties feed their babies, I had never considered anything else. The midwife watched me pick up Emily and guide her head to my breast. She got the idea pretty quickly, which seemed to impress the midwife.

'That's fine – textbook breastfeeding my dear. If only everyone was like you, my life would be much easier.'

I thought she could not have seen my name above the bed, or she would not have praised me. It said:

Miss Penny Wardman

So, despite the Woolworths wedding ring, which all St Mary's girls wore, nobody could be mistaken about my shameful status.

Mrs Ryan and her son had a terrible time with breastfeeding, the midwife spent ages with her, but she couldn't get the hang of it. At the two o'clock feed, (feeding on demand was an idea still way ahead in the future) I sat up in bed, feeding Emily and watched poor, recumbent Mrs Ryan, trying to get her nipple into the baby's mouth. Trying to be helpful, I said:

'Why don't you sit up a bit, Mrs Ryan, so that you're bending over the baby more, then it just goes in his mouth easily – see?'

'And why don't you shut your evil mouth, you little harlot! Of course it comes naturally to you. People like you, you do it like animals, it's all instinct to you, just like animals. Don't you presume to talk to me – slut!'

And she burst into wretched, heaving sobs. The nurses came and drew the curtains around her, and henceforth, young Master Ryan had a bottle.

Three days after Emily was born, the midwife asked if I would express my extra milk for the premature unit. I did not feel I could say no, and anyway, helping in this way seemed somehow to alleviate my shame. The midwife had noticed I was unmarried, but she told me it did not concern her. Britain was on the cusp of a huge shift in attitudes, and in ten years time unmarried mothers would be almost unremarkable. So while all the patients and most of the staff in Hackney Hospital made it quite clear that they held me in contempt, a few went out of their way to say 'There but for the grace of God, go I.'

The midwife was mainly interested in my milk. She said there was a shortage because more and more mothers went straight to bottles. Twice a day, after Emily's feed, she wheeled up a trolley, attached tubes to my breasts via suckers on my nipples and switched the pump on. I sat, watching my milk spurt rhythmically into a glass jar. As the milk flowed, so did the silent tears.

There were four beds in our ward, and at each visiting time, three husbands came with flowers and drew the curtains round. I really felt it then. Billie came once, halfway through visiting time, and while it was nice to see her, I really wanted Dermot. I wanted him to see her, now her eyes were open and she was so perfectly beautiful. There was a pay telephone outside the ward, but I had no money. I borrowed a shilling from a nurse with red hair, and called the Air Base. He wasn't there but I left a message, telling him the news of his daughter's birth. I returned to the ward, lay on my bed and wept.

The other mothers did not speak to me much. Once up and about, they would go over to each others beds, admire and compare their babies, but although I never heard the word 'bastard' spoken out loud, nobody came over to admire Emily and when I approached the other beds, I got tight little smiles and monosyllabic answers. I don't suppose my middle class accent helped.

Mrs Ryan's toenails clicked like a dog's paws as she walked barefoot on the wooden floor. She addressed the whole ward.

'When I was so big I couldn't bend to cut me toenails – look at them now!'

They were thick, yellow, and curled right over. I looked away when she said that, but every time I heard her click across the floor, I was forced to visualise them and retched.

All new mothers spent eight days in hospital after the birth. Despite the sustained heat wave in early June 1963, the large, plate glass windows at Hackney Hospital remained closed. I lay sweltering on top of my bed, reading the Manchester Guardian. June 2nd was the 10th anniversary of the Coronation, but also of Hillary's ascent of Everest, only apparently it wasn't, because the news had taken until then to reach London. We now learned that he had actually reached the summit on May 29th, and there were rumours that his guide 'Sherpa Tenzing' may even have set foot on the summit first.

This was a sharp reminder of ten years previously, when I had been just nine years old, and obsessed with the Coronation. Behind the large and kindly pages of the Guardian, I wept again.

Emily and I were getting on fine. After two days she opened her dark blue eyes. She didn't seem to mind the occasional teardrop on her head as she was feeding. She just fed, slept and gained weight. She yelled a bit before feeds, as all the babies did, but the staff were very strict about not picking them up until feeding time. Bad habits apparently.

When she was about a week old, and feeding enthusiastically one day, she suddenly stopped, let go of my nipple, her eyes wide with surprise. It was such an unmistakable expression, and I knew immediately what it was – the clip on her umbilical cord had popped off. When I changed her nappy after the feed, there was the detached clip, leaving behind it a neat and sweet little belly button.

I treasure that small moment as the first wordless understanding between us, a signal somehow that the close bond between mother and daughter was there, even if we would be compelled to ignore it.

The eight days in Hackney Hospital were very lonely, and I couldn't stop crying. I made no noise, the tears would just rise up, and anything would set me off. Especially the evening visit of The Husbands, sometimes with other family members, all admiring their babies, none of them nearly as beautiful as my Emily. The other mothers' bedside cabinets were piled high with flowers and fruit. Billie had brought a bunch of chrysanths, but no fruit, because it would 'give baby the squitters'. The visiting hour, between 6 and 7pm, was the most wretched part of my day.

After St. Mary's, where there was always company and everybody was equally disgraced, the semi-Coventry I experienced in Hackney Hospital was hard, and I thought this was why I could not stop crying. I did not learn about post-natal depression until several months afterwards. I just thought that I was going to be desperately sad like this for the rest of my life. On the morning I was to return to St. Mary's, I lay in the first bath I'd been allowed since the birth. The red-headed nurse came into the bathroom, and swept open the curtain which surrounded the bath.

'Where's that shilling I lent you for the phone?'

I lay before her, naked and humiliated.

'I don't know. I'm sorry, I haven't got any money.'

'Well, you shouldn't have borrowed it then, should you? Shouldn't borrow when you can't pay back.'

'I'm sorry. I can bring it to you next week.'

'You're going back to St. Mary's today, and I want it now, before you go, or I'll never see it again – what are you going to do about it?'

'I don't know. I'm sorry.'

'You unmarried girls are all the same, no responsibility! That's just typical. You just take what you can get, and never give a thought to anyone else. I need that shilling now, and I'm not going to see it again, am I?'

After several seconds, during which I began to weep, and she scornfully regarded my nakedness, she flung the curtain back, rattling the rings along the metal rail, and slammed out of the bathroom. If I had known her name, I would have returned the shilling to her as soon as I had it, but she did not give me that opportunity.

Emily and I went home on the bus. I wrapped her in the white, lacy woollen shawl it had taken me the whole pregnancy to knit, and carried her in my arms. I was so proud of her, and smiled self-consciously when people peered over to look at her. Sister Mary rushed out to welcome us home. She was completely besotted with newborn babies – and at last Emily received the kind of admiration which was her due. St. Mary's gathered us back into the accepting love of the all female community, only now we were on the Mother and Baby Wing. We had a room to ourselves, with a cot for Emily, so I could easily feed her during the night. During the day, the cots were all wheeled into the sunny Day Nursery, where we could go and pick our babies up any time, feed them and hold them for as long as we wanted.

Sister Mary was not so rigid about four hourly feeding as they had been at Hackney Hospital. Soon she would prescribe for us the little white pills, which would cease lactation, in preparation for relinquishing our babies. Who knew what feeding schedules the other, older mothers would impose? Some girls refused to breast feed at all, fearing that it would make giving the baby up even harder.

Tanya came to see Emily and me at St. Mary's. Now in her first year at St. Martin's School of Art, she was dressed entirely in black, and wore thick black eye make up. She looked so glamorous and bohemian - so grown up. She had been half a head shorter than me all our lives, and I noticed with shock that we were now the same height. When had that happened?

Then Dermot came to St Mary's and sat in the guests' waiting room. I brought Emily down and put her in his arms. There were tears in his eyes. He knew she was his. He said she was beautiful, kissed her, kissed me, said goodbye and walked away. I was desolate, but it was what I deserved.

Like a kitten, they took her at eight weeks. Billie and Walter did not want me to darken their doors with my disgrace, so it was arranged that Emily and I would go from St Mary's to stay with Auntie Marie in Streatham, and Frank would pick her up from there.

He came for her in a red car. He said he would not stay long, in fact he would not even come in, because he feared I would become emotional and he didn't want a scene. Besides, Auntie Marie would start talking and then he would never get away.

I carried her downstairs, wrapped in the lacy woollen shawl and handed my just weaned daughter to him. He had a carry-cot wedged between the two front seats. Entitled and expert, he placed Emily in the carry-cot, which had been prepared for her with sheets, a blanket and a bottle. He shut the car door, rolled down the window and said:

'I'm going to drive away quickly now, because I don't want any tears or fuss.'

I watched the red car go down the street, went up stairs and got out my make up bag. Just as Tanya and I had learned to do after saying goodbye to Billie each time she returned us to Reedham, I did not cry. I had not deserved to live at home with my own mother, how could I possibly have expected to keep my own daughter? Instead, I applied a layer of my new, Mary Quant foundation, and set to work upon making up my face.

Dermot and I were still writing to each other, and because I had discussed with him the possibility of Frank and Siobhan adopting her, they were terrified that he would come and take her away from them. Frank wrote out a letter for me to copy to Dermot 'she is being adopted away, I do not know where she will be, you must never contact me again.'

I wrote the letter, exactly as I was told, and he never contacted me again.

I needed a job and a place to live. Once again, my mother's idea was to get me out of the house. She told me that traditionally, a Residential post is considered suitable for a ruined woman, and I got a live-in job as Housemother in The Children's Reception Centre in Harlesden, a short stay assessment home for maladjusted children who were being taken into care. I felt right at home.

46

Epilogue

As soon as one friend finished reading this memoir, she said:

'You can't leave it there, it's so sad, that cannot possibly be the end. I want to know what happened next.'

But this is really all I want to write - about myself, anyway. For several years after I lost Emily, I walked around in a fog of pain. My family – especially those who had taken her - cast me as a Bad Girl, and I embraced that role.

Three things saved me: my sister, reading and writing. As we became adults, Tanya and I realised that we could rely upon each other far more than we ever could on our mother. The close relationship children usually have with their mothers had subtly shifted in both of us from her to each other.

From reading, I came to realise the important role the Black Sheep plays in a family; bearing sins for all other family members. Novels such as Bernice Rubens' *The Elected Member* opened my eyes. My parents' generation required a scapegoat for all kinds of bad behaviour, and I cheerfully obliged them for far too long.

I have always written. During my teens and twenties this took the form of long, emotional letters to various contemporaries. I still have one, written to a friend when I was 16. In thick black ink on thick blue paper, it is melodramatic and excruciating to read now. However, I began to realise that simply by setting things down on paper made them clearer somehow. It was a way of listening to my own voice and a route to self-understanding.

Men were a mystery. They did not seem human to me, and I had no idea how to behave with them or how to talk to them. They fascinated and terrified me. All I knew of men was shouting, hitting and sex. This last was the best way I knew of getting their attention for at least a short while. I enjoyed it. I became good at it. I became stupendously promiscuous.

If you know you have treated someone badly, an effective way of coping with this knowledge is to tell yourself that they deserved it. For a long time, the older generation of van Tinterens firmly believed that I was insane. They had a lot invested in this belief, too. If I was unstable and mad, obviously Frank, Siobhan and Billie had done the right thing by taking my baby from me. For most of my twenties I helped them out by acting up to these expectations. I did the kind of things that girls without fathers, brought up in care often do. Self-destructive things. Illegal and dangerous things. I was an embarrassment, an attention-seeking bore. I talked endlessly about myself, harangued complete strangers about the evils of the world, especially nuclear weapons. I was promiscuous, I married a decent, but unsuitable man and had my son with him, but I'd so often been told that I was no good as a mother, and had been so poorly mothered myself, that I had no idea of it, had never seen it done, had no confidence in myself as a mother.

The responsibility terrified me and I ran away to live in a squat. The next few years were a mess, moving from squat to squat, sleeping on people's sofas, living from hand to mouth. But I always saw my son regularly, and I always worked, usually as a switchboard operator – I never really mastered touch-typing. In 1974, two life-changing events saved me.

I got a council flat in Deptford, South East London. It was small, built in the 1930s and very close to a railway line. For the first six weeks I had no electricity and lived by candlelight, kept warm by gathering bits of wood from skips and burning them in the open fire. When I finally got electricity, I was overjoyed by the miracle, except the naked light bulbs revealed how filthy the entire flat was. But now I had a secure place of my own, I could have my son to stay with me at weekends. Until then, I'd had to see him at the houses of friends. In 1979 he came to live with me again. In 1974, I started a journal, which I keep to this day. Writing things down was - and still is - crucial to my personal growth.

The second life-changing event was meeting the man who is now my husband. I got a job as a telex operator at British Monomarks and there he was. He looked really grumpy and so I deduced he must be married. It turned out he was neither grumpy nor married, just shy. After an on-off-on courtship, we settled happily into each other. I cannot bear to think what my life would have been without him.

Another sort of person would have made this memoir a self-help book: *How I put my sad childhood behind me and found True Love.* But if you've read this far, you'll know that's not my style. And if you've read this far, you're entitled to have the loose ends tied up.

Reedham closed in 1974 and the building was demolished. Walter Gilmore died of lung cancer in 1972. Frank died in 2003 aged 89. Billie died in 2008 a few days short of her 93rd birthday. I graduated from London University in 1983 with a BA in English and History. My two children, Emily and Tim are healthy, happy and despite everything, we are all still close. Tanya is also on her second marriage also well, happy and still the best sister anyone could have.